Voices of Experience: narratives of mental health survivors

Edited by

Thurstine Basset
Basset Consultancy Ltd, UK

and

Theo Stickley
University of Nottingham, UK

WILEY-BLACKWELL

A John Wiley & Sons, Ltd., Publication

This edition first published 2010
© 2010 John Wiley & Sons Ltd.

Wiley-Blackwell is an imprint of John Wiley & Sons, formed by the merger of Wiley's global Scientific, Technical, and Medical business with Blackwell Publishing.

Registered Office
John Wiley & Sons Ltd, The Atrium, Southern Gate, Chichester, West Sussex, PO19 8SQ, UK

Editorial Offices
The Atrium, Southern Gate, Chichester, West Sussex, PO19 8SQ, UK
9600 Garsington Road, Oxford, OX4 2DQ, UK
350 Main Street, Malden, MA 02148-5020, USA

For details of our global editorial offices, for customer services, and for information about how to apply for permission to reuse the copyright material in this book please see our website at www.wiley.com/wiley-blackwell.

Library of Congress Cataloging-in-Publication Data
Voices of experience : narratives of mental health survivors / edited by Thurstine Basset and Theo Stickley.
　　　 p. ; cm.
　　Includes bibliographical references and index.
　　ISBN 978-0-470-68363-7 (cloth) – ISBN 978-0-470-68362-0 (pbk.)　　1. Mentally ill–
Biography.　　I. Basset, Thurstine.　　II. Stickley, Theo.
　　[DNLM: 　1. Mentally Ill Persons–Personal Narratives. 　2. Adaptation,
Psychological–Personal Narratives. 　3. Mental Disorders–Personal Narratives.
4. Survivors–psychology–Personal Narratives. 　WM 40 V8895 2010]
　　RC464.A1V653 2010
　　362.196′8900922–dc22

2010016190

A catalogue record for this book is available from the British Library.

Set in 11 on 13 pt Dante by Toppan Best-set Premedia Limited
Printed and bound in Singapore by Ho Printing Singapore Pte Ltd.

01　2010

Contents

About the Editors

Thurstine Basset

Thurstine Basset trained as social worker and worked as a community worker and social work practitioner, mostly in the mental health field. He is now an independent training and development consultant and runs his own company, which is based in Brighton. He works for national voluntary agencies, such as MIND, Together, Rethink, the Richmond Fellowship and the Mental Health Foundation. He is the Chair of the Mental Health Training Forum, Middlesex University. He is a Visiting Fellow at the University of Brighton. He has written mental health learning materials, many of which are published by Pavilion Publishing, with whom he works in an advisory role. He works as an educational writer for the Royal College of Psychiatrists. He likes to walk and watch cricket.

Theo Stickley

Theo Stickley trained in counselling and mental health nursing and practised in both professions for many years. He now teaches mental health at the University of Nottingham, where he is Associate Professor in Mental Health. He has published widely in the nursing and mental health press. The focus of his research is mental health and the arts, and he has led on a number of research projects in collaboration with people who use mental health services. Theo is a keen gardener, motorcyclist and artist (but has not yet found a way to combine all three simultaneously).

Contributors

Peter Amsel
Composer, writer and healthcare activist

Thurstine Basset
Independent training and development consultant
Chair, Mental Health Training Forum, Middlesex University

Caroline Bell
Groups Training and Development Manager, Self Help Nottingham and the
University of Nottingham

Timothy Bird
Member, CAPITAL Project Trust

Peter Campbell
Mental health system survivor and freelance trainer

Peter Chadwick
Psychologist, Author
Lecturer, Birkbeck College and the Open University

John Stuart Clark (aka 'Brick')
Political cartoonist, travel writer and member of Making Waves Ltd.

Sarah Collis
Director, Self Help Nottingham and the University of Nottingham

Joan Cook
User Involvement Development Worker, Self Help Nottingham and the
University of Nottingham

Ruth Dee
Trainer, Researcher and Author

Alison Faulkner
Freelance researcher and trainer

Thomas France
Member, CAPITAL Project Trust

Peter Gilbert
Professor of Social Work and Spirituality, Staffordshire University
National Project Lead on Spirituality and Mental Health for the National
Spirituality and Mental Health Forum
Visiting Professor, Birmingham and Solihull Mental Health Foundation Trust
and the University of Worcester
Chair, National Development Team for Inclusion

Libby Jackson
Member, CAPITAL Project Trust

Brice Jones
Chair and member, CAPITAL Project Trust

Laura Lea
Co-ordinator of Service User and Carer Involvement for the Psychology
Doctorate Programme, Department of Applied Psychology, Canterbury Christ
Church University

Richard Lilly
Member, CAPITAL Project Trust

Richard Love
Member, CAPITAL Project Trust

Mariyam Maule
Survivor poet

Jonathan Naess
Director, Stand to Reason

Clare Ockwell
Chief Executive and member, CAPITAL Project Trust

Howard Pearce
Member, CAPITAL Project Trust

Kay Phillpot
Member, CAPITAL Project Trust

Joy Pope
General practitioner, Bolton

Dave St. Clair
Member, CAPITAL Project Trust

Esta Smith
Survivor poet

Jude Smith
Member, CAPITAL Project Trust

Martin Snape
Member, CAPITAL Project Trust

Theo Stickley
Associate Professor in Mental Health, University of Nottingham

Premila Trivedi
Freelance Mental Health Service User Trainer

1

Introduction

Thurstine Basset and Theo Stickley

In this book people with experience of living with mental health problems talk about how they cope, survive, manage, recover, discover, struggle, combat discrimination, thrive, become liberated and grow – in essence, how they live their lives.

Their stories are about finding meaning and explanations. They are about their beliefs and their strategies for life – strategies that are rooted in deep personal experience. This experience is their expertise and offers a guide to others who may be struggling with living and surviving in the twenty-first century. If anybody can teach us about how to live in our modern, or postmodern, world, it is people who have struggled with the complexities of existence and found their own unique ways of surviving, learning and moving on.

Stories and Narratives

This book can be read on different levels. Certainly, it contains stories that may inspire hope and encouragement. Also, the book may be read as a textbook and the contents may be treated as research that can stimulate inquiry. Either way, what is central is the importance of true stories of people's lives. In textbook language, stories are often referred to as narratives. Some say that narratives have been fundamental to the development of human history, culture and individual identity (Brockmeier, 2001; Benwell & Stokoe, 2006). Thus storytelling provides meaning to events and enables people to make sense of their world:

Voices of Experience: Narratives of Mental Health Survivors   Edited by Thurstine Basset and Theo Stickley ©2010 John Wiley & Sons, Ltd.

> People dream in narrative, daydream in narrative, remember, anticipate, hope, despair, believe, doubt, plan, revise, criticize, construct, learn, hate and love in narrative. (Shkedi, 2005: 12)

The study of narrative is the study of the ways in which human beings experience the world, that is, through the recounting and retelling of experience. Narratives are present in every society. All communities have their local stories, mainly focusing on events that have occurred involving local people. Each civilisation has its own history of mankind. Wherever there are people, there are narratives. People from all walks of life, all human groups, have their narratives. Such is our unquenchable thirst for other people's stories that we become addicted to fiction and soap operas on television. In recent times, the study and practice of narrative inquiry has gained momentum in qualitative research and is illustrated with numerous journals, books and conferences focusing on the method.

In the psychological arena, psychoanalysis has championed the centrality of the person's story. The expertise, however, remained firmly with the analyst and the patient remained a case to study. It was much later, with the development of narrative research, that the storyteller became the narrator in terms of research processes. What is fundamental to narrative approaches in research is the notion that it is through the act of storytelling that people make sense of their lives.

It has been said that narrative has become essential for people to have an identity and that identity can be understood in two ways. Identity can be understood as something that is fixed (from the Latin root word for identical: 'idem') or something that is permanent but changing. It is this latter meaning from which we create our narrative identity (Ricoeur, 1988). Thus, the River Thames may have an historical identity, but is in a constant state of change. Narrative is therefore a way of balancing both the self that is constant and the self that is changing as we are able to make sense of ourselves through the stories that we tell ourselves (and others) about ourselves. The narrative, therefore, is a product of our constructing, deconstructing and reconstructing ourselves and our identities. It is fine that our stories change over time, and so they should, as we change and grow as people.

Narrative Research

Narrative research came to the fore with the work of sociolinguists in the early 1960s (particularly Labov & Waletsky, 1967; Labov, 1972). By the end of the 1970s narrative approaches in various disciplines had become established. Notably, Fisher (1984) observed the central role of narrative in politics and of narrative analysis in political sciences. Polkinghorne (1987) did something similar for psychology; Richardson (1990) for sociology and, by the 1990s, narrative inquiry had had also become common in various science studies (Silvers, 1995) and provided the foundation for research from a variety of other disciplines (Bertaux, 1981; Ricoeur, 1981; Mishler, 1986; Riessman, 1993; Elliot, 2005).

Whilst we do not locate this book in an illness narrative context, there is much to be drawn from the illness narrative literature. As narrative approaches gained momentum in the social sciences, some working in healthcare recognised the limitations of rationalist frameworks and sought to introduce similar approaches in healthcare. For example, Frank (1995) identifies three fundamental illness narratives: restitution, chaos and quest. Restitution narratives are those of the person anticipating recovery; chaos narratives are enduring with no respite; quest narratives are those where people discover that they may be transformed by their illness. What is common to all types of illness narratives is the focus on the centrality of the telling of the patient's experience. By gaining knowledge of a disease from firsthand experience and how people make sense of their illness, or how people extract meaning from their experiences, the reader may become hopeful in relation to their own experiences. These principles, based primarily on physical illnesses, are directly paralleled by experiences of mental distress. Narratives have become central to the recovery paradigm in mental health. Stories abound of people's recovery from mental distress. Naturally, these stories inspire hope in the reader. Belief in recovery is contagious.

In the UK, there is a medical research project that utilises narrative approaches: Health Talk (www.healthtalk.org). Researchers from the University of Oxford have built a massive database of personal and patient experiences through indepth qualitative research into more than 40 illnesses and health conditions. People's stories are communicated through text and mini-interviews. The idea is that patients, their carers, family and friends, doctors, nurses and other health professionals can access the site, listen to people's stories and learn from others' experiences. Historically, in health research, people's stories are considered to be the weakest kind of evidence. In Health Talk, however, people's stories are offered as expert evidence:

> These methods provide a high quality evidence-based approach to patient experience and ensure that a full range of patients' perspectives are analysed in terms of what someone might expect to experience when diagnosed with a particular condition or illness.

> (www.healthtalk.org)

The Department of Health has provided strong support to the Health Talk research. As far as we can tell, this is the biggest example of narrative health research being put into practice. Recent NHS guidance has endorsed evidence-based methodology and its importance to informed patient choice.

In their examination of the narratives of people who are deaf, Jones and Bunton (2004) have identified two camps: the 'wounded' and the 'warrior'. These distinct categories may also be interpreted as the deficit model or social model, respectively. The wounded are generally those who experience illness as a loss; the warriors are generally those who see themselves as a marginalised and oppressed minority group who need to assert their human rights. The wounded or warrior concept can illustrate people's responses to different forms of adversity, including mental health problems. There are those with serious mental health problems who seek cures (e.g. SANE: www.sane.org.uk) and those who are proud to be mad (e.g. Mad Pride: madpride.org.uk).

Illness narratives, however, tell us as much about society as they do about the people themselves. People are social beings and are constantly influencing and being influenced by the society in which they live. Often, sick people may relate to a sick society. Maybe readers need the capacity to look beyond the illness and examine the broader sociocultural contexts, which are inseparable from the experiences of mental health problems.

Experts by Experience

Narrative research focuses on the story of the individual and therefore provides opportunities for individual voices to be heard. As the previous example of the Health Talk research illustrates, people become experts simply on account of their lived experiences. Gabriel (2004) argues for the expert authority of the narrator on the basis of experience. Whilst, for example, the doctor may be considered the expert in terms of education and the experience of implementing that education in practice, doctors can never be fully expert until they have experienced the disease themselves. Thus, there are two experts – one by education and training, the other by experience. In this book, we deliberately give voice to the expert by experience in order to help inform those who may experience similar issues and those who have a caring role. The notion of the patient as expert is enshrined in recent DoH discourse (Department of Health, 2001).

If we are to acknowledge the expertise of patients, we must also accept the importance of the service user/patient knowledge that underpins this expertise. Very little work has been done to establish what service user knowledge is and how it might be incorporated as a key element in the overall mental health practitioner knowledge base (Basset, 2008). We need to build on the work of people like Branfield and Beresford (2006) in their support of service user networking and knowledge.

According to Gabriel (2004), the expert by experience is more vulnerable in terms of potential exploitation from the expert by education, for it is they that are more likely to understand research, publish and receive the plaudits and benefits of a research profile. Neither of us, as editors of this book, has experienced inpatient mental health care. We are therefore more in the experts by education camp. However, we feel that our relationship with the various chapter writers is that of colleagues with a strong desire to tell it how it is and publicise important narratives so that they can reach a wider readership. As regards the potential royalties from sales of this book, we have arranged to share these equally with two service user-led mental health organisations: Making Waves in Nottingham and CAPITAL in Sussex.

It has been our intention to create a platform for people's voices to be heard. When people have a voice, they have power. Reality and daytime television have created a platform for a confessional discourse that empowers victims to become survivors through acknowledgement of their suffering (Goldie, 2004). This is also illustrated by the growth of web logs (blogs) where people can tell their story to a global audience. It is estimated that blogs now exceed 60 million. In turn, it is now not unusual for authors of blog confessionals to secure book contracts. Thus a combination of narrative and twenty-first-century technology has the power to emancipate and liberate as well as provide a vast audience. Narrative research should empower participants and is one method that gives voice to the researched; this is especially powerful for those who have been oppressed.

A Platform for Stories

We would argue, therefore, that stories of people's experiences of mental health problems, survival, discovery and recovery are imperative to mental health research and practice. We hope that people from all walks of life will read this book and may understand more about what it is like to experience mental health problems. Many mental health problems are rooted within the society in which we live. A book such as this may do very little to bring about positive change in society, but if we can bring about some positive change in even a few readers, we will have achieved something important.

We thank all the contributors to this book. We shall refrain from commenting directly on their stories, as we believe that we should allow their stories to speak for themselves. We shall, however, attempt to draw out some themes that emerge from the narratives in the final chapter. There are only a few narratives within this book and we do not suggest that they are representative of the many. In this respect, it is important to state that everybody's story is uniquely different. We acknowledge that, throughout history, people have paid a great price for being considered 'mad', 'insane' or simply an outsider to mainstream society. The price may have been incarceration, loss of relationships, role and personhood, indignity and in some situations even death. By providing a platform for people's stories, we believe we are performing one small act of restoration. This book may shock, challenge or inspire; whatever it does for you, the reader, we hope it imparts greater understanding and harmony for the future.

The Policy Context

It is not our intention here to write a long piece about policy changes in mental health. Suffice it to say that the Conservative government in the 1980s and 1990s oversaw the running down and closure of the majority of the large Victorian hospitals with the subsequent media frenzy (often front-page news) about the perceived failures of community care. In their final days they came up with 'The Spectrum of Care' (Department of Health 1997), which, at 12 pages in length, was perhaps a little bief given the size of the task!

The 'New Labour' government, elected in mid-1997, could not be accused of producing mental health policy documents that were on the laconic side – quite the reverse. Placing mental health at the top of their agenda, in particular by publishing, and subsequently following up, 'A National Service Framework for Mental Health (NSF)' (Department of Health, 1999), a steady stream of policy documents poured forth in subsequent years.

The NSF was a 10-year programme running from November 1999 to November 2009. It would be churlish to be too critical of a government that has made an enormous effort to improve mental health services. Their focus on mental health was unprecedented in the UK. However, they always ran the risk of not knowing quite how much should be changed. They wanted to modernise services, but they also wanted to use existing structures on which to build this more modern approach. Hence the decade 1999–2009 can be seen as one which sent very mixed messages – with messages of social inclusion in the policy and messages of exclusion inherent in additional compulsory measures in the Mental Health Act 2007. These mixed messages, perhaps a product of applying modernisation in a distinctly postmodern age, were at times confusing, particularly to service users and grass-roots mental health workers.

A hopeful atmosphere was nevertheless created, based on an overall policy direction that championed social inclusion, fighting discrimination, mental health promotion, self-management and self-help, holistic approaches and recovery. These approaches see service users and their families working alongside mental health workers in partnership. The role of the worker is to enable and facilitate in assisting service users to live their lives to their potential, using their strengths and abilities. Finding ways of living with mental distress is a part of the picture. Fighting discrimination is everyone's task.

However, it is not always easy to graft new approaches onto old systems. These new philosophies of support and enablement could not be easily placed within an existing care, treatment and illness model. The idea that service users are experts in their own right does not always sit well with professional mental health workers, who have their own expertise. Nowhere is the difference more pronounced than when mental health professionals talk of their patients not having insight, when what they are really saying is that the patient has a different understanding of their experience and situation. Clearly, one of the aims of this book is to deliver insight from the service user's perspective.

The mental health service system has recent knowledge of the complexity of these attempts to change ways of working as a similar situation occurred when, in closing the large hospitals, the institutional practices in these establishments sometimes followed patients into the community.

Another reason for producing this book is to cast some light on the term 'recovery'. A close inspection of the NSF for Mental Health (Department of Health, 1999) reveals no mention of recovery. However, it does emerge briefly (albeit quite upfront in the title) in 'The Journey to Recovery' (Department of Health, 2001a) – this policy document was subtitled 'the government's vision for mental health care'. There are four short paragraphs on recovery, stating that a more optimistic approach is needed with 'the vast majority of those using mental health services having real prospects of recovery' (p. 22).

Eventually, after some key people involved at the National Institute for Mental Health in England (NIMHE) had pushed through a recovery agenda, NIMHE produced their Guiding Statement on Recovery (NIMHE, 2005). It was not long after that that many mental health services declared that they were moving towards recovery-oriented services.

We feel that despite the central position that recovery attained from 2005 onwards, it came in slightly by the backdoor, and so had even less chance than other approaches of being implemented properly. The NSF for Mental Health (Department of Health, 1999) has an underpinning message that services will be much improved with greater resources and a real effort to bring in evidence-based practices: assertive outreach, early intervention and crisis resolution across the whole service. As such, it is pretty much accepting that a properly resourced and modern medical model of service provision is what is needed. Of course, there is some emphasis on involving service users and their families as part of this. Nevertheless, it is just about possible to do all that is necessary within the remits of the NSF and for the power and expertise to still remain firmly with the professions.

This is not the case with recovery, which is much more of a challenge to the medical model and the status quo, with service users both taking the lead and having their expertise acknowledged alongside that of the professionals. As a result, we think recovery has struggled when put into practice because of the culture of most of the services, which could handle the NSF as not too great a challenge to the expertise of the professionals, but see recovery as a step too far. Sometimes they do take the step and end up thinking they are following a recovery approach when they are clearly not.

In essence this book contains accounts of recovery in that some contributors use the word to describe their experience. Others, however, find the word unhelpful and still others prefer to use the words discovery or survival, often aided by self-management and peer support. The word 'recovery' itself can mean many things and hence it is open to different interpretations. However, at root, recovery starts with and belongs to the service user so one cannot escape the conclusion that bolting it onto a mental health service which does not really celebrate and value the expertise of its service users, as has happened in various NHS Trusts, is simply not going to work. We shall revisit this discussion in chapter 16.

This book was written in the latter part of 2009 as the NSF for mental health programme reached its final days. As such it is both partly a celebration of what has been achieved during the era of the NSF and also partly a challenge for the future.

The Chapters

In chapter 2, Peter Chadwick explores his journey as one of 'total psychology' from cognitive neurochemistry to the sociopolitical and spiritual. He recounts the alienation he felt from within the culture in which he grew up. He sees his recovery as a product of science, art and spirituality.

In chapter 3, Peter Campbell explains how his experience of mental distress has been much more about 'living with' than 'recovering from'. He has found that coping with mental distress is partly about learning practical strategies to mitigate the worst aspects and partly about making sense of it through frameworks of understanding that can confer meaning and value. He explores how his involvement in survivor action has helped him progress in his life and combat the discrimination that is deep-rooted in society. He makes some important observations about in-patient services.

In chapter 4, Alison Faulkner writes about her work as a researcher and her belief in empowering service users and survivors through doing their own research. This includes her work as the leader of the 'Strategies for Living' project at the Mental Health Foundation. She also outlines her own strategies for living.

In chapter 5, Joy Pope explains and explores her own and other people's coping strategies, drawing on her experience of working as a general practitioner and journeying with and through depression. She elaborates on a number of ideas, but also stresses the importance of an individual approach, with each person having different strategies and things that work for them. She writes about facing stigma and staying well.

In chapter 6, a Canadian contributor, Peter Amsel, describes how he has coped living with bipolar affective disorder for 25 years. Peter is a composer of classical music and also a writer. He compares the impact of his mental health problems on his work with Beethoven's deafness and the impact this had on the composer. Peter describes a faith (not 'merely spiritual') that enabled him to continue his work. It has been important to him to understand his illness, his symptoms and diagnosis in order to protect him from the dragon that might snap off his head.

Understanding brings liberation. For Peter, mental illness has been an enemy. Ultimately, the enemy can be defeated by working in partnership with healthcare professionals and taking responsibility for oneself. Recovery is possibly if we really want to recover.

In chapter 7, Ruth Dee talks about how she has coped with the effects of childhood trauma for nearly all of her life. Having experienced horrendous childhood abuse she began to dissociate when she was aged three. In this chapter, Ruth describes in detail how dissociation was first a form of coping and then how she learnt to cope with experiences of dissociation. Ruth was not diagnosed with dissociative identity disorder until later in life, when she experienced health problems while working as a senior manager. Although Ruth's experiences might be considered extraordinary, she learnt very practical ways to cope. She describes the specific help she has received from healthcare professionals and explains the significance of each.

In chapter 8, Laura Lea gives a detailed account of how she gradually rebuilt her life after breakdown. She also gives some insight into how relatives/carers can feel when someone they love has a mental health issue. She describes some of the strategies and building blocks that have helped in her recovery and survival.

In chapter 9, Peter Gilbert recalls his personal pilgrimage and how his life's journey led him into and out of depression. He speaks of discovery rather than recovery and broadly explores the role of spirituality in its many forms and in relation to the human condition.

In chapter 10, Richard Lilly explains how the Holy Spirit and his Christian faith has sustained, nourished and helped him to make sense of his life, with nearly 40 years' experience of the mental health system.

In chapter 11, various members of CAPITAL (Clients and Professionals in Training and Learning) relate their narratives of coping, survival, discovery and recovery. The importance of CAPITAL as an organisation that supports and encourages is often central to their stories.

In chapter 12, Sarah Collis, Caroline Bell and Joan Cook discuss the ways in which people can help each other through self-help groups and peer support. Whilst there is clearly merit in professionally-led groups, self-help groups are defined, run and controlled by their members. The core activity of self-help groups is mutual support. Deep connections are made when members identify with the experiences, emotions and reactions of fellow members. Participants benefit from helping each other and by pooling coping strategies, sharing information and drawing on the collective wisdom of the group. The authors invited people from various groups to write letters to them describing the significance of the groups to their lives. People who have experienced the benefit of such groups have therefore contributed to this chapter. People have experienced respect, healing and found hope for their lives.

In chapter 13, Premila Trivedi delivers a critique of mental health services and illustrates how they can take service user/survivor concepts like recovery and mould them to fit their structures and frameworks, thus robbing them of their original ethos. She gives examples of how this has happened in her own experience. She raises questions about the current recovery model and questions whether it is relevant for black and ethnic minority (BME) service users. At least, it needs to address social and political as well as personal issues for it to be relevant to BME service users, who face discrimination through racism in addition to the stigma and discrimination that is linked to mental ill health.

In chapter 14, Jonathan Naess writes about his experience in taking a sabbatical from his corporate job in the City of London to set up Stand to Reason. Stand to Reason is a 'Stonewall' for mental health, being a service user-led organisation committed to fighting discrimination and stigma, challenging stereotypes and changing attitude. He explains how his experience of mental health problems led him to do this. He reviews the successes of Stand to Reason and talks about the organisation's plans for the future.

In chapter 15, John Stuart Clark (also known as the cartoonist 'Brick') employs a conversational style as he describes his mental breakdown. Escaping to China was not the answer, and back in England John encountered 'Atro', a giant lizard, white and cynical. Atro was to become an unshakeable nuisance in the coming years. John sensitively reflects on the impact his experiences have had on his relationships. He is on a journey: 'To travel hopefully is better than to arrive, and the true success is to labour.'

In chapter 16, Joan Cook joins the editors to revisit the concept of recovery and discuss the role of explanations, beliefs and strategies as part of people's journeys. The importance of self-help and peer support is again highlighted. The chapter ends with an exploration of the role of the mental health worker, and this is summarised in the form of a diagram, which illustrates key elements in relation to how mental health workers and service users can work together in partnership.

The poems that illustrate the text are broadly on the theme of living with and surviving mental distress. Mariyam Maule's poems are reproduced by permission of the Maule family.

References

Basset T (2008) You don't know like I know. *Mental Health Today* (March): 26–28

Branfield F & Beresford P (2006) *Making User Involvement Work – Supporting Service User Networking and Knowledge*. York: Joseph Rowntree Foundation

Benwell B & Stokoe E (2006) *Discourse and Identity*. Edinburgh: Edinburgh University Press

Bertaux D (1981) *Biography and Society: The Life History Approach in the Social Sciences*. London: Sage

Brockmeier J (2001) *Narrative and Identity. Studies in Autobiography, Self and Culture*. Philadelphia: John Benjamin

Department of Health (1997) *The Spectrum of Care*, London: DoH

Department of Health (1999) *A National Service Framework for Mental Health*, London: DoH

Department of Health (2001) *The Expert Patient: A new Approach to Chronic Disease Management for the 21ˢᵗ Century*. London: DoH

Department of Health (2001a) *(The Journey to Recovery. The Government's Vision for Mental Health Care*, London: Department of Health

Elliott J (2005) *Using Narrative in Social Research: Qualitative and Quantitative Approaches*. London: Sage

Fisher W R (1984) Narration as a human communication paradigm: the case of public moral argument. *Communication Monographs, 51*: 1–22

Frank A W (1995) *The Wounded Storyteller: Body, Illness, and Ethics*. Chicago: University of Chicago Press

Gabriel Y (2004) The voice of experience and the voice of the expert – can they speak to each other? (pp. 168–185). In B Hurwitz, T Greenhalgh & V Skultans (Eds.) *Narrative Research in Health and Illness*. Oxford: BMJ Books/Blackwell

Goldie P (2004) Narrative, emotion and understanding (pp. 156–167). In B Hurwitz, T Greenhalgh & V Skultans (Eds.) *Narrative Research in Health and Illness*. Oxford: BMJ Books/Blackwell

Jones L & Bunton R (2004) Wounded or warrior? Stories of being or becoming deaf. (pp. 189–202). In B Hurwitz, T Greenhalgh & V Skultans (Eds.) *Narrative Rresearch in Health and Illness*. Oxford: BMJ Books/Blackwell

Labov W (1972) *Language in the Inner City: Studies in the Black English Vernacular*. Philadelphia: University of Pennsylvania Press

Labov W & Waletzky J (1967) Narrative analysis: Oral versions of personal experience (pp. 12–44). In J Helm (Ed.) *Essays on the Verbal and Visual Arts*. Seattle, WA: University of Washington Press

Mishler E G (1986) *Research Interviewing: Context and Narrative*. Cambridge, MA: Harvard University Press

National Institute for Mental Health in England (2005) *Guiding Statement on Recovery*, London: NIMHE

Polkinghorne D E (1987) *Narrative Knowing and the Human Sciences*. Albany, NY: SUNY Press

Richardson L (1990) Narrative and sociology. *Journal of Contemporary Ethnography 19(1)*: 116–135

Ricoeur P (1981) Narrative time (pp. 165–186). In W J T Mitchell (Ed.) *On Narrative*. Chicago: University of Chicago Press

Ricoeur P (1988) *Time and Narrative*, Volume 2. London: University of Chicago Press

Riessman C K (1993) *Narrative Analysis*. London: Sage

Shkedi A (2005) *Multiple Case Narrative: A Qualitative Approach to Studying Multiple Populations*. Amsterdam: John Benjamin

Silvers A (1995) Reconciling equality to difference: caring (f)or justice for people with disabilities. *Hypatia, 10(1)*, 30–55

Minute by minute
we cope
And hope we can cope
One day at a time
Gradually we recover
And see the sky
And the clouds move
And the sea change colour
And the snowdrops
And the daffodils
Appear through the snow
And remember the snowman
And the Halloween parties
And the birthday parties
And the happy times

Libby Jackson, 'Recovery'

2

The Antidote to Madness: Crystallising out the Real Self

Peter Chadwick

The people in this city don't care what you do sexually as long as it doesn't involve children, animals or vegetables. (Ken Livingstone, Mayor of London, April 2008)

I do not see myself as having any family; I do not see myself as having any parents or any hometown, or as having been to any school. I do not see myself as coming from any supportive local community (*what* 'supportive local community'?!). No … not at all … instead I am 'The Man from Nowhere'.

Any sense of real existence only occurred in me, any sense that I was being a person who was me, a person in his own right, was when I went to Liverpool to study for my first PhD, which actually was in geology. I was 23. Psychologically, perhaps even in a sense spiritually, my birthplace was Liverpool. Never do family photograph albums command my attention, nor photographs of my parents, school photographs or photographs of my source district. The fact is: 'I wasn't really there'.

When *nothing at all* that one experiences mirrors what is within, all you become is a walking shell, an eggshell with no (alive) interior. Your behaviour may be strange, offbeat, tactless, ludicrous, childish or in various ways deviant, but what does it matter? Really you're a hole in space. You don't exist anyway!

From Nowhere to Nothing

Out of this brutal, sneering, utterly loveless swamp of my physical origins, I was like a released bubble enclosing a vacuum, looking for a chance to materialise into

Voices of Experience: Narratives of Mental Health Survivors   Edited by Thurstine Basset and Theo Stickley ©2010 John Wiley & Sons, Ltd.

something that could *be*. Psychosis could have overwhelmed me at 22 but my private reading of psychology somehow kept it at bay. Eventually the tide of madness came in, in 1979, when I was 33. Ambulance men (Peter and Paul) dragged me off the road after a suicide attempt when, deluded, I had thrown myself under the wheels of a double-decker bus. The bubble had popped. The fact-ridden, materialistic, atheistic world of academic psychology, to which I had turned at 27, had filled me with *nothing*. After all, what mirroring of what is within can a person obtain by reading volumes of impersonal mechanistic facts? All they'll conclude is that they're a bioelectrical information-processing device! A journey from Nowhere to Nowhere ... resulting in Nothing.

R. D. Laing, now dead, buried and scorned, probably would understand all this. In a more theoretical and less heartfelt way, it also would make sense to Jean-Paul Sartre. It's hardly surprising that Laing would refer to the schizophrenic as 'the living dead'. I'm sure he'd been there. As both Oscar Wilde said (and W. B. Yeats also knew): 'Give a man a mask' (in Laing's case that of doctor/psychiatrist) 'and he will tell you the truth'.

Alienation

I don't know that one really 'recovers' from crises such as happened to me as one recovers from a broken leg. Psychosis is an outgrowth of one's very life. To leave it behind like an oxbow lake of thought one has to grow further and out of it. One gets by, but also tries to get oneself some kind of life, some meaning, some purpose. One looks for love, for commitment to some endeavour, to someone. Love someone, build something.

Wherever I am and whatever I am doing, my heart is always in Liverpool or London. In total years, most of my life has been spent in West London where, really, I belong and where the mirroring without of that within fully gave me a life, an identity and a feeling of self-worth. I met my wife and taught psychology at the university there for over 20 years – *real* psychology, what we could call 'person psychology', not 'behavioural science'.

Regarding mirroring I must, however, acknowledge another West London figure, Oscar Wilde. When one reads a writer and finds oneself saying inwardly, 'Oh! He's noticed that too!' or 'Crikey! He's felt that too!' things start to light up inside that otherwise would remain dormant or paralysed. In a way, where I 'grew up' I was in an atypical kind of 'locked-in' state and it was only possible to dare to *be* as the years progressed and particularly after moving to West London in late 1979.

Feelings, trust, sensitivity and heartfelt intimacy of expression were like the plague to my mother and to the men in the culture in which I was born. A lantern-jawed, hard-facedness was all that seemed, really, to matter. Carl Rogers would understand this induced alienation from the Real Self and the distortions of the personality and feelings of utter life-meaningless that it produces. Always being something that one is not, saying things one does not truly feel, behaving at odds with one's deepest values and sentiments, laughing when one should not laugh, smirking when one should not smirk, punching when one should not punch – the childish, emotionally stunted, emotional *liar* that is the young British male. But there was one good thing in this parody of a life – at least I knew, in some remote corner of my mind, that it was ALL SHIT.

Getting Even

My basic problem was not to feel ashamed and worthless about being a feminine man. 'Getting better' has been about externalising – and having valued – that femininity within. But, of course, there is another issue: What do you do with your *anger*? How do you deal with your *hatred* of your abusers? You can't forgive people who are so self-righteous and so inflated with their own virtue that they don't feel they've done anything wrong. It's like trying to forgive Joseph Goebbels or Islamist suicide bombers; it would be utter psychological, and spiritual, hypocrisy.

But what one can do is turn the negative around into something creative, something productive. For example, many a short story has flowed from my pen, catalysed by the behaviour of the football bullying ring at school – they do well as Gestapo-style interrogators in Chadwick (2006) and one of them is the homosexual rent boy of Oscar Wilde's lover, Bosie Douglas, in Chadwick (2007). I've had them as the Incarnation of Sin in short stories and plays but have, so far, spared my mother, as I really don't think that she knew at all what she was doing. She really should have gone to see somebody.

Obviously, one cannot always get out of psychosis in 'nice' ways. Hatred and aggression are not all they're made out to be and have their uses, particularly in asserting one's identity and rights. The French Resistance understood when under the Nazis that this was not the time for Christian values. One doesn't treat nasties like the Nazis well; one treats them badly. The nasties themselves understand that; treat Hitlers and little Hitlers well and they think, 'Ah! We can take advantage of this one! Have some fun!' Even the teachings of Jesus are a short blanket; they don't cover all the trials of life.

As a pantheist, my beliefs have been important to me. We see the cosmos as necessarily having a positive and a negative side. This applies even in the realm of the materialistic, as in particles and charges, and of course in life there always are advantages and disadvantages, arguments, but then counterarguments. In Christianity, the Father, Son and Holy Ghost have as their opposites Satan, Sin and Death. Like it or not, some people are designed for the latter triad and relish bringing evil, suffering and pain into the world and thrusting meaning, trust and faith out of it. As Churchill realised in the 1930s, they are not the kind of people to be blown a kiss on the wind, but instead are to be bombarded with fire. It's sad, indeed it's dreadful, but it's just life. It's just the way the world intrinsically is.

Spreading Femininity

Hatred is not always in the service of evil and is not always weak. My own hatred for my abusers in my early years has helped me to proselytise and stand for everything in which they did *not* believe. In the 1970s and 1980s, I wrote dozens of articles for, and appeared in, a multitude of transvestite magazines that reached tens of thousands in Britain, Europe and America. I like to hope that what I did helped to ease self-stigma and encouraged many other transvestites to accept themselves and be true to who they are. The publications and photo-spreads also aimed to bring beauty into the world. For someone like myself, who does not see himself as possessing male beauty, to have had extraordinary female beauty was a gift that had to be shared. Beauty must show itself to the world, whatever the cost and however misunderstood.

When I was much younger I was indeed transvestite and also a trace bisexual – not at all in keeping with the football terraces/building site culture of my youth. In an analogous way to the Jews and race fascism I was, in turn, a victim of sex and gender fascists. Had Hitler won the war and successfully invaded the UK, I would have been taken to a concentration camp perhaps in the Cheshire countryside ... and gassed. And the people who would have informed the SS about 'the sissy boy in our school' would have been the football bullying ring and their hangers-on. 'Getting better' was about making my life worthwhile, finding people I could love, not hate, and coming to terms with sorrow. In many ways, it was creating a sense of self. London enabled me to do that.

In a way there was a sense in which the psychosis was a distraction, like treading on one's own shoelaces and falling over. Central in my life has been love, beauty and creativity. These have sustained me. I have never focused on 'staying out of hospital' or 'managing symptoms' or even replacing surrealistic thought with rational thought and logic. I looked ahead of all that, focused on the real root cause of my crisis, sex and gender fascism and lived a life as *opposite* to how I was 'brought up' to live as I possibly could. That's where my identity lay – not in 'doing as I was told', not in conformity, doing the done thing and boorish manly behaviour, but in a world of perfumes, poetry and silk. And every imagined sneer from my enemies of the past would make me stronger and stronger.

The Fighting Underdog

Even when transvestism and bisexual inclinations left me, as eventually they did, there was much to be done in favour of other victims of abuse. My work on the positive side of psychosis (Chadwick, 1992; 1997; 2008) has been energised by my wish to help the stigmatised and I have also done and written things in similar praise of black people, gay men and lesbians ('black bastards'; 'queers' and 'lessies' in the sleazy culture I came from). Perhaps out of hatred could come love, out of utter ugliness could come beauty, and out of doing the done thing could come creativity.

My life has very much been characterised by the fighting spirit of the underdog. I was stigmatised for supposed homosexuality in the 1960s and for transvestism – my real orientation – in the 1970s. Scandal and gossip followed me and clung to me like a cloud of magnetic gas. Oscar Wilde knew what it was like to be me, terror in front, horror behind; like him, the world was my prison. Is it any surprise I went psychotically paranoid? Throughout my life virtually all of my paranoid inferences have proved correct! Why not go a step or two further, as I should have done at school and in the neighbourhood of my youth, and I might *still* be correct?! I would have been then! In 1979 I was not correct … so, instead I went mad.

But it needn't and shouldn't have happened – and these days, with the more tolerant and accepting atmosphere we have now, it possibly wouldn't. But always there are underdogs, for one reason or another, gradually with time (if not in schools where bullying is still rife) the playing field of life is getting that little bit more level as we come to see ourselves as just one species with this singular planet as the only world we have. We really are recognising that somehow we need to learn more about how we can get on with one another.

The negative is the easy way. In Christian ideology Satan is seen as being near and easily accessed. God is more distant and more difficult to reach; one has to work harder for the positive. The genuine positive is to hike on the harsher path.

Reflections

I am effectively 'cured' of schizo-affective psychosis, but this would never have come about if all I'd aimed to do was think about 'how to get out of it' – which is the usual focus of professionals. I had to delve into causes, not only genetic (my brother George also was schizophrenic) but also cognitive, motivational, familial, interpersonal, socioeconomic, political and spiritual. In a way, nobody was to blame for what happened. The 1950s and early 1960s culture obviously was the product of heavy industry, two world wars (the second against the greatest evil this world has ever seen) and generations of biblically seeded hatred of people into alternative sexuality and cross-gender behaviour. Conformity was the order of the day; an ethos of never standing out from the crowd, never being in any way different. Such an iconoclastic, heterodox person as me might just as well have been born in Hell. The whole saga was perfectly understandable, maybe even, in principle, to some degree predictable. The socioeconomic, political and attitudinal ambiences of my early years were critical to disentangling how this crisis eventuated. Treating it as 'all in the head' or 'all in the brain' would have been dreadful folly. To recover, I didn't only have to change what was inside my mind but also what my mind was inside of. I had to change my circle of friends, both male and female, my place of work, the kind of work I did, the town I lived in, and how I lived and expressed myself. If anything, the changes were as much of things *outside* myself as of things inside myself. After all, people don't want to be changed, they want to be loved.

In this sense my recovery meant putting myself in the way of situations and people outside of myself who would bring out emotionally what was within – something my mother (and my late father) had no interest in at all. Their Edwardian ways only produced a mockery of my real personality. My life was like a trip from Bristol to Edinburgh, but via New York. My parents and source culture sent me off in completely the wrong direction. It must have happened to many in those days. What I found to be just as bad was that the human sciences and the psychoanalysis of the 1960s and 1970s shared the very same homophobic and transvesto-phobic attitudes and social representations as my abusers!! – from Nowhere to Nowhere, frying pan to fire. No wonder I ended up totally *alone* and feeling persecuted by all in the middle of a stadium of paranoid madness. Thank God for London people.

But speaking as a psychologist, my journey was one of 'total psychology' from cognitive neurochemistry to the sociopolitical and spiritual. Therefore, my recovery was a product of science, art and spirituality. The writings of poets, art critics, novelists, painters, playwrights and philosophers were all as important as the facts and theories of science. Discussions with Buddhists and Christians were as important as discussions with psychiatrists; going to church and visiting art galleries, as important as CBT and diet. For these reasons and many others I believe that a psychology that is a blend of science, art and spirituality will give us more insight into the human condition than the impersonal, fact-finding empiricism that currently dominates our subject. Psychology should lead, not just follow culture at a safe distance, as it has in the past.

Conclusions

I believe with Kaines (2002) that schizophrenia is such that it is as if the positive and the negative work together to orchestrate all that is. There is a touch of evil in schizophrenia. To me, evil is real, a semi-tangible force operating in the world, not just the verbal gas of a social construction or a convenient defensive attribution or label that we apply to people to distance 'them' from 'us'. The schizotypal and schizoid predispositions are in many ways good (see Chadwick, 2008): they confer tremendous sensitivity, spiritual sensitivity, imaginativeness, a resonance to detail, subtlety and nuance, emotions and empathy that are deeper than psychiatrists realise and a capacity to tune in to a level in life more profound than the average, 'normal' person can access. To have all this twisted and deformed into the agony of insanity is evil. It is the misappropriation of good.

Evil destroys; it is vile and feeds on fear. It destroys love, faith, trust, meaning and, most of all, hope. To overcome schizophrenia one must create, value beauty, seek love in one's heart and meaning and purpose in one's life. Reason and fact can help, but in the story of life they are the lesser good.

References

Chadwick P K (1992) *Borderline – A Psychological Study of Paranoia and Delusional Thinking.* London and New York: Routledge

Chadwick P K (1997) *Schizophrenia – the Positive Perspective: In Search of Dignity for Schizophrenic People.* London and New York: Routledge

Chadwick P K (2006) Critical psychology via the short story: On the masculinity and heterosexuality Thought Police (MASHTOP). *Journal of Critical Psychology, Counselling and Psychotherapy, 6(4)* (December): 200–209

Chadwick P K (2007) Freud meets Wilde: A playlet. *The Wildean, 31* (July): 2–22

Chadwick P K (2008) *Schizophrenia – The Positive Perspective* (second edition): *Explorations at the Outer Reaches of Human Experience.* London and New York: Routledge

Kaines S (2002) The bipolar originating consciousness, *Open Mind, 114* (March/April): 10–11

But what is the cause
Emotional insecurity
Financial insecurity
Harsh words or deeds of people we care about
or simply an illness
Like diabetes
Can we understand
Or should be try
Just try and live
And cope
But not alone
The isolation and pain
is too much to bear
We need kind words
Love and understanding
Of others and then
we too can be whole again
And not be afraid
And not alone
But able to cope
And be happy
And laugh
And cry
With others who may not understand
But care

Libby Jackson, 'But What is the Cause?'

3

Surviving the System

Peter Campbell

This chapter reflects my 42 years of using mental health services. Although I do not particularly care for the now fashionable expression 'expert by experience', I can certainly claim a great deal of intimate, firsthand knowledge of services, in particular acute wards. I have had more than two dozen admissions in 11 different psychiatric hospitals across the UK: Scotland, East Anglia, South West London, North West London. About two-thirds of my admissions have been under sections of the Mental Health Act and I have experienced some of the unpleasant accompaniments of compulsory treatment, like solitary confinement in a police station cell or in an on-ward seclusion room. While on an acute ward I have often done very little except eat large quantities of carbohydrate-heavy food and sit in the dayroom enduring the smoky atmosphere. While an in-patient or out-patient I have, almost inevitably, consumed large quantities of psychiatric drugs and these have been the mainstay of my care and treatment. Although 42 years seems, and is, a long time, I don't regard my story as being that remarkable or extraordinary. In many ways, I could be seen as a typical 'revolving door patient'.

Anyone who experiences continuous or episodic mental distress makes efforts to come to terms with it. These are not phenomena that can easily put to one side. Coping with mental distress is partly about learning practical strategies to mitigate the worst aspects and partly about making sense of it through finding suitable frameworks of understanding that give the phenomena meaning and value. The most readily available and, by some distance, the most influential framework for understanding severe mental distress is the 'medical model', which asserts that the problem is basically one of illness with genetic or biochemical origins. Most people will have this model thrust at them from the moment they enter services for help and notably as part of the process leading to a psychiatric diagnosis. Moreover,

Voices of Experience: Narratives of Mental Health Survivors   Edited by Thurstine Basset and Theo Stickley ©2010 John Wiley & Sons, Ltd.

the general progress of individuals and their possession of the highly valued (by professionals) attribute of 'insight' will often be thought to be significantly linked to the degree to which they accept the medical model as an explanation.

For a number of years, I accepted the medical model as a framework of understanding. During my second admission I remember the consultant giving me a detailed account of what manic depression was (including diagrams). I accepted this at the time and found it helpful. But I gradually came to appreciate drawbacks to the framework. My reading suggested the model might not stand up scientifically. The emphasis on distress as illness not only encouraged a resort to exclusively physical treatments (drugs, ECT), but pushed to one side any consideration of the content and meaning of my crisis episodes. Thinking of myself as having a chronic and incurable illness robbed me of power and agency and confined me within an essentially negative category. By the time I was entering my second decade of service use, the medical model, which I had initially found reassuring, seemed increasingly unsatisfactory, without the capacity to encompass the complexity of my interior or exterior life and give it positive value. As a result, I began to actively explore frameworks that better met my needs.

Today, I am happy to identify as a mental health system survivor. Although there are other aspects to my identity, this description helps me to convey and accommodate central elements of my life experience. I find the term 'survivor' a positive one, although I know some service users see it as too confrontational, too negative, too pessimistic. To be able to say 'I am surviving' certain very real difficulties carries a degree of pride for me. But the more important point is about what I am surviving: the mental health system. It is this that gives me a helpful and, I believe, realistic perspective on my situation.

As a starting point I take mental distress to be part of the mental health system. Because I speak of distress rather than illness and place emphasis on the importance of society's response to my distress does not mean that I am minimising its significance. It is mental distress that has led me into the mental health system. I do not believe myself, or the majority of service users, would be in that system unless we had experienced such distress. But I must survive much more than distress itself. In particular, the way services relate to me as they attempt to offer assistance presents a series of obstacles I must contend with. These range from compulsory care and treatment to institutional practices and an absence of real listening. Then, at the point when I return from in-patient to out-patient status, I must survive society's response to mental health service users – in short, discrimination. Although there have been some changes in attitudes and practices in the last 40 years, discrimination remains deep-rooted in our society and culture. Surviving prejudice and discrimination is a significant aspect of life for all mental health service users. Indeed, an increasing number now claim that it has a greater impact than the problems that brought them into services in the first place.

Identifying as a mental health system survivor makes more sense and is more helpful to me than thinking of myself as mentally ill, a mental patient or even a service user. It has parallels with the social model of disability, which emphasises social responses to impairment as disabling rather than impairment itself. Although I have never thought of my distress as an impairment (I now have severe hearing loss, which I do recognise as such), the focus on social processes rather than individual pathology rings true and has been empowering.

In recent years, an increasing number of service users have come to view, and been encouraged to view, their life experiences as part of a recovery journey. A number of organisations have solicited 'recovery narratives' in order to inform better mental health practice. This framework leaves me completely cold. I have never thought of my life in terms of recovery. I have never contemplated recovery, am not 'in recovery' or recovered. While there are some differences over what exactly people are supposed to be recovering from, there is a strong sense that it is something catastrophic. One often-quoted definition of recovery talks about 'the development of new meaning and purpose in one's life as one grows beyond the catastrophic effects of mental illness' (Anthony, 1993). I do not see my mental distress as a catastrophe. Although I have been confronting acute crises since the age of 17, I have never considered them as a catastrophic interruption to my life, a major loss or setback from which I am trying to recover. For me, it has been more like a process of adaptation to new realities, where the emphasis is on stumbling forward to make new discoveries rather than looking back to recover lost ground. Although I applaud many of the changes implicit in the introduction of a recovery approach to services, I could never supply a recovery narrative. My experience of mental distress has been much more about living with than recovering from.

One attraction of alternative frameworks is that they often allow more focus on the content of the unusual thoughts and perceptions that may accompany mental distress and make room for more positive valuations of the whole experience. Spiritual and religious frameworks frequently allow this, as do perspectives that see distress as an aspect of personal growth. A number of my crises have contained strong spiritual or religious aspects, although this has become much less evident in recent years. While I have never been able to integrate these experiences into a coherent spiritual framework and don't believe that they have given me any special insights into my life or life in general, I do see them as legitimate reflections of my character and everyday concerns. I certainly would not dismiss them as meaningless facets of a psychotic episode.

I believe there are very real difficulties in attempting to place a positive value on mental distress. Certainly, my own experience of living with recurrent crises is that they are overwhelmingly destructive events. Although I have been accused by a number of psychiatrists of 'enjoying mania' (as is the custom), my crises have almost always been nasty, brutish and short. I have never had the chance to ride the euphoric waves of mania for weeks in the way some people apparently have. For me, crisis has almost always been a rapid descent through unusual thoughts to confusion, fear and self-control lost or taken away. To suggest that it is enjoyable and to imply that I may in some way seek mania out is to completely miss the point.

On the other hand, I would contend that my capacity to enter crisis (psychotic episode) is inextricably linked to other personal capacities, which have more recognisably positive characteristics. Creativity is perhaps the most obvious of these.

All these capacities are integral to me. Perhaps, by losing my capacity for psychotic ideation and behaviour, I might become less of a person rather than more whole. It is notable that many people with a mental illness diagnosis do not want their unusual capacities removed from them, either because they have positive aspects or because they are so essential to who they are. I could not argue that mental distress has made me a better person, although I have learned a lot from living with it and gained immensely from knowing other people with similar experiences. In the end, mental distress is, as the phrase implies, essentially problematic. You can survive it, recover from it or grow through it. But the truth is, the majority of us would prefer to avoid it.

One of the difficulties facing people who are trying to make sense of their mental distress is not so much the availability of alternative frameworks as the dominance of the medical model. Accepting a spiritual framework may be helpful, but its usefulness can be limited if the rest of the world accepts a medical model explanation. And that, to oversimplify a little, is pretty much the actual situation. Although in more recent years I have found the company of friends and colleagues who have diverse understandings of distress, for the majority of the last 40 years I have been surrounded by people who believe that mental distress is an illness or disease. In particular, almost all my interactions with mental health services, which have been extensive and where I have been at my most powerless, have been carried through on this basis. Regardless of my own inadequately worked out understandings, I am in the hands of experts who assume an air of certainty, defining my crises as 'relapse' and placing social circumstances beneath 'non-compliance with medication' in the scale of causation. In these circumstances, without wishing to deny the value of minority perspectives completely, it is possible to detect their practical limitations. Like it or not, the vast majority of service users must make some accommodation with the medical model. It is too pervasive and its adherents too powerful to be entirely avoided. While those who break off from services may enjoy some ideological space, for those left struggling in the service system, myself included, it is much less easy.

The practical implications of living with mental distress vary considerably from individual to individual. One important general dividing line may be between those who are contending with quite high degrees of distress almost continuously and those, like myself, whose distress is essentially episodic. Although in recent years I have begun to experience bouts of depression that can last for weeks or even months, most of my difficulties have occurred in relatively short, well-defined and dramatic crises. I have not usually had to cope with distress on an ongoing, day-to day basis. Many of the strategies I have adopted to survive everyday life in these circumstances have been largely about healthy living and are applicable to the entire population. A good routine, a healthy diet, adequate ways of relaxing and proper amounts of sleep are chief among these. The last of these has particular importance and I have often been tempted to see my crises as being as much about an exaggerated sensitivity to lack of sleep as anything else.

Predicting and trying to respond sensibly to the circumstances that bring on a crisis has been a central part of my survival strategy over the years. In some cases, avoiding doing certain things has been useful, but the truth is that avoidance of stress is often neither easy nor desirable and if it came down to taking risks and having a fulfilling and challenging life or doing very little but staying out of the acute ward more, I have always decided to do the former. It is one sign of the greater sophistication of services over the last 30 years that they have tried to assist me in anticipating and preparing for difficult situations where they previously ignored the issue altogether.

Observers confronted with the frequency of my admissions in the last 40 years could well conclude that any strategy I have had for avoiding crises has not been particularly successful. It is hard to argue otherwise. Unfortunately, I have always had the capacity to move into a crisis extremely rapidly, often in only 36 hours, and this has made it very difficult for me or others to take avoiding action. Moreover, predicting the circumstances that bring on a crisis is by no means an exact science. Life is unpredictable and unexpected circumstances like the death of a loved one, the illness of a friend or a cataclysmic world event can upset the best laid safety strategy. At the same time, while many of my crises have occurred at times when I was vulnerable and so make a certain amount of sense in retro-spect, a few still seem entirely inexplicable and not clearly linked to what was going on in my life at the time.

For whatever reasons, crises have been a regular feature of my adult life and I have seen the inside of a good many acute wards. By and large, they have suc-ceeded in putting me back on the rails without satisfactorily meeting my real needs. In my opinion, this can be attributed to an approach that is essentially dehumanising. One aspect is the failure to respond to crisis holistically and, in particular, to help people come to terms with the content of the troubling thoughts and perceptions that often accompany extreme distress. To ignore these areas is to deny the full meaning and significance of the experience and leave individuals in an unsatisfactory limbo. Equally important, is the comparative lack of ordinary conversation between staff, particularly nurses, and patients. Interaction between patient and staff and, indeed, between patient and patient is often at a low level on acute wards. While staff frequently talk about their days in terms of 'fire-fighting' difficult situations, patients describe days of boredom and inactivity. My own impression is that, for a range of reasons, staff now have less time to talk naturally to patients than they used to, although complaints about nurses spending all their time in the nursing office were also a feature of services in the 1960s and 1970s. For me, coming to terms with a crisis has always been essentially a solitary task, although carried out in close proximity to others in the acute ward. Having developed a severe hearing loss ten years ago to which acute ward culture is in no way adapted has accentuated that isolation.

The deficiencies in the human response to crisis provided by the acute wards I have experienced are particularly notable in relation to the emotions that are aroused in the individual. Crises are frequently accompanied by traumatic events: detention by the police, restraint in handcuffs, solitary confinement in a police cell while awaiting assessment, compulsory detention, further instances of confinement or restraint. Inevitably, these have an impact on the recipient. Confusion, fear, anger and despair can result. Yet, in my experience, staff on acute wards are rarely very sensitive to these additional aspects or even to the emotional distress that has led to the crisis in the first place. While I would not accuse acute ward staff of being uncaring, I do feel that they usually place tight boundaries on the degree of caring and comfort they routinely offer to distressed individuals. Surviving a repeated failure of the caring imagination in the face of crisis has been a significant element in my career as a service user.

One of the feelings that frequently occur during a crisis admission and in its aftermath is shame. This may be attached to the strange, outrageous and uncharacteristic behaviours that accompany a crisis, but is also frequently related to a strong underlying feeling of personal responsibility. Thus, a crisis of mental distress is somehow always to a real extent my fault in the way a crisis of physical health characteristically is not. Viewing crisis as a failure may be exacerbated by professional attitudes (I have never been congratulated on handling a crisis better than a previous one) and by over-simplistic approaches to non-compliance with medication regimes, but is probably linked to something more profound. The idea that to exhibit mental distress is a sign of personal weakness, a character defect even, is one that has been known to me since childhood and is not easily thrown aside, despite our now living in times of disability rights and survivor activism.

I would not claim that shame at being 'mentally ill' has been an everyday feature of my adult life. Nevertheless, it is quite obvious that living with society's generally negative view of mental illness is an important aspect of the experience of almost all people with a mental illness diagnosis. Discrimination encountered while seeking employment has been one of the most hurtful and frustrating aspects of my adult life and there was a period when I found it almost impossible to be honest about my history of service use and succeed at job interviews, even for work that was a long way below my capabilities. On the other hand, I was able to work with pre-school children on and off for 15 years despite my history, and have been in some kind of employment for most of the last 40 years. While outright discrimination is a regular occurrence and should not be underestimated (it is striking how often students omit physical and verbal harassment of service users from their discussions of discrimination), it could be that the slow attrition of living in an uncomprehending society does even more damage.

Research has shown the impact of the anticipation of discrimination, even when discrimination is not actually occurring (Thornicroft, 2006). Stigmatising attitudes can be internalised. It is very difficult to be continually confronted by negative stereotypes of violence, alienness and incompetence propagated by the media without some erosion of self-esteem. Although there is now a greater degree of openness and tolerance about 'mental illness' among the public, in some respects this is not an irreversible progress and most people with a mental illness diagnosis still feel constrained to keep secret about what may be an important aspect of their life. This is particularly true if their problems are deemed to be due to psychotic illness. In my view it is not possible to counter discrimination by persuading society that there are no differences between people with a mental illness diagnosis and other people. Although there is a common humanity to which we must always return, the interior and exterior experiences are often substantially different, in particular in relation to the unusual thoughts, feelings and perceptions that may be experienced. The equal citizenship of mental health services must be built not on similarity but the positive valuation of difference.

Mental health services have played a basic role in helping me cope with mental distress. In particular, they have provided a degree of sanctuary and support when I have been in crisis. This has enabled me to continue returning to a reasonably full life over a long period and is by no means a negligible service. What mental health services or the mental health system as a whole have not done is improve the quality of my life. For transformation in this area, contact with other service users/survivors and involvement in service user/survivor action has been largely responsible.

In the early 1980s, I was really going nowhere in my life. I was significantly without hope, had low self-esteem, was isolated, silenced, struggling to stay on the surface while carrying the burden of 'mental illness' in secret across one shoulder. Although to an outsider I might appear to be coping with my predicament, had my own accommodation and was not dependent on benefits, in reality my life was on hold, without great meaning or purpose. Regular contact with other service users/survivors, particularly activists, from 1984 onwards slowly began to change the situation. Acceptance was a vital element. Although knowing other service users did not prevent me from continuing to have crises that necessitated admission to the acute ward, this was no longer viewed by those around me as an extraordinary or catastrophic event. Instead, mental distress was seen as an aspect of who I was, which did not detract from my character or competence. Unusual behaviour was unusual behaviour but everyone behaves strangely at times – that's life. Openness was important. Because we often had similar experiences, discussion of mental distress and society's response to it became a good deal easier. More often than not, other service users/survivors I met had the same type of responses to the treatment they had received in the system and it was possible to develop a critical analysis that placed our experiences in a more convincing perspective. The capacity for mental distress was not automatically devalued. In the late 1980s I was fortunate enough to be able to enter a positive community based on shared experience and to replace isolation with solidarity.

I learned a great deal about mental distress and the mental health system that I had previously never known, partly through contact with other service users/survivors and partly through study. I gained a better understanding of areas I was largely unfamiliar with, like hearing voices and self-harm, and this enabled me to appreciate my own situation more sensitively. At the same time, as an activist I was increasingly being asked to put my personal experiences of mental distress to constructive use in the attempt to change services and public attitudes. Through this process my relationship to my own distress began to change and I no longer perceived it as an unequivocal burden but as something that could have a positive value to others and could be used creatively. In certain circles, my mental distress ceased to be solely a secret burden that I carried about and became an asset that was sought out and treated with some respect.

Using a hitherto negative personal history in a positive way can be liberating. That has certainly been my own experience of involvement in survivor action. While some of my other activities over the years have been worthwhile and rewarding, in particular working with pre-school children, being a survivor activist has given me a particularly strong sense of purpose and self-esteem. It is linked more deeply to who I am and relates to goals to which I am particularly committed. It has become a way of life which, although by no means excluding continuing mental distress, is much more satisfactory than any I had achieved prior to the early 1980s. Whatever survivor action has achieved in changing the mental health system, and I do believe certain changes have resulted, it transformed my personal development. I gained new skills and new confidence, learned how to speak in public and how to organise voluntary groups. I learned how to teach. At the same time, I had the opportunity to travel extensively in the United Kingdom and, to some extent, outside it. I was able to develop a busy, interesting and purposeful life. While I don't believe the purpose of survivor action is to be therapeutic, there is no doubt that it changed me for the better.

Since 1990 I have been working as a freelance trainer in the mental health field. I think I was one of the first survivors to take this path. In a sense I have moved from being a recipient of services to a paid mental health worker, although I am not directly involved in service provision. Certainly, the role of freelance trainer would have been unlikely to be open to me without my personal experience of the mental health system. I have no formal teacher training or qualifications as a mental health professional. Nevertheless, being a survivor trainer is not simply about personal experience, and the mental health education field has moved some way beyond merely wanting service users to talk about their personal experiences in training sessions. It seems to me that a successful survivor trainer offers analysis and critique of the mental health system (often derived from the service user/survivor movement) that is informed and illustrated but not dominated by personal experience.

Personal experience undoubtedly has a huge immediate impact as an educational tool. This affects both the teacher and the student. In my early years as a freelance trainer I was frequently aware of how using personal examples of distressing situations like solitary confinement (seclusion) had a delayed effect on me, causing me to feel upset and destabilised after the teaching session was over. At the same time, students can be overwhelmed by the overuse or inappropriate use of personal testimony. There is a potential tyranny of personal experience that can pre-empt disagreement and make fruitful discussion and debate between teacher and student very difficult. On the positive side, the use of personal experience can undoubtedly open up a wider and more sensitive understanding of problematic issues. The generally enthusiastic response by students to input from survivor trainers is in no small part due to this personal element.

Developing a career as a freelance trainer has been important to me. One aspect of this has obviously been connected to finding an audience prepared to positively value personal experiences I had previously kept hidden. Doing something constructive with my life experience has been personally empowering. But I have also had to develop new skills as a teacher and communicator, to study, to keep up to date with developments in the mental health field, in a sense to turn myself into a professional. These were relatively new experiences in my life and brought their own degree of excitement, satisfaction and pride. As a freelance trainer I have not always travelled completely from the status of outsider to the position of insider in the educational field. The extent to which I have been involved in curriculum development has been relatively limited. I have more often provided one-off sessions on training courses than worked on their long-term development. Although this has sometimes been disappointing, I do not entirely regret it. My vision of survivor trainers is that they remain somewhat removed from the educational system rather than totally absorbed within it.

I have been very fortunate to live for more than 40 years with mental distress and have a fulfilling life for a good deal of that time. I still find the reasons why I have been able to cope and not 'go under' slightly mysterious, although the support I have received from services and from friends and loved ones has been crucial. Hope has been an important element. The point when I became convinced that mental distress would not destroy me or relegate me to the back wards of an institution was very significant and followed at a later stage by the belief that I could go on and have a constructive life. Being accepted in my full humanity, with my differences, has also been vital and something I have been more likely to find among fellow survivors than within services. Being treated with compassion when in mental distress has not always happened, but has not been forgotten when it occurred.

The mental health system changes very slowly. My mental distress, while episodic, is enduring. Services, particularly acute services, may have improved but still find it difficult to respond sensitively to individual needs and understandings. Society remains substantially uncomprehending. These are basic realities that I cannot change but must accommodate myself to. They are the reasons I still see myself as surviving the system.

References

Anthony W A (1993) Recovery from mental illness: the guiding vision of the mental health system in the 1990s. *Innovations and Research, 2*: 17–24

Thornicroft G (2006) *Shunned: Discrimination against People with Mental Illness.* Oxford: Oxford University Press

For example. How many questions
Are there. An endless stream
And answers?
What is a wall? How did it get there?
A constant factor. The separation between
A wall, and as myself comes and goes
Lodged in my mind are so many concepts
I don't know.
What process of thought should I abide by
Even if it is so old
Before. I arrived, did I know
Even to accept what I learnt in class
Just didn't work anymore
I had to switch off. Do what I have to
Go onwards into a place
A type of acceptance, a world in which
To live within limits
I take the same path home, visit the
Supermarkets, search for bargains
In second-hand shops
Sit down on the benches in the main
High street, smoke a cigarette
As I usually do and stare as hard as I can
At the coloured lines representing
Street signs or shops.
So much for advertisements, television news
And radio broadcasts. Email and websites
I only know as much as I know.

Dave St. Clair, 'They Come and Go'

Mardi Gras noon Somerset soon
a plastic red balloon
a spoon up your nose
a line or two
beneath the doom
addiction fruition
dying in need
fixing up

rapping outside in the morning
a craving
something happening
within my mind
reversal
stopping

in the woods of the past
a glass cutting
a broken window
voices screaming
in prisons and asylums
even on the streets
people freaking out
running like mad men and women
what am I doing here
and why is all this
happening to them

I wonder if
I might end up that way
the thought crosses my mind
for a second
then I too switch off
and blank out the thoughts
rather like not being able to forgive people
especially my parents
and siblings

Dave St. Clair, 'Fixing Dinner'

4

Measuring the Marigolds

Alison Faulkner

Inchworm, inchworm
Measuring the marigolds
Seems to me you'd stop and see
How beautiful they are
(Kenny Loggins, *The Inch Worm*)

All too often, clinical academic researchers in mental health are, in my opinion, trying to measure people inappropriately and failing to see the whole human being, which is why this song comes to mind. In this chapter, I am hoping to convey something of the beauty of the marigolds growing in the mental health field. For much of my life, I have worked as a researcher and latterly sought to enable other mental health service users to take an active role in research, thereby taking more control of the research process. The word 'research' covers such a wide range of activities, methodologies and investigations that it is a wonder we have only one word for it. In many ways, my personal search has been for coalescence between my identity as a 'researcher' and my identity as a 'mental health service user'. We all have a number of hats, or labels, by which we may become known privately or publicly, and these are just two of mine, although they are the most significant for the purposes of this chapter.

Researcher

I fell into research by accident, never having had a clear idea of what I wanted to do or be. Following a psychology degree and an MSc in Applied Psychology, I

Voices of Experience: Narratives of Mental Health Survivors   Edited by Thurstine Basset and Theo Stickley ©2010 John Wiley & Sons, Ltd.

was offered a nine-month contract in the psychology department in which I had studied for the latter and subsequently went on to work for MIND (NAMH). From my own experience of mental health difficulties and an admission to psychiatric hospital as a student, working for MIND seemed like a natural step to take. I became research assistant on a project researching section 136 of the Mental Health Act (1983) and was fortunate enough to have some fascinating experiences during the course of the following two years. These included sitting in the custody office as observer in Tottenham Police Station, North London; going out on the beat with a young PC; interviewing psychiatrists about their assessments of people picked up by the police; and, finally, attempting to interview patients held under section 136 in Claybury Hospital.

From there I went to work for a social research institute as a qualitative researcher. Qualitative research is about finding meanings and understanding people's behaviour and motives; it is not about attempting to measure people or to fit them into preconceived categories. It still means being rigorous, however, and analysing the information gathered very carefully. This appealed to my need to make sense of the world, to understand more about what was going on for people through research but without the artifice of measurement.

Using scales and questionnaires to measure has an attractive simplicity about it, which fits neatly with the need of the medical model to diagnose, to place people in boxes and put labels on them. The simple fact that mental health professionals often have to rely entirely on self-reporting in order to reach a diagnosis is fraught with the wonderful complexities that render us human. Measuring the diameter of a marigold tells you nothing about what it looks like as a whole bright-orange flower.

In reality, practising professionals often do realise the complexities of lived experience; my own psychiatrist has been reluctant to place a label on me. It is often the researchers, the clinical academics, who rely so much on people fitting into boxes in order that research can be carried out on people who fit into the required diagnostic categories. They persuade themselves in this way that they are carrying out true scientific research. Even they are not responsible for this though – it is the whole Western approach to science and research, the positivist crew who steer the ship at present. The current push towards evidence-based practice within our health and social care services emphasises this need for 'scientific' research.

If I could make any difference to the research world, it would be to finally raise the status of good quality, rigorous, qualitative research to meet that of clinical trials on an equal basis, to do away with the 'hierarchy' of research, which places randomised controlled trials at the top as the gold standard of acceptable evidence.

Doing Research Differently

My first opportunity to do research differently came whilst working at the Mental Health Foundation in around 1995. Believing in the importance of bringing service users into the research agenda, June McKerrow (the director at that time) put resources into a project, of which I was the leader, with a steering group entirely of service users. The Mental Health Foundation was a strange place when I first went there; it acted as a series of committees giving money to predominantly medical researchers, many of whom could not understand the concept of service user researchers or research.

It was a challenging project, but a good one. We had a great team of people, including Andy Smith, David Crepaz-Keay, Marion Beeforth, Linda Smith from the African Caribbean Mental Health Users Group, people from Brent User Group, UKAN, the Hearing Voices Network and London Voices Forum. During the course of this project I came to understand that I, too, was an ex-service user. As a student, I was admitted to hospital for a month and attended a therapeutic community day hospital over the summer between my first and second years. It was a strangely difficult concept to come to terms with at the time, and it was not until a couple of years later when I found myself in hospital again that I fully embraced the idea of being a 'service user', or person with mental health problems.

The research, which came to be written up as 'Knowing Our Own Minds' (Faulkner, 1997) was entirely user-led. We were given the freedom to design our own questionnaire and to decide on the topics and questions in it. We decided that we wanted to know what service users thought of different therapies and treatments, how helpful they found medication and talking therapies, and what other things they found helpful in their lives. At times, designing a questionnaire by committee was a bit of a nightmare, and it led to a decision towards the end of the project to select an editorial group from members of the steering group.

The research uncovered some of the subtleties of the ways in which people viewed their medication, their positive and negative experiences of talking therapies and what people found helpful in a crisis (not surprisingly, someone to talk to). We began to hear about the role of religious and spiritual beliefs in people's lives, and the ways in which many diverse things could be helpful to people (in giving a structure to the day, the importance of being listened to, being treated as a 'whole person', the role of peer support, finding ways of expressing feelings). 'Knowing Our Own Minds' demonstrated the importance of understanding the full context of people's lives: how it is that people find ways of coping on a day-to-day basis and what alternatives they seek when conventional treatments do not solve all of their problems, or indeed create new ones.

Strategies for Living

'Knowing Our Own Minds' formed the foundation for our proposal to the National Lottery for 'Strategies for Living', a programme that became my best job ever. However, its publication in 1997 coincided with the death of my father in a year that became my own *annus horribilis*. Later that year, my relationship of seven years came to an end; I bought my first flat and turned 40. I began 1998 in psychiatric hospital.

Over the coming weeks, months and years, I found myself living with the feeling that I had no future, alongside finding that I was working on a fantastic project that everyone seemed to want a piece of. At times that in itself could be overwhelming, but we were a close and supportive team and one of our most vital strategies for surviving was humour. There are so many incidents now that I can look back on and smile about. As before in my life, I found that work was an essential part of my own strategies for living, and the team at the Mental Health Foundation became my day centre, giving structure to my day and a purpose to my life.

The core Strategies for Living research project, which became the report published in 2000 (Faulkner & Layzell, 2000), found out nothing that can be described as new or groundbreaking, yet it was both of these things. Service users interviewed service users; people with mental health problems interviewed each other and others with sensitivity and care. Some people had never been asked these kinds of questions before and were moved by the experience of being interviewed by someone who came to them with honesty about their own experience.

We described it as 'user-led' research; it was led by a team of service users who designed and carried out the research, interpreted and wrote it up (ibid.; and see Nicholls, 2001). The research was part of a new movement towards empowering service users through research. In some ways it did not go far enough, but it did go a long way (see Nicholls et al., 2003, for further developments) At the same time, the User Focused Monitoring project was developing at the Sainsbury Centre for Mental Health under Diana Rose, and we saw ourselves as sister projects, taking forward the ethos of survivor research and user-led research.

Our approach followed in the footsteps of emancipatory research, as written about in, for example, Barnes and Mercer (1997) and by Peter Beresford and Jan Wallcraft (in Barnes & Mercer, 1997; and others). It felt exciting to be part of a movement for change, as beautifully described by Viv Lindow:

> Research has its part to play in developing solidarity among psychiatric system survivors, and helping to raise the expectations of those who have been 'educated' to live with an unacceptable quality of life. Survival research can be a small but key part in the move to seize freedom within an oppressive and excluding society. (2001: 145)

What it means to me to work as a service user/survivor researcher is to try to turn these experiences into new ways of working that endeavour to equalise the relationship between researcher and researched, to empower people to say 'no' if they want to or to take more control over the research if they want to. I have worked with many people over the years since the start of the Mental Health Foundation's Strategies for Living programme and I have continually been amazed by people's capacity to change and grow in the carrying out of research. It is not just about developing skills that research offers us as service users; it is the opportunity it gives us to reflect and to think about our personal experiences alongside the experiences of other people. I do believe that it has the potential to empower people, in that it gives us the opportunity to, as it were, reverse the 'research gaze' and to use research for our own purposes. I am fortunate in that I achieved a professional life through doing research alongside using mental health services. Sometimes I feel as if I fall between two stools – being too 'professional' to be a 'real' service user and insufficiently 'academic' to be a 'real' researcher – but often feel that I am both things and that it is good.

The Strategies for Living research findings (Faulkner & Layzell, 2000), by their very ordinariness, somehow became groundbreaking. It seemed that people with mental health problems were human beings like everyone else. People valued relationships with other people in their lives, whether they were mental health professionals, friends or family, and often they were fellow travellers on the mental health journey, such as people encountered in day centres and self-help groups, wards and user groups. Other strategies identified by interviewees included finding their own strategies, religious and spiritual beliefs, physical exercise and medication. These form the 'first-level' findings from the project.

Strategies for Living: findings

- **Relationships with others**
  Friends, family
  Other service users
  Mental health professionals
  Counsellors, therapists
- **Personal strategies**
  Peace of mind
  Thinking positively, taking
    control
- **Medication**
- **Physical exercise**
- **Religious and spiritual beliefs**
- **Money**
- **Other**
  Hobbies & interests
  Information
  Home
  Creative expression

More important, perhaps, were the 'second-level' findings: the feelings, beliefs and meanings beneath and behind the strategies that people discovered or chose for themselves.

Underlying themes

- Acceptance
- Shared experience ... shared identity
- Emotional support ... 'being there'
- Reason for living
- Finding meaning ... and purpose
- Peace of mind ... relaxation
- Taking control ... having choices
- Security ... safety
- Pleasure

It is these themes that provide us with a more fundamental understanding of what we are all looking for in our search for 'recovery', survival or for a meaningful life, following the onset of mental health problems. And we find them in different places, with different people and different activities, because we are all individuals with our own stories to tell.

My Own 'Strategies for Living'

During the course of the research, we asked ourselves and each other about our strategies for living, and so I share these with you now. An observation that we all made is that some of these 'strategies' change over time, and move in and out of focus. Also, we don't always choose to do what we know to be most helpful for ourselves; at times of distress, we may be unable to find or to see those things we otherwise know to be helpful or, in anger or despair, we may cast them aside.

My first thought about what has helped along the way is therapy. I have been in therapy for long periods in my life, and it has been a vital lifeline in many ways. My first experience of therapy, which I have written about elsewhere, was less than helpful, but I still maintain a belief in therapy as a way of making sense of my inner world and of allowing someone to travel alongside me, particularly at times of relative isolation and distress. I have struggled with it at times, struggled to find the words to say what is going on in my mind, but ultimately it is and has been of immense value.

> We sit silently,
> measuring the space between us.
> The second hand circles and swoops,
> counting time.
> Light slants across the wall
> painting shadows of distraction.

Words loom large behind my eyes,
roll up over my tongue,
falter at the last hurdle, and
fail to breach my lips.

A chasm opens up in the space,
slicing it in two, and
folding us back into islands of self.

A few words falter and shift,
smoke signals seeking
some distant translation.
A sigh, a murmur of understandings,
a feeling creases my brow and
passes like a ghost stalking my grave.
I shiver.

And then —
She catches my dream
as it rips through the air between us, and
holds it there for us both to see.
Carefully,
She passes it back to me —
Lighter than before, and
Stripped of the need to terrify.

The mock leather creaks and sighs
As we reposition ourselves.
I wonder what she thinks of me.

'Dream Catcher'
(For S.)

Secondly, there is swimming. Swimming is my passion and my outlet for energy, anger, love, relaxation, competitiveness, strength and power. I first started swimming regularly in my early twenties, almost taught myself during a period of unemployment when I lived near a pool. I watched good swimmers and imitated them, perfecting my breaststroke and breathing rhythm. I learnt to put my face in the water first by doing it in the bath with goggles on, and then graduating to the swimming pool. I can even swim under water now for a short distance. Swimming gave me a wonderful sense of strength and power, a good feeling about my own body. I had, like many women, spent many years in my teens denying myself food and being obsessed with my weight. Now I had a strong and good feeling to associate with my body. My arms and legs became stronger and my breathing too. Swimming can lift my mood; it helps me to think things through as I swim up and down, sometimes almost becoming a form of meditation as long as there are not too many people in the pool. It is refreshing, cleansing … invigorating. It can also be a marker of my distress; if I cannot get to the pool or find that it does not help, then I know that things are getting difficult and that I need to seek some additional support.

Thirdly, though not necessarily in this order, there are friends and, to a lesser extent, family (I say this latter because there is a limit to what I share with my family about my mental health). Some friends are valued because they have been there over a long period of my life and they give me a real sense of continuity along with friendship and support. Others I have met through my personal experiences or my work in mental health, often people who can offer a reflection of my own experiences, an understanding that runs deep and forms a strong bond. And, then of course there are the friends who are just fun to be with.

Amongst the mental health and other professionals who have helped along the way, the one who stands out the most (apart from my current therapist) is my GP in Haringey, Dr Stock. He was the person who took me to hospital in 1998 and explained what he was doing and why he thought it was a good idea. Subsequently, he would always agree to see me at the surgery when I was having difficulties, and always managed to seem pleased to see me. It was a sad day indeed when I moved house and left his catchment area.

I feel obliged to mention medication, which I do use now and have done for over ten years. It took a while to find something that I found helpful, and I feel forever ambivalent about taking it. I am always talking of reducing it or stopping it altogether, but somehow the time is never right. I actually increased it last autumn with the onset of new events in my life.

My work, and in particular writing, is another important and invaluable part of my strategies for living. Just as many of the interviewees told us in the research, a sense of meaning and purpose is essential. And I have often written about the difficult experiences I have had in relation to mental health services as a means of taking control and dealing with them.

I cannot write a chapter like this without mentioning the role of cats in my life. Xena, the Warrior Princess, is the boss, and frequently supervises my work at the computer. Boris is the young interloper who eats everything in sight, catches mice and sleeps a lot. I first invited Xena into my home in October 1998, a short time after my more recent 'breakdown'. At first I could hardly bear her intense affection; it was almost too much for me. For a time, I was unsure about keeping her and could not take the cat carrier back to the Cats Protection League in case I would need it. But eventually she nudged her way into my heart and has remained there ever since. She has never fully accepted Boris into our lives, but I am still hoping …

What Does It All Mean?

I have no doubt that my personal story and my explanations of my own mental health will continue to be rewritten and retold until my story comes to an end. So this is by no means a conclusive explanation. I trace some of my emotional issues back to childhood and to the type of parenting my mother learnt, or didn't learn, from her mother, who herself had severe mental health problems. It was an upbringing couched in the view that negative feelings of all kinds should be swept under the carpet, perhaps for future generations to find. I was an angry child and a high achiever; in primary school I was good at everything (except sports). I was an angry and depressed teenager, desperately jealous of my much-loved younger brother, and in addition I was in two road accidents between the ages of 12 and 17. I began self-harming at about the age of 15, and my story is testimony to the fact that self-harm is not primarily about seeking attention – no one knew about it for several years. Finally, I was admitted to hospital for the first time at the age of 20 and to the Marlborough Day Hospital therapeutic community at the end of the first year of my degree in 1978.

In those days, too, coming to terms with my sexuality formed a large part of the difficulties I was experiencing. Some years later, at the age of around 26 or 27, I was able to embrace my identity as a lesbian, but it took a long time to achieve that (Faulkner & Sayce, 1997), I cannot emphasise enough how new and terrifying all of these things were to me at the time: being gay, having therapy, being seen as 'mentally ill'. I was doing a psychology degree, but I didn't understand about therapy. It was easy to associate my sexuality with mental illness, and to confuse therapy with having a relationship. It is very important to remember how vulnerable a person is when they make that very first contact with psychiatric services, whether it is voluntary or forced on them. I did not speak in therapy for weeks – or was it months?

What it all means to me now is that I get great strength from the work that I do, especially when I feel that I am enabling the voice of other mental health service users to reach the people who will hopefully act on what they hear, or enabling them to gain new skills and insights through research. I am aware of being vulnerable, but I also feel strangely resilient in some ways.

I guess I'll never be invited to do jury service and I have to make decisions about travel insurance every year. I have never taken out life insurance of any kind and I do not have a pension because I haven't worked in any one job for long enough. I chose to become freelance in 2004, partly because I imagined that the lifestyle would suit my variable mental health – and I was right. It does suit me very well, but again I have no pension and occasionally have too many days at home alone with the cats at the computer.

Rather like I imagine life as an alcoholic or a compulsive gambler to be, I still regard myself as having the potential to self-harm. Currently, it is a few months since the last time I did so, and hopefully the time will continue to extend. I adopt certain strategies to reduce the likelihood of doing so, such as collecting my medication one week at a time so that I never have too much in my possession. My feelings about self-harm took a huge knock when my friend Helen Blackwell died in October 2007. All of a sudden, it all became too real, which is not to say that I stopped immediately, but it began to take on a new meaning. The eternal challenge is learning to live with the feelings – of fear, depression, guilt, anger, sadness – rather than turning them into another opportunity to harm myself.

Strategies for Living, Self-management, Recovery and Measurement

If 'Strategies for Living' was originally conceived out of the need for people with mental health problems to have our say about what we find helpful, it was also formed at a time when organisations supporting people with HIV/AIDS were beginning to talk about 'people *living with* HIV and AIDS'. Hence the birth of our title 'Strategies for Living with Mental Distress'.

For some people, however, the concept of 'living with' is not enough; they want to soar above, recover and thrive. For other people, the concept works well because it reflects their ongoing lived experience. Either way, the language and meaning of mental health, illness and distress, finding our own strategies, self-management and recovery are all too often fought over by professionals and service users alike.

The word 'recovery' has not had an altogether easy journey. Despite the efforts to explain 'recovery' as non-clinical in its ethos, the word does imply an underlying medical model. The fact that people often start their presentations about recovery with statistics about the number of people who do 'recover' from schizophrenia (in a clinically measured sense) further muddies the waters. On the one hand, it is about people's individual stories, their goals and aspirations. It is about recovering a meaningful life, working with your strengths and encouraging hope and optimism; it is not about 'cure' or recovery in the traditional sense. This means that everyone is included, not just those who can achieve a clinical recovery. All of this sounds good. I am a great believer in the importance of personal narratives. Many people I have interviewed over the years have never had the chance to tell their story before; too often they are silenced by mental health professionals who have little time to listen and aim to make a diagnosis as quickly as possible.

However, if recovery is to be an entirely individually defined concept (as its origins suggest), then how is it that we are placing themes and elements and stages on it? And, similarly, how is it to be evaluated? With a person-centred approach to goals and outcomes, recovery presents a challenge to those who wish to assess the effectiveness of a particular service or intervention. How can you collate outcomes or measure effectiveness in an aggregated way if outcomes are to be personal and particular to each individual? A similar argument might be made about psychological therapies.

And so we come back to the difficulty of measuring the marigolds. I am deeply frustrated by the way that everything has to come back to measurement and outcome in order to demonstrate the evidence for an 'intervention'. It seems to me to be very much like trying to place a tape measure across a flower, trying to measure our lived experience. What I think we need are new ways of assessing the value of different approaches, not just a combination of qualitative and quantitative methods but rigorous, 'emancipatory' and user-focused methods. I am not even arguing for (solely) user-controlled research, because I believe that we can all bring our expertise to the table in an effort to be more creative. The methods are out there, but the system is either too short-sighted to see them or too blinkered to believe that anything other than a randomised controlled trial will do the task. We need to understand what the marigold looks (and feels) like and how it grows, not just measure its diameter and circumference.

The Future

Research is by no means the only way to bring about change – indeed, it is a particularly slow way of changing the world around us, and is not guaranteed to have any impact at all. Therefore, I also put my energies into talking and writing about things that I believe need to change (Faulkner, 2008), and to user involvement in its many forms and to carrying out consultations with service users if I believe that they will reach the ears of people who will make changes to improve services.

Mental health services continue to need improving in some significant ways, despite initiatives such as Recovery, new models of crisis resolution and support, and greater access to psychological therapies. Acute inpatient care still remains the Cinderella of our mental health services; no one has yet found the glass slipper that fits, so it still cannot go to the ball. Research does not tell us that being hospitalised, sitting around watching television and getting bored, and generally becoming the passive recipients of an institutionalised routine, assists our mental health in any way. Feeling safe and supported is important, but there must be other ways of achieving our own and other people's safety (Faulkner, 2005).

Much of the difficulty facing us continues to be people's attitudes. As I write, there are a number of initiatives to combat stigma and discrimination, not the least of which is Time to Change. Everywhere I go, every piece of research or consultation I carry out, people talk about the pain and the fear associated with the stigma and discrimination they experience in everyday life. I hope that attitudes are improving, but they have a long way to go.

Despite the many difficult and sometimes humiliating experiences I have had over the years as a result of my mental health problems and the services they give me access to, I feel a tremendous sense of friendship and companionship with the many people out there with whom I share this crazy life. In many ways I wouldn't have missed it. Even being an inpatient has given me intense understanding and insight into the experiences of others, who are on both parallel and divergent journeys.

One of the threads that have wound their way throughout my working life and my lived experience is that, despite some common themes, each of us is ultimately individual and different. I remember very well writing these sentences in the Strategies for Living report:

> In one of the early discussions with the interviewers, it was suggested that a key finding of the study might be that 'everyone is different'. It is certainly true that the complexity of things that people find helpful in their lives, and the reasons they do so, suggests infinite variety rather than easy categorisation. (Faulkner & Layzell, 2000: 90)

The challenge for all of us involved in mental health services and mental health research is how to acknowledge and hold this individuality, rather than always to choose the simpler option of 'easy categorisation'.

References

Barnes C & Mercer G (Eds.) (1997) *Doing Disability Research.* Leeds: the Disability Press

Beresford P & Wallcraft J (1997) Psychiatric system survivors and emancipatory research. In C Barnes & G Mercer (Eds.) *Doing Disability Research.* Leeds: The Disability Press

Faulkner A (1997) *Knowing Our Own Minds.* London: The Mental Health Foundation

Faulkner A (2005) Institutional conflict: the state of play in adult acute psychiatric wards. *Journal of Adult Protection, 7(4):* 6–12. Brighton: Pavilion Publishing

Faulkner A (2008) On the receiving end. *Healthcare Counselling and Psychotherapy Journal, 8(1):* 29

Faulkner A & Layzell S (2000) *Strategies for Living: A Report of User-led Research into People's Strategies for Living with Mental Distress.* London: The Mental Health Foundation

Faulkner A & Sayce L. (1997) Disclosure. Ponder the politics of 'coming out' as a user. *Open Mind, 85* (May/June)

The Inch Worm, lyrics by Kenny Loggins © FRANK MUSIC CORP; © 1951, 1952 (renewed). FRANK MUSIC CORP. All rights reserved

Lindow V (2001) Survival research. In C Newnes, G Holmes & C Dunn, *This is Madness Too.* London: PCCS Books

Nicholls V (2001) *Doing Research Ourselves.* London: The Mental Health Foundation

Nicholls V, Wright S, Waters R & Wells S. (2003) *Surviving User-led Research: Reflections on Supporting User-led Research Projects.* London: Mental Health Foundation

An unfathomable well of emotion
I find within
Silent soliloquies I shed
Drowning in infinite sorrow
That only the solitary magpie knows and understands.
Clear milky droplets
A discharge of hurt and misery
Collect and coagulate
Then slowly trickle down
My battered and bewildered cheeks
Ever increasing
Burning the windows of my soul
A scorched earth policy
Stripping me of my dignity
My very humanity.
The torrents overwhelm me
Sadness overtakes my limp, dishevelled frame
Pockets of pain and torment
Reappear on the surface
Manifested in deep despair.
Tiny encapsulated messages
Of unknown sentiments of happiness and joy;
Of even being glad to be alive
Or certainly wanting to be dead
A discreet form of communication
That says so much
Yet is seldom heard or listened to
Secrets shared and divulged
Soon overtaken by feelings
Of shame and disgrace
To be replaced by hatred of my entire being.
The tears I cry
A soothing and calming secretion
A process necessary
To replenish and cleanse mind, body and spirit
The tears I cry.

Mariyam Maule, 'The Tears I Cry'

5

Coping Strategies and Fighting Stigma

Joy Pope

A woman is sent home from work with a feverish cold. She phones her partner and mother to arrange childcare. She looks out tissues and paracetamol. Pouring herself a jug of water, she collapses thankfully into bed and lets herself sleep.

By coincidence, a few months later, the same woman is sent home again, this time because she is so anxious and low in mood that it is affecting her work. She leaves in a daze, and when she reaches the house she simply stares into space for many days, too guilty to admit she cannot meet the needs and expectations of family and friends, let alone her own. Finally she speaks, but is given conflicting advice, leaving her trapped and unable to move. She feels as if in the fog and smog of the following:

Fog	**Smog**
smog	fog
polluted	distorting
foul	distracting
making all that is in it	the traveller from
and all who walk in it the	all roads and ways
same.	ahead.
Fog	**Smog**
smog	fog
blindfolding	darkening
confusing	filtering out
lest paths become clear	sun's light and warmth
and decisions a	and the hope of a journey's
possibility.	end.

Voices of Experience: Narratives of Mental Health Survivors   Edited by Thurstine Basset and Theo Stickley ©2010 John Wiley & Sons, Ltd.

Fog
smog
heavy
dense
growing more so
into the
night.

The woman's story is no one's story, and yet it is one that I have witnessed over and again in my professional life as a general practitioner, and one to which I can relate from my own journey with and through depression. We have ideas for how to help ourselves through physical illness, particularly acute infections, but may have little concept of how to do the same when facing deep personal pain, apart from the belief that we should 'pull ourselves together'. Add in stigma and differing advice from colleagues, managers, family and friends, and we have a recipe for deteriorating health and long-term illness.

But, and it is a big but, we are discussing the human race, and people have a tremendous resilience in most situations. Eventually, the fictitious woman above will find things to take her through the most difficult of times, despite her fear and belief that such a way does not exist. Finding her own path is a major part of recovery.

It is a strange fact that in recurrent depression people may forget the thoughts and activities that helped in a gently positive way in previous episodes. I certainly found this and began to develop a simple list. Joining the Doctors' Support Network (www.dsn.org.uk), a support group for doctors with mental health problems, led me to a much broader range of ideas, which someone suggested we publish. *Doctors as Patients* (Jones, 2005) still proves helpful for doctors. My chapter in that book ('Ideas for the Dark Days') was written with doctors in mind. However, much of it is relevant to people from all walks of life and I found myself using suggestions not only for myself, but also for my patients.

Soon it became obvious how important it is for people to make their own lists. For example, mine includes doing jigsaws. Many will not find this appealing, and my suggesting it will be of limited use. Ultimately, the goal is for each to find their own way through the fog – or snowstorm.

They came gently at first,
three snowflakes floating on a light breeze.
Dusted off
the journey continued as before.

The next valley carried the wind
As on the through train from the North Pole.
Skies scowled at the intrusion
then covered their faces
as the blizzard began.

Determination took the traveller over.
Rucksack opened,
contents used with good effect,
resources to maintain the ever-slowing journey,
used until
Gone.

Only the mobile phone remained.
Help requested, much advice given -
'Stop', 'Don't stop',
'Find shelter', 'Don't give in',
'Keep going, walk on as if the snow's not there.'

Not there?
An increasing and numb exhaustion
warned the storm might not be the first to die.
The rescue party could not come too soon.

Unsure now if nightmare or reality
three possibilities floated
around the mind.
Return home,
find a snow plough,
or fly South with the swallows for Winter.

'Snowstorm'

It was not until I was writing this chapter that I remembered this poem, and realised that the traveller did not ask for help until a long way into her troubles. Contrary to popular belief, this is very typical and people may struggle for a long time before asking friends, family or professionals for help. The rucksack full of ways to cope in difficult times is one we all carry, although for all manner of reasons some are much better equipped than others. When a request for help is made it is usually because the rucksack seems empty. However, there is then the risk of receiving so much opposing advice that the person remains stuck – I was given all the advice of the fourth verse above. This emphasises the need for people to find their own individual ways through the storm.

This chapter is about people who are distressed, particularly from anxiety and/ or depression, and also about finding that way to get through each day and the whole episode. All the ideas mentioned came from real people struggling with real issues and/or illness. None came from professionals, although I am aware that therapists and others use some, maybe all, of them. They are certainly not put forward as a replacement for therapy or medication if either is needed, but they form a demonstration that those with distress or mental health problems can retain qualities needed to help themselves, at least to a degree. They are grouped according to the point in the journey where someone might first find each suggestion helpful.

Early on – Using Our Senses to Bring Comfort

There are many books and television programmes that remind us how our environment can affect our mood. However, people under stress may often find that things that are big, bold or very intense can be hard to cope with. Reducing to a simple level may give some comfort. Consciously thinking of the five senses can help people find ideas which will help them, especially on those days when other activities are curtailed by low mood and limited energy.

Starting with the sense of sight, someone who loves to go to local beauty spots may suddenly find that it is all too much, too beautiful, and this may be accompanied by the feeling that s/he is not worthy to enjoy it. This unexpected reaction is itself distressing and there is a sense of loss and disappointment to add to the original low mood. But there are still ways to appreciate visible beauty in a gentle way. The person in the example may find s/he can cope with watching nature programmes or DVDs instead, or sit and gaze at just one flower.

Other things to look at include candles, favourite posters, old holiday albums or photos of those who are supportive. The last can be helpful popped in the pocket or purse to bring out when feeling anxious and unsupported. The dark of winter is depressing for many. The full use of lights in the house as well as a light box may help, as does avoiding dark situations such as eating by candlelight, beautiful though such settings may be.

The sense of hearing speaks at once of music. It can have a powerful effect on our mood, a fact that most teenagers know instinctively! People with depression have often told me that their families tell them not to play 'such sad music'. It may be sad to the more upbeat listener, but if it matches the person's mood it can make someone feel heard, understood and comforted. It would be sensible to avoid anything that seems darker than that, but ending with something gently more positive can work well at a time when really cheerful music seems so alien that it drags the person down. Comfort from listening is not limited to composed music. Birdsong, including the dawn chorus after a sleepless night, the sound of the wind, waves or running water are all caressing, soothing sounds. For those living away from the coast and countryside, they are available on CDs, the internet, or even via a small indoor water feature.

Using the sense of smell brings thoughts of a long soak in a bubble bath, of perfume or of scented soap. I keep some fragrant hand cream and room spray at work for use after difficult consultations to clear the air – or just because I want to. All of these for the right person are much loved and used comforts. But there are many other aromas, such as fresh coffee, new-mown grass, the earth after rain, flowers or new bread.

Savouring food can be difficult for those whose appetite is lost and also for those who comfort eat during difficult times. Reasonably priced, ready-prepared vegetables are now available and can be very helpful in maintaining a healthy diet when motivation is low. The wide choice of ready meals in supermarkets may help for a short while, though the amount of fat or salt that most contain is rather alarming for long-term use.

Pets that can be hugged or stroked invite the use of touch, even for people whose past experience has limited their receptiveness to touch from humans, and animals give that wonderful side-effect of unconditional love. A self-given foot or hand massage can be a start to experiencing good touch for others. A favourite old jumper can be comforting in cooler months, as can a pair of cosy slippers. A soft throw over a chair feels good and gives a sense of security when wrapped around tightly. And I know I am not the only one to find furry toys essential!

All of these senses can be used to pass time and enhance the day, but it takes practice to remind oneself that the softness of the blanket or the smell of the food is there to be savoured. Deliberately working through the list of senses allows someone to work out what they might find comforting even on the most difficult of days. Eventually they can come to be enjoyed.

There is one other 'sense', which needs mentioning. Humour is a great gift, but can induce panic. There is a common fear among people with mental health problems that they are fakes underneath, 'non-copers' who could snap out of their mood if they tried. That they can laugh at a joke and have suicidal thoughts a few minutes later seems incredible to them and their family and friends, but it happens. Laughter often comes harder the more unwell someone is, but watching a comedy programme or reading a funny book may bring a brief holiday to a troubled mind.

Activities to Move on with – Hobbies and Creativity Kept Simple

I often ask people in my surgery about the hobbies they use against the normal stresses and strains of life. A common response is 'gardening'. If the person is currently distressed from major stress or depression, then this may be followed by 'But I just cannot do it at the minute because …'. Tiredness, a feeling of the task being too great or overwhelming, may all combine to keep someone from what they normally enjoy. This is where some lateral thinking needs to come in, enabling the person to find something related which is simple, small and doable at that time. It may be looking after just a small area of their garden. Another person might buy a hanging basket and nurture that, plant a few bulbs in a planter in autumn or purchase a small indoor pot plant to watch it grow. More possibilities are to forget one's own garden and walk around the block looking at everyone else's. It partly depends on what it is that the person gets out of their hobby. So, with the example of gardening, s/he can consider whether it is the cultivation with hands in the earth, watching new life appear or simply the end result that satisfies. What will work for one may not for another, but finding a way of keeping in touch with the things one normally enjoys gives a small thing to do each day and provides a springboard to expand into fuller activity in the future.

So serious crosswords may be left behind for a while for simpler puzzles; normal reading let go for familiar children's books where concentration is no longer required; craft-making and other artistic skills become children's colouring books (also good for sleepless nights!), and so on. Social hobbies may be more difficult if being with groups of people feels threatening, but people-watching in a reasonably quiet shopping centre or a shared coffee with one other person can be a start. Working with all the possibilities means that choices become possible once more.

However, some people do not find this approach helpful. They feel they have lost so much and at the moment cannot see that they can ever recover, so a 'tamer' version of their favourite hobby simply reminds them of their loss. They may find that something totally different is possible and can lead to change. Creativity may be new to workaholics and others who have never had hobbies before, but the things people can do seem limitless! Writing, crafts, sculpting, art, poetry, a new language, music-making, not to mention sport and a whole variety of collecting hobbies represent a tiny fragment of these possibilities. Once a new activity has been established there may be classes available at a local college, or groups which meet nearby. There are often adverts in a local library. Starting slowly, however, is again the key to making a success of a new activity at this time.

For Completing 'Must-Do' Tasks – Aim Small, Hit Large

Things that comfort and those that start to move people forward are good, but the basic activities of life still need completion and that can present a problem for someone who is struggling. Keeping appointments, completing forms, even having a wash can seem overwhelming and impossible, yet the distressed will often berate themselves each day that the task is not done. I remember being like that over some bills which needed paying. Finally, I did one. I expected to get at least momentary elation from completing it, but was disappointed. The amount of energy used seemed totally disproportionate to the size of task, which made the others grow in size in my mind. I gave up. But then I walked past the bag which contained my cheque-book and I realised I could at least pick it up and put it in the same room as the bills. I had no idea until then how many tiny steps are involved in paying a bill, but over the next two days I put a pen with the bill and cheque-book, added an envelope, added a stamp, wrote the cheque, wrote the envelope … and so on. Each element was done in the knowledge that that was the only thing I had to do at that moment in time and was achievable at that moment. This quelled panic and made it relatively simple. That feeling of elation finally came, not only because I had achieved my goal, but also because of the discovery that here was a way of making tasks non-threatening. The result could have been predicted – a third cheque was written in far less time. By aiming at small enough goals I had definitely 'hit large'.

For some tasks there is not the time to break things down over such a long period of time, but there may be ways to help make life easier. The difficulty of getting going in the mornings felt by so many with depression can be helped by eliminating morning choices so that clothes are chosen and put ready the night before. A few alarm clocks around the bedroom going off at different times can help get someone out of bed. More difficult tasks can be deliberately done at the best time of day, although I think it is important to use some of that time for the comforting and creative/enjoyable things in life as well.

For other tasks things can be spaced out over a much longer period. So the toilet and kitchen sink are kept spotless and the rest of the house left while the new routine becomes the norm. Then a small area in one room is made pleasant for one person to sit in, with space, of course, for a mug and a soft blanket. Further progress is easier once a start is made, provided small enough steps are taken.

Tidying the whole house, a common problem when emerging from depression, requires the task to be broken down again. One room is enough at a time. There are many suggested ways, particularly for the sitting room, such as putting one or two items away every day, or asking all members of the family to remove their belongings from that room NOW. My favourite is to use two boxes. Into one go things that simply need putting away or filing, with no action or decisions first. That goes into the hall and I try to put one item away every now and then during the day. The other box will have things that need some sort of non-urgent action or decision-making about them and one can be tackled every day or so. That leaves furnishings, which stay in that room, and a very small pile of those items or papers that need urgent decision or action.

Some people become very withdrawn when mentally ill or distressed and may retreat to bed. They may try to force themselves to do one activity each day, but if it seems too great, then the result can be a negative experience. Aiming to just wash one's face may be enough to do each day for some, and each time it is done it gives a tiny sense of success, and, as with all the other ideas suggested, can lead on to greater change.

Starting to Emerge – Starting Again

> Delicately strong,
> their bells of greening whiteness
> call a reveille to a sleeping Spring
> while joyfully tolling the demise of Winter.
>
> Their welcome work done
> they, too, will slowly die.
> Why should I mourn?
> There will be lilies at Easter.

> 'Snowdrops'

It was a great relief to discover that I was not the only one to find emerging from a low patch almost as bad as the patch itself. There is thankfulness for a little light returning, that things are not as bleak, but motivation and energy remain poor and do not match the things one begins to realise need doing. In addition, the small things that have comforted and helped in the worst of times may no longer appeal. For example, I rarely do a jigsaw except when on holiday. Yet, as mentioned, jigsaws are on my list of things to do when unwell. As soon as my mood picks up then, like the snowdrop, my desire to do them dies. There is a strange grieving for activities left behind which can occur at this point – something I have noted in others as well. The whole set of ideas above has to be revisited, possibly a few times during the person's whole journey, until the 'Easter lilies' are found which need to remain for our ongoing health.

Getting Back to Normal – Facing up to the Future

Back to work? Take your bag!

The prospect of return to work takes up a lot of time and discussion in GP surgeries and occupational health clinics. Return too soon and the person risks not coping and feeling such a failure that it takes even longer to be properly ready. Leaving it too late, however, also seems to reduce the chance of success. If part of the cause of the original distress was work-related, then those issues need facing first, ideally via Occupational Health, Human Resources or at least the line manager, and possibly the trade union.

The person at their readiest for work still has many things to face and most find the prospect scary, even though they want to return. It can be hard to remember that the people and things that have been supportive so far are still there. Once I realised this, I devised in my mind a bag full of those little things that had made me feel better while absent. There was a photo or two, a bunch of flowers I had been given along with some cards, a family dog, and so on. I decided that, after each patient I saw that first day back, I would make myself look in my hypothetical bag and remind myself of one of the items in it. Doctors' bags are traditionally black, but as yellow is my favourite colour, I decided that is what it would be. The 'yellow bag' idea took off well among members of the Doctors' Support Network, though I hope the resultant carriers ended up in an array of colours!

Other ideas are similar but more concrete – something in the pocket or handbag which is a reminder of one's support structure, a photo, a tiny soft toy or other object which is a reminder of someone, or even wearing teddy-bear socks can help. These ideas can also be used for appointments or other scary times.

Facing bullies, facing stigma

The world of physical pain is little understood by many, but the world of emotional and mental pain generally fares far, far worse. There is the apparent belief that if you do not talk about it, then you cannot be feeling it, but if you do discuss it, then you must be attention-seeking. There is the theory that since everyone has bad days, which we grit our teeth to get through, then the person with the most severe problems should be able to do the same. These two beliefs, together with fear and a host of other factors, easily lead to a culture of stigma and bullying. Regretably, the National Health Service is by no means exempt, especially where the 'us and them' attitude between clinical staff and their patients has led to extremes. Thus some doctors and their families have been told by NHS professionals that their careers were over simply because they were depressed, even though most, thankfully, make a successful return to work. I am grateful that my own partners and fellow professionals have been incredibly supportive. They have challenged me at times, but always in a supportive way – the two are not incompatible. Things have moved forward over the years, but there are still too many stories of stigma and frank bullying from within my own profession. We must practise what we preach before we can expect others to do the same. Meanwhile, there are line managers to discuss with and trade unions to advise. If there is no union, then it is important for someone to take a trusted friend to official meetings, even if s/he has to wait outside.

One of the most difficult things to decide is how much to tell other people about our diagnosis. Telling those colleagues who do not need to know is scary, but not telling them can lead to difficulties. The pressure gets harder when we realise that it is in telling people that we ourselves can help break down stigma. It seems that it is the more vulnerable who have to take this task on. However, this can only be done when a person feels ready and willing. For some people simply telling family or friends is one ordeal too far, and no one should be placed under any obligation to tell all, although any negative consequences of not telling will have to be carried and should be thought out beforehand.

Facing dips, finding meaning

I grew.
For a summer
I grew,
watered by the melts of Winter's snows
nourished by the decay of last year's Fall.

So as I wait for the renewal of another Spring
I will accept the little losses of Autumn,

the chilling wind
the shortening day
and leaves falling like tears.

'Tree in Autumn'

The path out of depression or other distress is rarely straightforward and dips are discouraging. It helps to find some form of meaning in them. Discovering that the last one brought a wealth of insights cannot make the depths of a severe depression worthwhile and I stress that is not my point. However, a form of meaning can help someone start their helpful strategies a little earlier. Other meanings come from realising that one has become a better friend or met a significant soul-mate or discovered a new hobby or skill.

Special times, special planning

There are times when we know in advance that things may be difficult. Certain anniversaries and the first Christmas after a bereavement are classics, but advance planning helps. There may be reasons in the person's past to make them dread Christmas, but in any case the extreme busyness and expectations of Christmas can make it a nightmare for those with mental health issues. Keeping goals realistic is a huge step and sharing practical tips with friends can kick-start someone's imagination. Encouraging any children to dress the tree or do the decorations often goes down well with the young people even if the end result is less than perfect. Presents are a nightmare. The person could decide to buy them all in one internet department store, or use tokens, give money or use charitable giving, at least for adult gifts.

School holidays may be difficult for a parent, as a doctor's certificate is no excuse from childcare! Meeting with other parents to go out together and so share responsibility helps and gives some company if wanted. Looking out for holiday clubs can pay dividends. They may be advertised in school, library or local clinic.

Staying well, using analogies in difficult situations

Finally, the person feels well. The return to work, if available, has gone smoothly, therapy and medication may be complete and relapse-prevention plans formed and put in action. But there may still be some lingering issues to face, some ways of approaching life that leap up and threaten the balance, and the counsellor may not be there any longer. Looking out for 'analogies' is not easy for everyone, but for those who can do so it can be a very valuable way at looking objectively at life. Here are just two on the subject of selfishness:

- *Should I love myself or not? Isn't this selfish?* This is a common issue to get tied in knots over. One way round it is to think of a mother and child. No loving mother wants her child to grow up to be selfish; this is not part of the agenda for love. Instead, she nurtures him/her, teaches him/her to care for herself – and also have compassion for others. Loving ourselves does not mean sitting around drinking coffee all day, although it may result in that occasionally.
- *Should I let others walk all over me? Isn't that what is meant by being unselfish?* This is where I like the analogy of the doormat and the red carpet. A doormat collects another's dirt but does nothing else for the person who walks on it, who does not learn to shake their feet before entering the house. It is permanently at the door apart from when it is being shaken or beaten to get rid of the excess it has collected. In contrast, a red carpet is only laid down for special occasions. It makes the person walking on it feel important, gets them across a rough patch following which it is carefully cleaned and rolled up ready for next time. So we may do things to cover up for others daily but it makes no difference to them. But if, instead of using our energy in that way, it is saved for the emergencies of life – a sudden illness, accident or other out of the ordinary trauma – then the person feels special and is enabled to get better or grow so they can look after themselves another time. And they learn to clean their own dirty feet.

These 'analogies' are stories of the imagination and there are so many to be had in life. The natural world provides many and often it is in the making of them that answers are found or we realise what it is we really think at a time when normal logic seems to evade us.

The overall theme of this chapter has been that people in times of stress, distress or in the throes of mental disorders have the same gifts of resourcefulness as the rest of society, although their capacity to start themselves off may be reduced. The ideas quoted have all come from people with mental health problems and there are many more, which have not been mentioned. Those of us who have dealings with people going through difficult times, whether professionally or as one human being to another, may or may not also find new thoughts here. Direct suggestions may help, but equally may not appeal to the person struggling, whereas using more general ideas which enable the person to find their own comfort and way forward can be the most rewarding of all.

References

Doctors' Support Network at www.dsn.org.uk

Jones P. (Ed.) (2005) *Doctors as Patients*. Oxford: Radcliffe Publishing

Day by day
We have a cross to bear
Can it be seen?
Not by others
A glimpse can be seen
By those close to us
But because it's hard to see
Some people blame
Do not care
Do not sympathise
Or try to understand
but we have to be brave
And when we can
Understand the sufferings of others
Who also have a cross to bear

Libby Jackson, 'Day by Day'

6

Living with the Dragon:
The Long Road to
Self-Management of Bipolar II

Peter Amsel

After living with an affective disorder for over 25 years one might assume that I would be living a symptom-free, healthy and 'fully functioning' life. Given the fact that I am a reasonably successful composer of contemporary classical music and that I am presently writing a book about living with mental illness, the story is not all that it appears. While I am able to project a veneer of normalcy to many, people do not see the full story of what I am experiencing: they do not know how much pain I am in all the time, nor do they have any idea about the anxiety that grips me when I am away from home; they are unaware of the savagely swirling emotions that threaten to rise to the surface without warning. Most of all, people do not understand that I am living with a dragon: a beast that seeks to devour me at every opportunity, seeking to destroy my spirit by taking away the things that are important to me through the manifestations of this pernicious affective disorder. Those things are my ability to be creative, the ability to create a sculpture with sound or paint a picture with words; these are my passions, my reasons for living. While I am still currently in treatment for the management of bipolar disorder, it has not been possible to eradicate all of the symptoms that I experience at any given time, nor has it been possible to fully control those symptoms. If it were possible, I could well find myself in a situation where I was rendered unable to compose or write at all due to the close link between creativity and this often malicious disease. This situation has been explored in much greater detail by many writers exploring the relationship between the disease and creativity, including a chapter in the seminal work on the illness, *Manic Depression*, by Goodwin and Jamison (2007) and a chapter written for the book *Learning About Mental Health Practice* (Amsel, 2008) which also explored the challenges of treating creative individuals.

When it was first suggested by my family doctor that I might benefit from taking an antidepressant, my reaction was to stare at her in disbelief: I sat in her

Voices of Experience: Narratives of Mental Health Survivors   Edited by Thurstine Basset and Theo Stickley ©2010 John Wiley & Sons, Ltd.

office feeling stunned and scared, completely unsure of what my future held. An antidepressant spelled out only one possible thing: *mental illness*. Surely my doctor had not suggested that I had a mental illness, I thought to myself, how can this be happening to me? At the same time I was struck by the thought that if I denied my doctor's suggestion of treatment, I might never find a solution to the problems that had been plaguing me for so long. It was this inner voice that drove me to look at the evidence confronting me with the blackness that had descended on my life like a dark storm that would not dissipate. Yes, it was true, I thought to myself, as my doctor read the conflicted emotions on my face and tried to comfort me. My life had been led down a path of darkness by something that I did not understand beyond the periphery; beyond the engulfing darkness of its seething hunger, my own life was being consumed and robbed of the few things that had not only given me joy but had provided me with my identity. If I only knew one thing about depression at that moment it was that it could kill: if not physically, then spiritually. The truth was, it was in the process of killing me and if something was not done to stop that from happening it was only going to be a matter of time before the disease won the day and the job was completed.

My reasons for going to see my doctor had not been trivial in any respect: I was truly in desperate shape. Aside from being unable to sleep for more than a few fitful hours at a time, I was experiencing extreme, debilitating migraines, and I was in the midst of a creative block the likes of which I had never known before: I had not been able to write a thing or compose a note for several months. In truth, it was this block in my creativity that I found to be more disturbing than anything else, even more than how I was physically feeling. When everything finally became too much for me to bear, when I could not stand another day without being the creative individual that I had been born to be, I was ultimately led to seek the help of my doctor. It must be understood that being unable to express myself creatively in the ways that had become so important to me had begun to make the thought of living unbearable. For as long as I could remember there had been music playing in my mind, not what you would think of in a bad sense or songs that I had heard on the radio, but rather the music that I was composing and would eventually work on, the music that would ultimately become the foundation for each of the pieces that I had worked on over the past 20 years. This 'soundtrack' was now gone and with it my desire even to *listen* to music; the prospect of living without my music was something that I had difficulty even imagining, it was a life that I simply did not want to live. How could I continue to call myself a composer if I could not *compose* or even *listen* to music? How could I be a writer that *could not write*? These were questions that pained and tortured me as I tried, for naught, to rekindle the creative flames that I was certain were still buried somewhere inside, just waiting for the right time for it to once again be revealed.

Patience is often a difficult virtue for someone to maintain when dealing with healthcare practitioners who give the impression that your care is not the most important thing in the world, an impression that can be gained when the process of diagnosis seems to take longer than it should; an impression that often arises out of legitimate frustrations, but can also be based on a purely subjective assessment. It is difficult to imagine how much I can appreciate the complexity involved in the process of untying the knot of pathologies involved in what I was experiencing considering the symptoms that I presented: a doctor, after all, can only work with what they are given. While an initial diagnosis of major depressive disorder, otherwise known as 'clinical depression', began my path towards a correct diagnosis, it also began a period of intense inner battles as my moods vacillated even more rapidly than before and the migraines that I was experiencing became almost paralysing in their intensity.

What I could not have known at the time was that my doctor had only diagnosed half of my problem. After taking the antidepressants that had been prescribed for about a year it was decided that my progress on the medication was not what it should be, and my headaches were posing issues that needed another medical perspective, so I was referred to both a neurologist and a psychiatrist. When I saw the psychiatrist – a psychopharmacologist – I was told that my problem was not depression. 'You do not have clinical depression,' he told me, which I could not believe, especially since I was still struggling with some very difficult, very dark episodes. 'If I am not depressed,' I countered, 'how come I want to jump off of my balcony?' This was delivered with a laugh and a smile in order to make sure that my 'threat' of self-harm would not be taken too seriously. It was not, but it managed to elicit an answer that I had not expected: 'No, no,' he said quickly, 'you *have* depression, just not *clinical* depression. You have *bipolar affective disorder*,' he paused and then quickly added, '*type II*'.

Bipolar disorder, type II, whatever that meant; I knew that it was also known as 'manic depression', something that I had seen in all its 'glory' while in university when a flute player experienced a full-blown manic episode and ended up hospitalised for several months. I knew what this meant: I really *was* crazy. Having spent a year reading about depression and its related conditions, I had thought that I actually knew something about what I had been experiencing, but I was wrong. After we had spoken for a while the psychiatrist put it perfectly when he said, 'You possess a great deal of knowledge but not very much insight about the illness.' Nothing could have inspired me more, nothing could have driven me to become better informed, more insightful regarding the nature of what I was experiencing, than the words of that psychiatrist. After all, who could become a better expert about my own mind and body than me? Understanding the nature of an illness was one thing, understanding its manifestation in *my* body and mind, on the other hand, was something that I could relate to better than any textbook. It was then that I decided that I might in fact be crazy, but I most certainly was *not* insane. Doctors may know about the mental illnesses, but precious few of them know what it *feels* like to experience the various aspects of those illnesses.

With the loss of my ability to create came the feeling that I had lost a great part of who I was as a person; I had lost my *identity* as an individual by not having what had always been perceived of as a 'gift': the music that had been my constant companion since before I began taking guitar lessons when I was a child. Consider how devastating it was for one of the greatest composers of all time when he began to experience the gradual loss of his hearing, one of the most important of the five senses to a composer. Rather than retiring into a world of silence and aural darkness he still managed to compose, even after he was totally deaf. When Ludwig van Beethoven was completely deaf he was still able to compose some of his most celebrated works for the simple reason that he was still capable of 'hearing' his music *internally*, using his gifts and knowledge as a composer to 'imagine' the sounds that he wanted to create with his pen. To lose this ability, as well as the ability to hear, would have been an overwhelming blow to a man who had already experienced an extraordinarily difficult life. Given that Beethoven contemplated suicide out of the frustrations from losing his hearing and the subsequent depression that this triggered, while still maintaining his ability to compose, it is not difficult to imagine that the loss of this facility would likely have pushed him towards a more effectively conceived plan to end his life: such is the importance of this gift.

As Beethoven struggled with the loss of his hearing he grappled with the difficulties that the handicap caused: he withdrew from society and became reclusive, his demeanour changed and he developed the now famous reputation for being an irascible, grouchy character when he still wanted to remain part of his beloved Viennese society. In 1802 Beethoven recorded his thoughts on these ideas in what has become known as the 'Heiligenstadt Testament', a letter addressed to his brothers, which was found in his room after his death in 1827. For those interested in the mind of the man behind the music the 'Testament' is a document of rare importance, providing firsthand insight into the feelings of a composer as he came to the heights of his creative power. Shortly after writing this letter he composed some of his greatest compositions, including the Symphony No. III in E-flat major, the *Eroica*, as well as the Piano Concerto No. III, in C minor. Within the next few years Beethoven would compose, arguably, some of the most beautiful – and most important – music of his time and of all time. All this from a man that had been so depressed from his ordeal he could not stand to live.

When I first read what Beethoven had written I did not relate to the words in the same way as when I was struck by the darkness of depression and found that I could not compose. Then the words that he wrote spoke clearly of his agony, an agony that I now shared in a different way. After I lost my ability to compose I had often been asked 'what are you composing?' by friends, and I found myself responding with lies and half-truths, out of shame. I could not admit that I was experiencing 'composer's block'. It became easier to avoid people rather than having to answer embarrassing questions. As Beethoven himself wrote:

> Ah, how could I possibly admit an infirmity in the one sense which ought to be more perfect in me than others, a sense which I once possessed in the highest perfection; a perfection such as few in my profession enjoy or ever have enjoyed.

Oh I cannot do it; therefore forgive me when you see me draw back when I would have gladly mingled with you. My misfortune is doubly painful to me because I am bound to be misunderstood; for me there can be no relaxation with my fellow men, no refined conversations, no mutual exchange of ideas. (Beethoven, 1802)

Was it enough of a loss to consider death? Would I end my life if I could no longer compose or write? It seemed like an overly dramatic response but, when you perceive your entire life as being related to the work that you do, it is difficult to suddenly recast the image of your life without the presence of those things that have, until the worsening of the illness, been of such importance.

Ultimately, it was faith that saved me: not merely spiritual faith, but the belief that my creativity would return and with it, my ability to do the things that made my life worth living. I knew that faith meant that you sometimes believed in things that could not necessarily be seen or proved to be true, but if I did not believe, how could I stand another day without my creativity? The choice was simple – I could either believe that I would be able to compose and write again, and that I would produce things that were beyond anything that I had done in the past, or I could give up and surrender to the illness. The choice was made: I have never surrendered. There were many pieces remaining to be composed, stories, poems and books to be written, and so much more I could not begin to make a list. Once I began to think of the music that remained to be written, when I stopped thinking of all that I had lost and began to focus on all that remained to be done, the inner soundtrack that had been gone for over a year returned, softly at first, but it was back: music was once again flowing from my pen.

Ah, it seemed to me impossible to leave the world until I had brought forth all that I felt was within me. So I endured this wretched existence – truly wretched for so susceptible a body, which can be thrown by a sudden change from the best condition to the very worst. – Patience, they say, is what I must now choose for my guide, and I have done so – I hope my determination will remain firm to endure until it pleases the inexorable Parcae [from Roman mythology; the fates] to break the thread. Perhaps I shall get better, perhaps not; I am ready. (Beethoven, 1802)

My Journey Had Truly Begun

Describing what it was like to live with bipolar disorder seemed to be difficult considering that the more I found out about the disease the more I realised that I had actually been living with it for many more years than I had initially believed. Unlike what I had seen as a university student, when I witnessed some of the classic symptoms of mania, bipolar disorder, type II can manifest itself in many subtle ways that often makes diagnosis very difficult. Episodes of depression, for example, are common elements to both types of bipolar disorder (American Psychiatric Association, 2000) which often leads to individuals being diagnosed with depression first, before receiving a more accurate diagnosis when other symptoms are brought to the attention of the doctor. One of the main difficulties in diagnosing bipolar disorder is that it is not always easy for the person experiencing the illness to recognise that something is wrong when they are not feeling depressed. Very few people are likely to go to their doctor with the complaint that they are 'too happy' or that they have 'too much energy', which are often characteristics of hypo-mania, or simply not being depressed.

While there are many clinical distinctions between the two types of bipolar disorder, with subtypes within the main types, the essence of the illnesses are quite straightforward: it is important to point out that the main difference between the two is that the condition of full-blown mania only manifests itself in bipolar, type I while people with bipolar, type II may experience what is known as hypo-mania. It should also be noted that individuals with bipolar, type I may also experience episodes of hypo-mania (American Psychiatric Association, 2000). In essence, hypo-mania is an episode that does not reach the heights or breadth of a manic episode, making it 'small' or 'less than' full-blown mania while it can also be similar in many ways, without being as dangerous, self-destructive or lengthy in duration.

If asked to describe the difference between mania and hypo-mania I often offer the following scenario: a person experiencing a manic episode may decide to run down the middle of the street naked, singing some Beatles songs at the top of his lungs. Someone experiencing an episode of hypo-mania, on the other hand, might look at the person experiencing mania and think to themselves, 'That looks like a *really good idea*'. The person experiencing hypo-mania might write about it, draw pictures of it, obsess about it and tell friends about how it looked like a really brilliant thing to do, but the likelihood of their going through with it would be extremely low. By the time a person experiencing hypo-mania gets around to doing something about it the episode may already have ended. While hypo-mania may sound similar to mania on the surface, there is a distinctly qualitative difference to the 'energy' that one experiences and what that energy is able to drive the afflicted individual into doing, as well as a quantitative difference. Manic episodes can last for over a week, and often longer, while true hypo-manic episodes last a minimum of four days (American Psychiatric Association, 2000). Mania is generally associated with behaviour that severely impairs one's ability to function in both a social and a professional environment. Another characteristic of manic episodes may be the presence of psychotic features and the need for hospitalisation. It must be remembered that this is an illness which has, when left untreated, led to the death of individuals as a result of exhaustion.

The energy that I have occasionally experienced through an episode of hypo-mania, unlike the debilitating nature of a manic episode, was actually something that could be enjoyed on many occasions. Unfortunately, there are often other symptoms involved with my hypo-manic episodes that make it difficult to harness the potentiality of the creativity that is regularly associated with the energy of hypo-mania. Symptoms such as free-floating anxiety and feelings of angst seemed to be particularly fond of expressing themselves at the same time as the various hypo-manic episodes, as well as a general irritation that was either manifested as a short temper or simply extreme irritability. It turns out that it is extremely rare for me to experience an episode of 'pure' hypo-mania, far rarer than the episodes that began to make up what I began to call the *rollercoaster ride from hell*. The worst part about this ride is not so much the ride, but what awaits me at the end: each twist and turn ultimately leads me inevitably closer to the dark tunnel that signals the end of the ride and the open mouth of the most terrible giant dragon, waiting to devour me once the ride comes to a halt.

When living with bipolar affective disorder, especially the type II variant which has brought a whole new meaning to the term 'rapid cycling', you get a great appreciation of the proverb *what goes up must come down*. Life often seems to be defined by the ups and downs of an unseen, mad conductor, who is wildly beating out an oddly syncopated piece of music for an invisible orchestra that nobody can hear … except those few who have been granted the 'backstage pass' that comes with having this illness. Having these diverse mood swings takes on an entirely different meaning when you find yourself cycling through various mental and emotional states in rapid succession. When cycling becomes what is euphemistically called 'rapid cycling' – a term which hardly encompasses the turmoil that exists – where moods alternate between everything from depression, agitation, hypo-mania, anxiousness, and several combinations thereof – things take on an entirely different complexion. I have found this to be especially true when tracking my own mood swings or 'shifts' and discovered that there were often 17 or more episodes in a day, something that is not only psychologically exhausting, but physically exhausting as well, leaving me drained of both energy and a desire to do anything constructive. It often feels as though I am racing through the tunnel at the end of the rollercoaster ride towards a solid brick wall.

Hitting that wall translates into a frighteningly rapid plunge into a dark depressive episode, barely escaping the jaws of the dragon as it tries to snap off my head. These depressive episodes can sometimes last longer than others, often for days or even weeks at a time; but soon enough the cycling resumes and the rollercoaster ride begins all over again. Perhaps the oddest times for this illness takes place when I am in a depressed state and still experience rapid cycling; with moods ranging from deeply depressed to varying states of agitation it is impossible to predict how I am going to feel from one hour to the next, let alone one day to another. These cycles merely avoid the 'higher', or elevated affects associated with the illness.

This may be where you can find the one silver lining about having bipolar disorder, particularly the rapid-cycling variant: you can always be certain that an episode of depression will end at some point, usually of its own accord and without the need for any emergency interventions. Unfortunately, on the other side of the coin, there is the likelihood that there will be many more episodes of darkness than would be experienced by someone living with clinical depression and no other underlying affective disorder. However, this should not be seen to imply that there are measurable or somehow qualitative differences between the intensity and potential seriousness of the depressive episodes experienced by people suffering from either bipolar disorder or clinical depression. It is not practical, possible or ethical to compare the seriousness of one's personal suffering with an illness such as depression based solely on something as transient as the duration of the illness or the number of episodes an individual has experienced during their life. Ultimately, the relative comparison of suffering that one may experience to that of another is both entirely impossible and meaningless on the grounds of the experiential subjective relationship between each individual and the manifestation of their illness.

While one person may find that certain symptoms are virtually impossible to live with, these same symptoms may not be as bothersome for someone else living with the same medical condition; the experiences are purely personal, with one caveat: while these comparisons become purely subjective and, as such, meaningless, they do provide the opportunity for individuals living with similar illnesses to be able to relate to each other under the umbrella of common suffering. People find it easier to relate to someone who has experienced a similar ordeal even if the path to where they presently are is not the same one as that taken by the other person; it is somewhat like comparing scars and boasting about how many stitches it took to sew up one's flesh. If a scar is covering a laparoscopic procedure it could be hiding something much more serious than the scar across a knee that came about from falling down a hill. Both are scars, but they have entirely different stories and, subsequently, totally different meanings. The result, however, is still a scar, and that will allow for common ground to exist, a point from which sharing can begin and where healing can begin. People who realise they are not alone are less apt to feel the desolation that can come with the diagnosis of a mental illness; feeling as though you are the only person in the world going through what you are experiencing. Being alone against the world is not a place you ever want to be, believe me, I have been there and it is a very scary place.

Having spent nearly a year studying depression I was now totally unprepared to start again on the journey towards understanding what I was now facing, or at least, I thought I was; once I began studying bipolar disorder I began to realise that it really was – in essence – depression *plus* the extra components of the illness. Of course, it was those 'extra' parts that had been making my life so interesting for the past few decades, and even more so over the past year since I had been taking the antidepressant prescribed by my doctor. As someone who experiences rapid cycling, the antidepressant that I had been prescribed before the final diagnosis was made could well have worked against my condition. The medication came from the SSRI (selective serotonin reuptake inhibitor) class of medications and seemed to cause me to cycle even more rapidly than I had been before seeking help. After seeing the psychiatrist a different SSRI was recommended, along with some mood stabilisers.

Before Things Get Better They Sometimes Get Worse

Very few things can make you feel as helpless, or as desperate for help, than when you are embarking on a new treatment protocol for an affective disorder and you happen to be alone. My doctor had referred me to a psychiatrist at the Royal Ottawa Hospital with whom I was able to make an immediate connection, and he decided to change my medications for the simple reason that I was not having the desired effects (or affects) on them, and I was experiencing extreme insomnia. We discussed the proposition of my becoming an inpatient but, in the end, decided that it would be better for me to remain an outpatient. Part of this decision was based on the idea that I am, ostensibly, a 'high-functioning' individual for whom being an inpatient would be extremely difficult. Unfortunately, this also meant that at those times when I ended up needing support the most, in the middle of the night when I could not sleep and was alone, trying to outrun the snapping jaws of the dragon, I had nobody to talk to, nobody to get advice from or anything supportive … so, I read, I read almost anything and everything that I could find relating to bipolar affective disorder and what I was experiencing, including new studies that I was finding through medical journals on the internet.

Aside from seeing my new psychiatrist regularly in the hope that we would find a pharmaceutical cocktail that would help me the most, accompanied by the fewest side-effects, I became involved in the Psychiatric Rehabilitation programme available at the hospital at that time. This consisted of offering different groups which were designed to provide both psychiatric rehabilitation and education to those living with mental illnesses. The different groups focused on providing the necessary tools needed to prevent the relapse of serious episodes of illness and to recognise the most disturbing stressors in our environment that influenced our wellbeing, and which may exacerbate our illnesses. They also assisted in the planning and completion of goals, allowing us to achieve as much as we are willing to believe that we are capable of achieving. These groups proved to be extremely helpful for my recovery process, not to mention the many others who participated in them over the many years that they ran, long before I came into the programme. The groups offered by the Psych Rehab programme that I took included Goal-Setting, Symptom Self-management, Thoughts and Feelings, and Stress Management. Each group contributed its own set of tools which allowed members to become better prepared at dealing with our illnesses. While the programme was heralded by visiting members of the medical community for its effectiveness and it became a model for the treatment of mental illness, it was cancelled due to the hospital taking a 'new direction' in 'client care'. For those fortunate enough to have taken both the Goal-setting and Symptom Self-management groups, the tools acquired and the support received will be impossible to replicate, but they will still be able to use those tools for the rest of their lives. These were ongoing groups that allowed people to continue to work on their 'wellness', or 'recovery' goals, discussing their concerns with both the group members and the group facilitator.

Since my lack of sleep was an ongoing and important symptom for me I began to monitor how much sleep I had, leading me to discover that there were many nights where I slept as few as one or two hours, or less, if you include the occasional night where I did not sleep at all. The several weeks that I monitored at one point averaged between 11 and 15 hours' sleep over a seven-day period. When this was reported in the group the response was unanimous: 'How can you live like that?' This was a question that I had asked myself on more than one occasion, but I could not allow myself to listen to such questions for the simple reason that they drew on the sense of hope that I was clinging to for recovery. Losing hope can be very easy, especially when you experience a cyclical condition such as bipolar disorder, and that can become crippling. Hope can be lost over virtually anything, no matter how seemingly insignificant; had I allowed myself to enter that stream of hopelessness I may well have lost my battle with this illness altogether, especially with the negative feelings associated with not being able to sleep. This could very well have become an overwhelming burden, creating an avalanche of self-pity from which I may not have been able to recover.

If you do not think for an instant that learning about your enemy is one of the most important things you can do if you have any hopes of victory, believe me, it truly is, for knowledge is power. If you believe that living with a mental illness is anything less than a war for your mind, you need to reconsider the power of these diseases. These are illnesses that can drive the strongest individuals towards the unthinkable; people who would ordinarily never consider hurting themselves or anyone else can be driven by these diseases to commit acts of self-destruction that you would never have thought possible, including that one, final act of desperation that cannot be undone; an act that speaks of such anguish it can only be the result of the darkest side having claimed victory over yet another desperate soul. Many people find it difficult even to discuss suicide, thinking it a shameful thing, a dark secret, something that must be concealed from the prying eyes of the public, but it is a part of this illness, whether you like to admit it or not. Thinking about suicide, often referred to as 'suicidal ideation', is a very common symptom of bipolar disorder and is something I have frequently experienced. Thinking about something, however, does not necessitate acting on those thoughts. It is only when we give power to those thoughts that they gain control over our lives. Suicidal ideation does not have to lead to suicide.

The truth of the matter is that suicide will only lose the power that it holds over us when it is exposed to the light; it thrives on the darkness that is secrecy and shame, allowing people who have treatable illnesses to take their lives for the simple reason that they did not have someone they could talk to in their deepest moments of need. In many ways it can be said that society induces individuals to commit suicide, encouraging the pursuit of that which is unattainable by most through the idealised version of 'perfection' that is marketed to the world through what is generally identified as 'American' culture, and which is clearly seen through the representations in the popular media and the constant depiction of the 'good life', as reflected in the possession of money, fame and the power to influence others. Some people get so caught up in the very idea of this 'rat race' that they are unable to extricate themselves from it, even when that is something that they desperately desire. While we may think that this is a too simplistic dismissal of the myriad contributory factors to suicide today, it is difficult to deny that one of the main stressors on contemporary youth, and of those identified as being members of generations 'x' and 'y', are bombarded with cleverly crafted media marketing campaigns that deliver specific socioeconomic messages regarding what success is, and that anything else is, by inference, a failure.

The starkness of this truth, and its importance to my life, was something that was made more real to me than I ever wanted to know when there came a knock on my door three years ago. At the time I was living near a pizza shop and had become friendly with one of the cooks. It turned out that his girlfriend was the sister of a very dear friend of mine from high school whom I had not been in touch with for several years. On this cold December night the delivery boy from the pizza shop gave me a message from his boss: his girlfriend's sister was dead. After I called the restaurant her sister called me and told me the entire story; it made me want to curl up in a corner and die. She was one of the sweetest women you could ever hope to know, the type of person that could make you smile even if you were in a lousy mood; and through all of that she was living a life that left her feeling miserable. Unfortunately, it turned out that she and I had far more in common than I could have ever imagined when we first met in high school. Through the intervening years time had made us closer through pathologies if not distance. Like me she also had fibromyalgia and suffered from severe migraines; instead of bipolar disorder she lived with repeated bouts of major depressive disorder, or just plain old depression. She did not want to go back into the hospital, according to her sister, and had been in a great deal of physical and emotional pain. All she wanted was the pain to end, a sentiment that I can certainly relate to given the chronic pain that I find myself in from fibromyalgia. Without the type of medical support that I have received – including a family doctor who has been willing to help me control my pain – my friend decided that she had experienced enough and it was time for the pain, and everything else, to end.

I had never understood why some people called suicide a 'selfish' act until I was told that she was dead; it hurt so much to hear those words, it felt as though a part of me died that night – part of me wanted to die that night – but I knew that I had too much to do, too much to live for. Death was not – is not – an option.

While I say that death is not an option for me, for my friend – well, I cannot pretend to understand what she was experiencing; part of me was angry that she did not call, part of me was angry because I thought that she *should have known* that I would understand her problems, that I would be willing to listen. I then realised that I was being just as judgmental about her as those who condemn that act of suicide without looking at the people who are behind the word; the only difference was that I was couching my judgement in the things she 'should have done' rather than focusing on the obvious state of despair that she must have been in to have allowed herself to be overcome by something that she had been seemingly able to defeat in the past. Of course, people do not call if they do not want to be talked out of something, which leads me to believe that she *really* wanted to end her life. I could not help but imagine her small form being engulfed in the jaws of that sinister dragon, its mouth seemingly curled into a smile as it raised its head to allow the small but precious parcel of food to slide down its gullet.

As My Eyes Meet Those of the Dragon it Realises that I Am Going to Kill it and, for the First Time in My Life, it is Scared

With increased understanding of the nature of my illness came a new level of liberation that had previously not been possible. While it was important to take the information provided by the groups and put those tools into practice, it was equally important to combine what I learned there with what I had already learned from other sources, from books, articles and resources found online, and use them to become more than an ordinary 'patient'. In many ways I was fortunate in that the philosophy at the hospital promotes the idea of a 'partnership in care', as well as 'clients' working with their 'healthcare team', so it never even occurred to me that there was anything wrong with taking up the position of patient advocate for myself and others. Perhaps my background in teaching and my facility with communication opened the door for my decision to become so involved in my care, but it all seemed perfectly natural; the fact that I was encouraged by my psychiatrist certainly did not hurt.

While I had become an advocate for mental healthcare I was also becoming more involved in my own care. Rather than being a passive recipient of medical care, as I had been for many years, I was now able to take a more active role; much to my surprise I discovered that the members of my healthcare team were not only not opposed to my proactive approach to my health, they were enthusiastically supportive. Apparently, or so it would seem from the responses I received, doctors would rather have patients that take an active interest in their own care than those that rely on them to make all of the decisions. In the end, the final decision regarding medical care is going to be made by the doctor, but it is the right of the patient to be involved in that decision. The burden of making those decisions is not as difficult when the doctor is not struggling with a patient who is not being open with them. Developing this type of doctor–patient relationship is not something that can be created after only one or two sessions; it must be cultivated through open communication with the doctor, demonstrating that there is a genuine desire on your part to be an active participant in your care. The best way to accomplish this is through asking topical, relevant questions relating to your treatment and about what you could do to learn more about your illness. Doctors are usually more than willing to recommend something to read, and many are gifted teachers who welcome the opportunity to share their knowledge. It is important to understand that there is a distinct difference between being active in your care and merely asking your doctor for different or more drugs. More than anything, it is essential to demonstrate that you are interested in recovery: that may sound odd, but some patients are not ready to recover at the beginning of their illness; they are more interested in being sick than working at what is entailed in the recovery process.

There is a distinctly different healthcare paradigm involved in a true partnership rather than with the conventional healthcare model with which most individuals find themselves entrenched. Most partnership-based models have the benefit of featuring recovery as a central component of the treatment plans. Without approaching recovery as something more than a vague concept, the idea that one day the symptoms of illness may go away is not enforced through the interactions between the healthcare professionals and the client. In order to foster the idea of recovery we must first be ready to *work* on recovery. In the case of other illnesses, such as measles or pneumonia, the process of recovery is quite straightforward: once the illness has been diagnosed, medication is prescribed and, after a certain period of time, there is the expected recovery. Things do not work that way in the case of mental illnesses such as bipolar disorder. You must be an active component of your own recovery process, otherwise there is no chance that it will work.

On the surface it sounds as though I am saying, 'You've broken your leg, now hop on over to Urgent Care and get yourself a cast.' But that is not the case at all; it is simply that the recovery process for an affective disorder requires a personal investment from the individual that is seemingly not as essential a component when dealing with the other realms of medicine. Of course, we have all seen, or heard, of how someone who has a positive attitude will tend to recover faster than someone with a negative attitude. Is this a function of genetics at play or merely a response to the power of 'positive' energy? Perhaps it is more a response to the fact that when we make a connection between our minds and our desire to recover we connect with a greater power than is necessarily understandable at this point in contemporary science. It is certainly a concept that made itself known to Dr Frankl when he was imprisoned in a concentration camp during the Holocaust and saw people who had said they would die do so right before his eyes. Others said they would survive, and they did; testament to the power of the human spirit to survive when there is a *why* to continue (Frankl, 1959).

Therein lies the crux of the recovery process: why do you *want* to recover? If you can answer that question, you are on the *road* to recovery. It is simplicity itself, if you can understand the idea that your recovery is predicated on the idea that you must be actively involved in every aspect of your recovery, as though you were fighting the battle of your life; you will then have a better chance of succeeding than were you merely passively receiving treatment for the same condition. Remember, when battling affective disorders we are talking about the *mind*, not treating a back injury or a broken leg, but an illness that is influencing the way we *think* and *feel*. In order to be able to overcome these wretched illnesses we must first believe that it is *possible* to achieve some level of recovery, otherwise, why bother? If you do not believe the pills you are taking are going to help, why take them? If you think they are poison, why swallow them? If you want them to work, believe that they are working, even as they slide down your throat and begin to dissolve in your stomach.

When I look at what could be called my 'recovery process' I sometimes laugh; I still cycle, still get depressed, still get irritated … and sometimes I still feel downright awful. However, I am able to compose and write, and I am not thinking about killing myself, most of the time. If I do have a moment where those thoughts creep in I simply start thinking of all the work that remains and well, quite frankly, I have far too much to do to die; perhaps in 50 years or so.

Poetry has been a constant companion and source of solace for me during the darkest times. When I was unable to compose or write anything else, poetry remained, sometimes being the only thing that prevented me from losing all hope of recovering my ability to create anything of substance. Writing poetry has always paralleled the composing of music for me in that you are creating a composition of words and tones, painting a picture with words that must convey as much as possible with brevity and conciseness of expression. With that in mind, please read these poems aloud if possible, listen to the rhythm of the words, feel the language as it rolls from your tongue, and enjoy the experience of performing the works for yourself.

Angel

Long nights have I waited
conjuring the memory of your face
desperate for the image not to fade
relying on the fickle passions of memory
ravaged by the passage of time

I must confess: there have been times
not many, but … nevertheless
when I have tried to whisper your name
in the silence of the night
and there came no sound

There was simply no trace of you to be found
desiccated memories seemed more shadow than substance
no details could be seen ...
even your smile was obscured beyond recognition
dissolving into a cloud of sorrow and grief

Not all things are forgotten though, and those that are
I fight to reclaim, to remind myself
of who you are ...
of who you
were ...

What never fades from memory, alas,
is the night I was told
that cold winter's night
the night I was told
you had taken your life.

In memory of my dear friend, who will always be an Angel.

Trust Me

When you hear me say
'I know how you feel,'
trust me,
for it is the truth
you cannot imagine
the burden that comes
when you feel everything –
not only those things
having to do with my own life
but everything I look at,
everything I touch,
everything I hear –
it all becomes as real to me as though it were my own wounds
being inspected – opened for all to see.

Not a pretty sight, one might think,
but not my choice – how can I stop this
when I am powerless to change the way
I feel – enslaved by the seemingly
endless variety of moods that flow
like a stream flowing over the rapids

Can you begin to understand when there are times
that I am overwhelmed by emotion –

where everything is so acutely intense,
it is difficult to articulate anything
that doesn't end up sounding like a deranged babble.

Why would you believe me? Can you believe that
someone can feel the pain of others?
That somewhere, deep inside, there is a
power that comes from my pain —
my pain which has allowed me to
feel so much
for so many
to never question whether compassion was
the right thing to feel
to know that everyone can be
afflicted — there is no distinction between
rich and poor when it comes to
pain

Just remember, when I say I understand
how you feel
through the torments of your pain
no matter how you feel
trust me.

What have you to lose?

© 2007 by Peter Amsel

This photograph is an extreme close-up of a retaining wall near the Rideau Locks behind the Chateu Laurier in Ottawa, Canada. I find it reflects the idea of strength in imperfection, for even with the crack in the wall, the wall remains intact, capable of completing its job. It is something like the struggle that people with a mental illness face every day of their lives: people do not understand that we can make substantive contributions to society – that we can be bricks in the wall – even with our cracks and imperfections, and it will not cause the structure to crumble. There is great beauty in diversity.

Acknowledgements

There are many people who I would like to thank, but the first should be my long-suffering editor, Theo Stickley, for inviting me to be a part of this project in the first place. I must also thank my healthcare team, Drs Bamford, Miura and Surko, whom I used as sounding boards for concepts and questions in this chapter and who were always generous to a fault with their time and knowledge. I would be remiss if I did not thank my parents for providing a place for me to write without worrying about anything. The generosity of their spirits is made manifest on a daily basis. Finally, to Dr Seuss, TDC, the most incredible cat someone could ever hope to have adopted them as their human. Your companionship has inspired me and helped me through the darkest times, thank you.

References

American Psychiatric Association (2000) *Diagnostic and Statistical Manual of Mental Disorders*, fourth edition, text revision. Washington, DC: American Psychiatric Association

Amsel P (2008) Treating creatively: The challenge of treating the creative mind. In T Stickley & T Basset (Eds.) *Learning about Mental Health Practices*. Chichester: John Wiley & Sons

Beethoven, Ludwig van (1802) *Heiligenstadt Testament*. Heiligenstadt

Frankl V E (1959) *Man's Search for Meaning*. New York: Washington Square Press

Goodwin F K & Jamison K R (2007) *Manic Depressive Illness*, second edition. New York: Oxford University Press

Five long years spent in silent exile incarcerated, banished away
Societies exterior invisible
Locked up, hidden from the view of the world;
Incommunicado, freedom of speech,
Expression, negated, nullified, punitively pathologised.
Abused, persecuted for my beliefs
A prisoner of consciousness, ignored, where political objectives are
Superseded by the mainstream collective.
Rights, rationed at great expense
Privileges withdrawn at every opportunity
Manacled by a liquid provision
Cruelly rejected, injected
So infected by the overarching social malaise.
Depleted, defeated by an entangled web of deceit
Sinister motives administered by a coercive regime
Oppressive tools, cultured and reinforced.
Behaviour controlled, monitored hourly, modified conditioning
Dehumanised, nothing more than experimental cargo
Endurance tested to maximum extremes
Dreams stolen, unsafe
Grand theft in the night
Enshrouded in deep dark secrecy.
A rational of mind imperialism
A daily realism, systematically enslaved
My only grave, monotony in this torturous brutal vacant landscape.
Living in inhumane deprivation and squalor
Surroundings inescapable with impregnable derision
Respect and dignity, not given.
Five long years
A sense of unease and hopelessness overtake my tired weary spirit
But a fierce conviction drives me on
That one day I will be free of the chains that bind me
And my only decree that finally
I will be given my liberty back
I will be free
And no longer living
A life of misery
In exile.

Mariyam Maule, 'In Exile'

7

Coping Strategies

Ruth Dee

Coping strategies are essential to any person's survival in daily life. They are even more important to us in times of stress and mental illness.

I believe that the majority of us are born with coping strategies and then adjust and further develop them throughout our lives. For me, coping means being able to have as great a quality of life as is possible at the time, to maintain good relationships with my family and friends, to be integrated into my community and to feel life has a purpose. I also want to be as independent as possible, to feel I can do things with less and less support from family, friends and professionals.

I began to use the coping mechanisms that I believe we are all born with at the age of three to survive mentally and physically. I did this without even knowing I was doing it. It was an automatic response to danger. I began to dissociate on a regular basis. We all have the ability do this; for example, it happens when we become so absorbed in a film that we don't notice the passage of time. In a life-threatening situation, like a car crash, we feel as if we are watching ourselves, temporarily relieving us from the trauma of the event. As children we use this skill often, but lose the ability as we get older as most of us don't need to use it in our daily lives.

I used the coping strategy of dissociating because of severe trauma and abuse on a sustained basis from the age of three. Dissociation allowed me to disconnect my mind from my body. During this dissociative process, thoughts, feelings, memories and perceptions of the traumatic experiences were separated off psychologically, allowing me to continue my daily life as if the trauma had not occurred. As the abuse and trauma were repeated regularly and over a sustained period of time my dissociation became an automatic coping strategy. As it was such an effective coping strategy I used it whenever I felt threatened or anxious.

Dissociation can be as simple as completely forgetting the event, or the personality can separate into different parts. These different parts then become the

Voices of Experience: Narratives of Mental Health Survivors   Edited by Thurstine Basset and Theo Stickley ©2010 John Wiley & Sons, Ltd.

individual, additional personalities, or 'alters', as they are often called. However, when the personality has split into different alters, each one can take control of the host. This is called dissociative identity disorder (DID). I developed DID.

The process of developing and living with alters and dissociation is a complicated one and inappropriate to this chapter. However my full story about developing and living with DID can be found in my book *Fractured* (2009).

During my adult working life I had already realised that I was mentally ill but didn't know what was wrong with me – nor did I understand the symptoms and behaviours of DID that I was experiencing; in fact they frightened me. The coping strategies I had unerringly developed as a three year old had enabled me to successfully progress to adulthood, raise three children, have a good long relationship with my husband and a career as a senior manager in education.

In DID all the feelings, memories and thoughts about the experiences of abuse and trauma are stored in the alters and therefore hidden/shelved from the child's daily memory allowing the child (me) to continue to live as if the trauma had not occurred. My mind developed separate neural pathways to deal with different aspects of the traumatic experiences. Nowadays, brain scans can show this to be an observable reality.

With my DID the memories of my early abuse and trauma eventually started to come through. I began to lose a lot of time – I was unaware of the passage of time and what I had been doing during the hours I had missed – even though I had apparently still been working. I started to talk out loud to myself, or rather to my alters. I was petrified of being 'found out'. I knew I was mentally ill, but couldn't make sense of my symptoms. I didn't approach my general practitioner for many years as I didn't know what to say. So I had to keep going on my own or completely give up.

At this point I think it may be helpful to describe some of the coping strategies I developed and used to cope with my mental illness at work and to enable me to be able to function generally. It shows that I was able to develop my own coping strategies even though they did eventually fail me. Surely this ability could be tapped into by professionals when I eventually went for help.

I developed a whole range of coping strategies:

- I was embarrassed by the fact that I was talking out loud and was concerned about how it would be viewed by my colleagues, so I always hummed a tune when walking from office to office. People interpreted this as my being happy; and I encouraged this. Humming also kept the internal chatter in my head quieter, allowing me to focus on a single issue.
- I would end up in unknown places when I dissociated when driving home or to a meeting. This really frightened me and I would panic, which in turn caused more dissociation. So I agreed with myself that I would always drive to the next roundabout or crossroads and take the road to a place I knew, even if it wasn't where I was actually going. This calmed me sufficiently to be able

to think logically and I could then often read the road map before needing to travel too far out of my way.

- I began to dissociate through the entirety of meetings I was chairing and therefore had no memory of what was discussed. But it was obvious that no one realised that anything was amiss. I was in the fortunate position of having a personal assistant and I insisted that the writing up of meeting notes was a priority. A strong filing system was developed so I had ready access to information that I had missed. My recording system became famous and was often used by my colleagues because of its quality.

- I used memos with all staff at all times. I wrote memos as soon as I knew I needed to see someone or wanted some information. (I carried them with me at all times at work.) Staff were then asked to bring the memo with them when they came to see me as I knew there was a good chance that a different alter would be in charge and not know what was going on. Because of my elaborate systems, I was considered efficient.

- I developed a relationship with my senior staff and secretaries that they considered eccentric. I had to be lively and outgoing at all times. I also said I had a poor memory and had too much to remember so they humoured me, apparently willingly. I was already humming, so it was easy to build on this. Being seen as an eccentric enabled me to cover up my unusual behaviours, such as talking out loud, forgetting my way round a very familiar building, completely and constantly forgetting the names of people I worked with every day and jumping at the slightest sudden noise.

- I would arrive at a meeting in a dissociative state and not know what the meeting I was obviously supposed to be chairing was about. Therefore, meetings invariably began with my asking people in turn what they wanted to achieve by the end of the meeting. This was usually enough for me to 'catch up'. People also felt they had a substantive say in the outcome of the meeting.

- As my talking out loud to my alters became more erratic and unexpected I had to attempt to cover this up. Initially, I tried to say that I wanted to say something, but this understandably annoyed people as I was interrupting them. So I covered it up by apologising and saying I had thought of something and needed to make a note of it. From then on I always had a notepad with me. I used this to just write down any words I said as I realised that if I did this, I was less likely to lose time/dissociate/switch. I couldn't doodle, as people would think I was uninterested in what they were saying. I therefore pretended to make my own notes.

- An advantage with DID is that the host is totally unaware of stress and tiredness. As a result, my capacity for work was enormous. The disadvantage is that my body became exhausted, but I was unaware of this until my breakdown.

The above coping strategies at work all seem to be very small things, but they allowed me to function as a senior manager in education without anyone becoming aware of my problems. I know I succeeded as, even on the day I left work to enter an acute psychiatric unit, no one even realised I was mentally ill (except the one person I had confided in). I had needed to keep working as it helped me focus, with the result that I didn't dissociate as much and I could keep the raging fear I felt for much of the time at bay. It also gave me a real sense of purpose.

During these years I developed a coping strategy for each little problem that arose. Life seemed to be all about having to get over one hurdle after another. It became harder and harder to cope with my alters and the memories and feelings of the abuse and trauma that had taken place over the first 16 years of my life. I became more and more depressed and dissociative and began to feel I couldn't cope. Finally, I had a breakdown and entered the secondary psychiatric services.

The coping strategies that I had unerringly developed as a child, and that had saved my life, had eventually become inadequate and inappropriate. I had tried adding to them on a daily basis as new problems arose, but I was fundamentally using the same ones. Now a whole new coping strategy was needed. This time I wasn't alone. I had my husband, who was now aware of my disorder and what it meant, and I had a care team who cared enough for me to help me develop new coping strategies. It has been their determination that I should have a good quality life and lead as independent a life as possible that has encouraged me and my husband to develop a whole new set of coping strategies. Unfortunately, it took a complete breakdown to reach that point.

It has not been easy to develop new skills and strategies and there have been many setbacks. In the seven years since the breakdown to the time of writing (August 2009), there have been several stages in developing coping strategies, each requiring a different level of input from professionals. What has been vital to my ongoing recovery is the way my care team have worked *with* me. They have supported me, encouraged me and, at each stage, made it clear they want me to recover and believe that I can. It is their 'we *can* do' approach that has helped me so much. They supported me when I felt I couldn't go on, when each new stage of my recovery was frightening, and they always helped me find a new way through.

I want to spend the rest of this chapter describing a few of the ways in which the professionals in the mental health services helped me develop new and appropriate coping strategies since my breakdown which have helped me progress so far.

The Mental Health Physiotherapist

I was referred to the physiotherapist (the physio) as soon as I entered the acute psychiatric day unit. At this point I was dissociating and switching into different alters constantly. One of the effects of this is to make me feel that I am floating and I can't feel any of my body. The physio initially worked on me so I could gain some level of feeling in my hands and feet. Once I began to gain some feeling when grounded, she worked with me to develop strategies I could use daily to ground myself. I learned to rub my hands together vigorously, to stamp my feet, to feel the arm of the chair that I was sitting in, to feel the heat from a warm drink. (I didn't know to feel these things before.) I would then practise these with the physio there to remind me to do it and then I would go through the activities when I was alone if I needed to 'ground' myself. They began to make a difference and often helped me to stop switching so often. Note that the physio used a graded strategy – first doing the work for me up to my being able to use the coping strategy on my own. I still use it today.

The Mental Health Occupational Therapist

I had once been a very independent woman, but during my breakdown I lost my independence. I wouldn't go out. I was referred to the occupational therapist (OT). I will use the example of catching a bus to my nearest city so I could go to a café or shop. Initially the OT visited me at home and we planned what I would like to achieve. On her next visit we went to bus stops, the route the bus would take and then the shops I wanted to visit. On the next visit we took the bus together to the city and stayed in the bus station for 15 or so minutes discussing where I would walk the next time. On the next visit we went on the bus together and then walked round the shops together. As can be seen, she was taking a staged approach of support with me. A few weeks later I caught the bus on my own, did some shopping and came home – I was delighted.

I added some strategies of my own to make me feel even safer – I bought a watch with the day and date on it so I could check this when I was getting anxious and repeat the day, date and time to myself. I would get anxious and would feel as if I was going to switch/dissociate as I was walking round the shops and on the bus. I also used the hand-clapping and foot-stamping strategy to keep me grounded. I made sure my husband's mobile phone number was the first on the speed dial. And I would write on my hands where I was going. In addition, I always take the same route round the city, the idea being that as all my alters use the same route even if I did switch we would all know the way home – it worked for me. Again, a staged approach had been used by the OT from full support in doing something I really wanted to do in order to improve the quality of my life to my being independent.

My Care Coordinator

My care coordinator has always made it clear that in graded steps I could develop new coping strategies. Even during my relapses he has said that I could get through the difficult times and then move forward again. This is an enormous support to me. He gave me hope even in very dark times. The immediate support may be going into a crisis day unit for a while or even onto a ward. This was to help me get through the immediate problems, but we still looked forward to when I could be discharged. He could tell me what progress I had made over the years and remind me what the next steps we had agreed were. I can't stress enough the power of having a professional who reminds me that he believes I can make progress, who tells me often of the progress I have already made, who wants me to be independent and who is there for me when I need support.

Together, we developed an advanced directive that I carried with me at all times as at this point I was often switching into a different alter and getting lost. The directive explained my condition, how to speak to me and whom to contact if I was found. It has worked with the police and the Accident and Emergency department after I had been found wandering. Having this gave me the confidence to try going out. As I am now at a different stage in my recovery we are just renewing the directive.

My care coordinator worked with me on developing a daily chart when I was very depressed. I made a time chart with targets such as: what time to get up and get dressed, when to have a meal, what activities I was going to undertake each day and for how long. It was very practical. I would tick off the things I had done and on his next visit we would look at it together. He was very careful to praise me for what I had achieved and then discussed with me how we could add more of the tasks I hadn't achieved. This step-by-step approach with a chart on my kitchen wall to tick was very motivating. We have drawn up other working charts for different situations over the years. The charts themselves are a coping strategy.

He also developed a relapse signature with me. We spoke about early warning/ sign scale identifiers; marked or daily signs; moderate signs and sources of help. We discussed these over a couple of sessions and then he had them typed up and they are hung on my kitchen wall. Because we worked on it together I feel it is a valuable document. I said what I thought and he raised points for me to consider and to agree to or not. As it holds both our opinions, I trust it.

Another little but significant strategy we have developed together to help me overcome the embarrassment of talking out loud to myself and having people stare at me was for me to wear earplugs. I can plug them into my ipod or pretend I am using my mobile. This really works for me and I feel more able to be in public without being embarrassed all the time.

Importantly, I feel we problem-solve together. He has said often that his role is to enable me to live successfully in the community as well as to coordinate my care. It is the working partnership that looks at problem-solving in a positive way that is so helpful and encourages me to take risks and to develop new coping skills.

The Psychotherapist

It is a little harder for me to describe the new coping strategies the psychotherapist and I have developed together as they are very personal and most are related to my DID. What I can say is that anyone who has DID has a good imagination. They have created a whole range of coping strategies and worlds in their head that has allowed them to survive horrendous abuse. My psychotherapist has used this ability to enable me to cope with the fears my alters held, to bring them into the present and to enable me to communicate effectively with them every day. For instance, when a child alter first expressed her fears out loud in therapy it was frightening for me and for the alter. We both needed a way to cope. Through discussion we agreed that I would create a bubble around the child alter that would inflate and shrink as she wanted. I put a rainbow between her, me and the past to block it out. I tried to hold this image in my head every time we were scared. Over the next couple of weeks this worked. We were both calmer, and gradually I was able to talk to her and finally she integrated. This may be difficult to understand, but the key points are that my psychotherapist used a strategy that built on my known existing skills; she needed to make sure I could cope on my own and not just when I was with her; she needed to move my knowledge and understanding of my DID along at my pace and with some encouragement to take risks; she ensured that I was in control of the strategy and we worked out one together. After some initial difficulties it proved to be a strategy we have used again and again over the years, though obviously the imagery changes to meet different alters' needs.

She referred me to a sensory-motor psychotherapist to help me through the dreadful fear I felt constantly as we were working through the alters' feelings. This is a period people with DID need to go through. I was still seeing my psychotherapist as I trusted her absolutely and was very wary of the new one. However, by using a sensory-motor approach, which entailed knowing how my body was feeling, what I was thinking and then managing my fears, together we increased my ability to cope with my fears. After six months I was far better able to cope with my fears. She had used my knowledge of my body, added some theory and together we made huge progress. She always gave me the confidence that I could make progress. In this case it was explaining the biological theory behind fear and anxiety that helped to move me on. I then stopped seeing this psychotherapist and continued working with my long-standing one. An important factor here was my psychotherapist's ability to say she felt someone else could better work with me on a particular issue. I didn't lose confidence in her and she was able to make the suggestion in a professional manner.

Later in psychotherapy we began looking at how to manage my DID in the here and now. After much therapy and discussion I now have strategies that enable me to cope far better with my disorder on a daily basis. I can now talk to my alters to ensure each of them has their needs met, that we can live together in relative harmony and each is present at the appropriate times. All of these are essential new coping skills that enable me to live comfortably. They have taken years to develop. It has been the trusting relationship with my psychotherapist that has developed over the last five years that has been so crucial in this. She is there to support me and to challenge me to move forward. She has used the abilities I have and built new coping strategies with these as the foundation. She has ensured I develop coping strategies that allow me to survive in the community and that don't rely on her to work. She ensures I know she thinks I can make good progress, which is so encouraging to me. Above all, she has given me *hope*.

A controversial coping strategy I have is the possibility of suicide. To me it is a logical strategy. If I can't find a way of keeping going, of making progress, and lose that sense of hope, then I could always die. It isn't a dramatic gesture or thought; to me it is realistic. Having this escape route enables me to think about and develop new coping strategies. I can keep going as long as I have an escape route if my quality of life is too poor and I can't make progress. It gives me the strength to keep trying. I want to get well and work hard with my care team and my family to have a good quality of life; having an ultimate escape route — death — helps me. This is difficult for people to understand as suicide is often seen as cowardly, a cry for help or a dramatic gesture. Nevertheless it can be seen as something else: a coping strategy.

Conclusion

As a child my body and mind had found an extraordinary mechanism for allowing me to survive unbearable trauma and abuse. I was too young to do this knowingly; it happened automatically.

My breakdown was the start of learning a whole new range of coping strategies. This time I had professional support. I am lucky enough to have a care team who support me to be as independent as possible, slowly, step by step and always looking to the future with me. At the same time I receive enough support and care when I am really struggling. I believe this model of patient and professional working together is one that may lead people to be able to find new coping strategies, at their own pace.

Whereas in childhood I was unaware that I had developed coping strategies I now *choose* to develop new ones. I use the word 'choose' because it is a choice. No professional can develop them for you; it has to be an active partnership and one where trust exists. It requires real caring and creativity on the part of the professionals to ensure the coping strategies developed together are appropriate to each individual's needs and build on skills they already have. The patient needs to trust the professional enough to take a huge risk and try something new when they are at their most vulnerable.

As can be seen from what I have written, the smallest coping strategy has tremendous potential for helping someone in their daily life.

A puppet to the mother's strings,
Dances hard to the weary tune,
It's a circle.

Pull them here, bow up and down, and jump,
There's the mark – oops over she goes,
Call the tune.

A life moment, still ... still ... silent ... wait ... ,
[Her or those of my choosing?] Wait ... ,
Defend him and his issue.

No contest; Cut through the lines,
'Look, sunshine through the window!'
Rejoice the view – I have the reins.

'No more knots and feline cradles,
Or demandings met from across the stables,
Our arguments may be fodder for fables,
But I now know that I'm enabled.'

Puppeteer now fully broken,
Trots nicely along with the rider, sitting upright.
Proud; we both know the rules to stop bolting.

Esta Smith, 'Puppeteer'

8

What's it Like Having a Nervous Breakdown? Can You Recover?

Laura Lea

Introduction

The mind forms the landscape of our lives, but until something goes wrong we don't take much notice of what this might mean. Perhaps we know enough about ourselves to see we have an odd habit here and there; we drink a bit too much and we go fuzzy; songs go round in our head too much; or we comment on ourselves when we do something wrong. However, generally, we ignore our internal world. It's like a landscape we never notice.

When serious mental ill health struck me, I found myself living in a foreign country, in a different mind, with no idea how to speak the language. Inside my head I was lying wounded on the floor, with a dark nightmare taking place all round me. At its worst it was close to hell, like being on fire, or in ice, as painful as that – physically painful, but in the mind. There was very little to show on the outside and no way to describe it to the people who were around me.

The world changes colour and is no longer the familiar place it used to be. When your mind becomes different, then so does everything else. Inevitably, you not only become a problem to yourself, but a problem to your family, friends or work. Finally, if it's really bad, you find your way to the mental health services, entering the world of treatment, theories and interventions.

Most of all, from that time I remember the feeling of losing the person I thought of as myself. It was a journey into a strange and very frightening world.

The House of Despair

Even now despair can warp my mind. Depression is something that pretends to be me. It sets up thoughts about hopelessness, death, being alone, being

Voices of Experience: Narratives of Mental Health Survivors   Edited by Thurstine Basset and Theo Stickley ©2010 John Wiley & Sons, Ltd.

unlikeable, never being able to achieve goals and is either deeply sad (crying for hours and hours) or completely numb. In it, I feel tired. I don't want to speak. I am fuzzy. For a long time I believed that this was who I was; it became my identity. But this is not me, this is depression. Depression pretends to be me.

These thoughts, moods, lack of moods, great fears, are the illness. Because of this, because I notice that at its worst these thoughts carry me to a different view of the sacredness of life and whether it's worth living, it's my personal view that depression is dangerous and that the legislation that allows us to be compulsorily detained is necessary. Mental ill health at its worst tips us away from our balanced self and when we are in that place we can't see as clearly as we do at other times.

Severe mental illness is being foreign, apart, in pieces. It's a lonely place and it was my belief that because of it I was 'abnormal'. I was treated by a psychiatrist who treated 'abnormal' people. I didn't realise that one in four of us at any one time will be experiencing a mental health problem. Now, years later, I wish that I had known more about what other people who have mental health problems experience and how they manage. More knowledge from people who had lived through their difficulties might have shortened the journey of recovery. Finding out that I shared experiences with others was finding out I wasn't in this new world on my own and that there were ways of doing things that helped. There are also things that don't help, and there is a language that I needed to develop to help me describe what was happening to me and negotiate a route round my mental landscape.

Breakdown came upon me suddenly as a result of having been given too high a dose of an antidepressant administered for fatigue. Within three days of taking it, I was asking myself if it was my voice that came out of my mouth. I became afraid of my thoughts, my own voice and everything around me. I put the problem down to the drugs and stopped taking them after a week. I then rebounded and plunged even deeper into this new world. It is definitely important to tell people about the terrible side-effects of taking psychotropic medication and then stopping suddenly. This is part of the basic knowledge and language that the community lacks about mental ill health.

I struggled on for three months – terrified by my own self, frightened I'd crash the car, feeling as if I was wearing sunglasses or grey-tinted glasses, sleeping less and less until, in a very organised fashion, I told my dad I was going to have a breakdown and the day after my birthday referred myself to the community mental health team. Those were the days you could walk in off the street and get help. Within an hour, I had seen a community psychiatric nurse and the duty psychiatrist. The psychiatrist wanted to prescribe tranquillisers but I wasn't having them because they were addictive. We reached stalemate. My request for clomipramine, an antidepressant (I had done my homework), was rejected. Seven weeks and an eternity later (that's another thing that happens, time warps and doesn't flow normally any more), having seen a consultant psychiatrist, I was put on clomipramine. In those seven weeks, I experienced the psychotropic drug experimentation trial that many of us go through. In that time I had a serotonin crisis and was very, very ill. During this period the seeds of my marriage break-down were sown. Even now, over ten years later, this is painful to talk about.

On the Outside Looking in

It would be nice to think that this beginning phase of contact with the mental health services is smoother these days. But from my own experience and from talking to people in the community I know that accessing help can be difficult and the response of the services at this beginning stage can make matters worse. These early days of recognising a problem, accepting that something has to be done and finding something – usually medication, but sometimes talking therapy – to sta-bilise the situation are fraught with pain for the family who see something (but often don't know what) going wrong. The care (or lack of it) that a person receives when they first access services sets them on a path which might lead to their maintaining a place in the world of friends and family and work, or losing every-thing. It's not just the illness that changes lives, using services changes the life of the person concerned and their family. At that entry point to secondary mental health services healing can begin. But I know that a person who seeks help can also be damaged by the workers they meet and the system that delivers mental health care. If you are a person who loves someone with a mental health problem (the government call this being a 'carer'), then you'll be able to count the number of hours you spend wondering if there is anything different that could be done that might make things work more smoothly for the person you love. I am aware that there is plenty of theory in circulation in the mental health system that tells workers that it's the family that creates mental health problems. People who love someone with a mental health problem automatically come under suspicion as being part of the problem, so the system impacts on the family. It might be that as a carer your experience is positive, perhaps you have a constructive relationship with the mental health team, being seen as a partner, being offered information and support that keeps you well and helps you relate to the situation in the best possible way. But carers get a bad deal. They don't sign up to have a mental health issue in their life and it's hard to understand as the person who looks in from the outside. There seems to be no one there to guide you, to help you help the person and tell you what is the best thing to do. It's easy day after day to spend time hurting because of the ill person's pain, angry because it can't be fixed and shut out by services and isolated from the rest of the community. Families often remain silent because of the stigma associated with mental ill health. It keeps everyone quiet, silencing the discussion, preventing each of us from learning the language necessary to talk about what happens when the mind changes.

If you love someone who has a mental health issue, most likely you desperately, sincerely and deeply want to see peace, pleasure, wellbeing and resilience flourish again in that person. It is true that some of us are more skilled than others at knowing how to help. It's human to make mistakes but somehow as a carer the mental illness and probably the mental health service magnify the mistakes. Being a carer can send you off balance. Mental illness is not normally expected. A new situation requires different ways of doing things, but so often, as the carer, not the person who is directly involved, the information isn't there, its not provided by the service. It is my belief that this is a serious failing. It leads to family breakdown.

Left with Something to Work with

Experiencing breakdown is to experience something unpredictable, but then there's the reaction to the experience. It's different for everyone. Some people entrench in denial; some people find a straightforward answer and move quickly to recovery; others, in an attempt to find a solution, roll over and do exactly what the doctors, nurses and therapists say without finding out or questioning. Some of us shift identity and become a 'mental health service user' with a sense of isolation from what is 'normal'. Identities shift not only for the person, who labels him/herself a service user, but also for their family. Relationships are put under strain. As I adopted a label of service user, which at least gave me an identity, I also experienced hopelessness and family stress. There appeared to be no choices open to me. My experience of mental ill health defeated me.

But – Recovery Does Happen

I'm not sure how it happens, maybe by luck, with medication, with the right mental health professional, by reading a book, becoming part of a group, by determination, by courage, by finding something 'other' that inspires. Among these and other things, people find recovery. There came a point when I could see that the new landscape of my mind had landmarks, islands of solid ground amidst the chaos of mental distress, which offered respite from what was a relentless and devastating illness. These islands of respite were the beginnings of finding a path around the landscape of mental distress. They are the building blocks of recovery.

Getting the right medication

Getting the right medication was essential and I consider myself lucky that it only took a couple of months. What would I suggest to anyone who finds they are playing medication lotto? Talk to your GP, be calm, take someone with you and ask for a second opinion.

Having a break and finding a place to find peace

Two months after my breakdown I went to stay in the country. I could rest and I could talk. It was what I needed. But maybe, being apart from my family at that time, contributed to my family breaking down, I was travelling a different path from them and nobody seemed to be reminding us that this could be just for a short while and about us all needing to repair.

Being honest

Being honest is the hardest thing, but I think – and this is a very personal opinion – that for recovery to occur there has to be some honesty. It has been said that anxiety is disguised depression. But it's really difficult often to work out what you might be anxious about and what you might be sad about. With this type of illness we are often alienated. Starting the process of owning the problems, revealing the secret sorrows and accepting that it's me that has the illness (no matter how significant external problems have played a part in causing it) and that I have to begin the search for recovery is – for want of a better way of describing it – sickening. After all, who wants to have to be honest about all the pain, all the little lies we tell ourselves and the things that make us hurt. How and where to be honest and who to be honest with is another matter. It is only safe to be honest when it's safe.

Taking one step

Starting to do something that reflected who I was helped me find something outside my mental ill health. I joined an adult education writing group. The first exercise on the first day was: 'Imagine you are a tube of toothpaste and write about it'. This was challenging. I thought that there might be a vague possibility that I might become a tube of toothpaste if I wrote about it, and that was a bit scary! This type of thought and the fear it creates seem bizarre to anyone who is mentally well. But this thinking demonstrates the loss of identity that people feel in breakdown, where thoughts seem more powerful than just thoughts and where the connection between speech, thought and action is no longer the easy, unremarked experience it was before. Of course, that is how it feels and it is not how it is. One of the most important things to learn about thinking when you feel this way is that thoughts are just thoughts, they arise, they hang around, they disappear. (Magic thinking when someone believes that their thoughts will cause a specific outcome in a way that is scientifically impossible is an illusion and sometimes a delusion.) Thoughts have no immediate power to make a difference to the real world. It is our actions that change us and the things around us. But it was almost as if this lesson, which small children often need to learn, had to be learnt again.

Having managed the 'mad' moments, this group and writing became something concrete and new that emerged from the rubble. Some of the creative writing ideas were too demanding and sometimes it was difficult to cope with the constructive criticism. On the other hand, it was nice to air some wilder ideas in fantasy and safely on paper (always bearing in mind the group's tolerance). But there was muddle. My mental health worker got very confused at one point because she couldn't tell whether I was writing and in control, or writing and out of control. Talking freely to a mental health worker can be a dangerous thing! This was a good example of normal behaviour (writing creatively, passionately and unusually – and admittedly with a little too much energy) being assessed as mad. It's no wonder we become guarded in what we say to workers.

Finding ways to manage mental health/ill health

I began to attend relaxation classes provided by the community mental health team. Six months previously I had turned them down on the grounds that they wound me up and made me think bad thoughts. The programme taught autogenics, a form of self-hypnosis and deep relaxation, the body scan and mindfulness (Buddhist meditation techniques). I don't use autogenics much now, although it was really useful at the time. But the exploration of mindfulness as a tool for finding ways to find peace is one that continues today. It was one worker giving me some information with some references that led me to a bookshop, then to a Buddhist centre, and eventually to finding out how to meditate carefully and usefully. Information is the key to recovery.

Following a hidden path

It was like picking up one little clue, following it for a while until the next clue came along, until I found that I was travelling more hopefully, with more tools in my kitbag to help me handle the problems – autogenics, writing, trips to the Buddhist centre. It wasn't easy to believe that a path existed. When it became obvious that I was on the road to some form of recovery, I could feel myself becoming so frightened at the possibility that there was a light at the end of the tunnel I wanted to slam on the breaks before I hit daylight.

Not sabotaging yourself

I carry my GP's words 'don't sabotage it' in my kitbag of ideas. Every time there is something new to try, I have to say 'don't sabotage it'.

Finding a way to start to reach my goals

I needed to fill my days with something more meaningful than daytime TV. I needed to meet people, learn, volunteer, think about work, work.

I was out of work for eight years due to ill health. Finding work involved driving to a distant town to a job agency, only to be told they couldn't help. Then I drove to another town to see someone from the 'Pathways to Work' scheme and was told they couldn't help either, but they gave me a phone number for CAPITAL (Clients and Professionals in Training and Learning), a service-user group in Sussex. I travelled halfway across the county to a CAPITAL meeting and found that they were talking about things that I could relate to, that there were people who had experienced similar things. I attended their training course once a month for a year, learnt how to present the service user perspective in order to train and educate mental health workers. I soon found that things I knew from before I was ill and things I found out at CAPITAL were coming together in me to enable me to speak out about mental ill health.

Taking some risks

There were people who saw some potential in me. They saw my strengths and offered me a chance to develop. I think they thought I could make something out of what felt like nothing. With the opportunity and support of people who saw some strength in me, I was prepared to take some risks. It's interesting to me that these people were not based in the mental health teams but were working in training, education and the voluntary sector. Within a year of joining CAPITAL, I began work at Brighton University as part of a team teaching the Certificate in Community Mental Health Care. It was great. The other member of CAPITAL and I and were treated as equals, taught as equals and even got access to the inner sanctum of the lecturers' offices. We group-marked the assessed work. I found my voice. I discovered I could respect myself. My ideas were listened to and further work around the importance of spirituality emerged.

Seven years on, I sat in a conference run by the NHS Partnership Trust where national speakers, representatives of different faiths, service users and carers, and many Trust workers talked about the next steps in spiritual care for people accessing mental health services. All of that came out of a conversation I had while teaching at Brighton University. Not knowing how spirituality related to mental health care, I had run a session on it for the students. Hearing me speak, the training officer for West Sussex asked me to work with him to develop a training day for staff. As a result of those developments, West Sussex Health and Social Care Trust subsequently became a NIMHE spirituality project pilot site. Hundreds of workers who need to nurture their own spiritual and working lives and many service users have benefited. Sussex Partnership Trust now has a spiritual and religious care strategy, which promotes holistic care.

Being involved in the service user movement has changed things for me and for other people. The identity of a service user has a lot of negatives, but it also gave me a group to belong to and a voice. That respect I received when someone gave me, a service user, someone with a serious mental health issue, an opportunity, and then listened to me and then made some changes, was what put me back on the path to contributing to the world.

In the end I went back to work. I still can't believe that I managed it. It feels like I struggled, crawled and clawed my way into a paid job, then to paying National Insurance and then to paying income tax. Work still presents me with huge challenges. For many years, I had truly and absolutely believed that I would never work again. The lack of access to the normal world of work did me great harm. But things did change, I did get a job – and I kept it.

Leftovers

Sometimes workers discharge people and think that's it, it's all better. But it's not. True, some service users believe in cure. I was recently challenged when I listened to a service user talk about thriving and not surviving. He said he believed he could be cured. If I'm being honest, I don't believe it will happen for me (but I have been wrong before).

We all have to manage our demons and I get very tired of managing mine. It seems that if I take my hand off the rudder, the ship goes off course and sails towards the rocks, so I restrict my life to stay well. I am isolated because I restrict my life. I hate it that if I stop taking the drugs, I will become ill. I loathe that sense of the mind overworking, the panic in the pit of the stomach and the threat of depersonalising. I tread very carefully around depersonalising. I have a whole set of strategies: talking quietly, reminding myself I must cry, trying to get to crying, getting involved with people in my everyday routines, guarding my sleep, using earplugs. These strategies have taken years to develop.

I still have no real language to talk to my family about what I live with. I pretend in order to avoid their condemnation. They don't remember things about me – the things I can't do. They tell me to pull myself together. 'You're overreacting,' they say, even when terrible, sad things have happened to me. I suppose I have given up trying to talk to them about what all this means. I also pretend to my friends to protect the people close to me who have themselves experienced mental ill health. But, recently some of them have understood words like anxiety and depression. There is more tolerance between us of what that might mean in everyday life, the battle that is being fought inside. As yet it's a vague, shared idea, not a full understanding, where we really know what we mean by mental ill health. There isn't yet a real acknowledgment that it's OK to be a bit broken round the edges. But it's progress. And I must remember that the illness itself will tend to blind me to the progress that has been made.

If you ask me where I am now, I would say that I think there is only one thing you need to start the journey of recovery. That is to be able to learn. For me, that's all you have to try to believe, that learning is all that's required, and then set off to find the way.

A journey beyond silence
A rising sun appears invigorated, excited
Enthusiastically ushering in a new beginning
Inspiring dreams to chase after
Life's pleasures apparent and audible
My surroundings surrender to comprehension
And reason, no longer afraid and undesirable
As grains of sand greet my hands
In a cathartic, sensitive show of affection
Each mere mortal testifying to time.

A journey beyond silence
The waves emancipated, free from their cruel master
Which they once had to obey, submit their complete personality
No longer lost at sea
Talk softly in a soothing reassuring way
Ameliorating the pain of the ocean's loneliness
As the tide reaches its zenith in its topsy turvy career
Singing beautifully, melodically. A soprano
Performing a rendition of Auld Lang Syne

A journey beyond silence
The wind rejoices, reverberating echoes of hope
Whispering the dulcet tones of joy
Happy to be re-acquainted with old friends
Reminiscing over old times and far off places
Circulating a refreshing upbeat mood
Heralding a triumphant crown over creation
As the seagulls bring glad tidings
Messages from above of the love of life and its merciful ways
Gathering at the universal feast. An age of plenty

A journey beyond silence
Vivid images collect. A collage of perceptions and ideas enthuse
Language colours the landscape
A reunion of tangible syllables and sounds
Which were once sadly missed, unable to fathom amuse my senses
Entice my curiosity reach out calling, waiting patiently
To be listened and answered to
The journey beyond the despairing silence
I begin to speak

Mariyam Maule, 'A Journey beyond Silence'
(*written following a SIMBA trip to Margate*)

9

The Bridge of Sighs and the Bridge of Love: a Personal Pilgrimage

Peter Gilbert

Through a Vale of Tears

'Nobody has ever cried with me before.' The young Asian woman fixed me with her earnest brown eyes and we sat looking into each other's souls as though time seemed of no import. She had come into the seminar room (where members of a faith community had arranged a meeting with a mental health trust), as people were streaming out for lunch, and sat down opposite me. Clearly needing to say what she had to say, and say it quickly, Devinda [not her real name] began to tell me her story. She was a single parent, abandoned by her husband, and feeling abandoned by God as well. She was highly intelligent and articulate, but had begun to lose faith in herself. She felt disconnected, devalued and depressed. Her mother, a member of the faith community, was very supportive to her and her child, but Devinda felt estranged from the community and cut adrift. Faith had been partially restored, however, when she'd seen a notice, saying that the community was going to be talking about mental health issues with the local mental health trust. She felt that this gave her permission to come and tell her story, and she was at the end of her tether, her journey had brought her to the edge of a chasm, and she looked in to see the darkness and contemplate falling into it. Perhaps all that held her back was the love for her son and her sense of responsibility to him.

Voices of Experience: Narratives of Mental Health Survivors   Edited by Thurstine Basset and Theo Stickley ©2010 John Wiley & Sons, Ltd.

What she told me was very painful and intense. I felt a great desire to reach out to her, but being aware that physically touching an Asian woman could be very inappropriate, I simply stretched out my arm and laid my palm of my hand upwards. Devinda gripped my hand and continued to talk more and more intensely, looking into my eyes, her eyes filling with tears. Since my own experience of depression in 2000 and 2001, I cry more easily. A cartilage between my heart and my eyes seems to have dissolved, and my emotions spill over. As tears filled her eyes my eyes filled too, and that's when she said: 'Nobody's ever cried with me before.'

I am a qualified and registered social worker. I am very much aware that there needs to be a sense of professional boundaries and distance. I also feel that at times we need, as one of my students put it, to step 'onto common ground' with those we are working with, to share that sense of our own uniqueness but also our common humanity. Whether we have a humanist perspective, that we are all human beings on this earth together; or whether it is more of a religious perspective that we are all children of God, we are all of us on this earth together to make of it what we can.

Because this story was told not in a professional interview situation, but in a seminar room, which would fill again after lunch, I took the risk of saying something perhaps I wouldn't normally say, and it went something like this: 'I am convinced that you were *meant* to come to this place, at this time, and I was here specifically to hear your story. You are on the edge of a chasm, and we were meant to be here to lead you back from the edge and to help you reconnect with your community, if that's what you want, and for you to know that you are not alone, and don't need to continue your journey in isolation.'

Later, we were able to connect her with those who we hoped could offer appropriate help in the future. This particular faith community in Birmingham (see Parkes *et al.*, 2010) is a remarkable community because over the years it has built not only its place of worship, but also a health and education centre which is open to all members of the community, various employment outlets and a new education centre, and created links to assist impoverished communities overseas. A sign of the community's maturity and courage is seen in the fact that they have identified the negative stigma of mental health, what Erving Goffman called a 'spoiled identity' ([1963] 1990). This is a major issue for this body. It would be easy to ignore this, but the community have engaged with the mental health trust, who have a commitment to work with faith communities, and a workshop was set up specifically to address these issues. The advertising for the workshop gave a form of 'strategic permission' for this issue to be discussed, and the result was inspiring.

After many years of rather mechanistic target-setting in health and social care, which certainly may have been necessary initially, in the later 1990s people seemed to be coming back to the words 'dignity', 'identity', 'empathy', and so on, and phrases such as 'the essence of care'. It is said that when Margaret Thatcher was prime minister, she criticised the word 'compassion' as being 'patronising'. But of course, this is exactly what it isn't. All the 'com' words are about being *with*: 'companionship' comes from the Latin – literally, one who takes bread with someone; 'community' is about fellowship; 'communion' is to do with mutual participation; and 'communication' is about talking *with*. 'Compassion' is not about giving easy sympathy, but is *suffering with*, and we cannot do anything purposeful in this life without working *with* other people.

It was the Russian Orthodox, Metropolitan Anthony, who used to say: 'Every time we reach out our hand to another to shake their hand and ask the question "How are you?", we open ourselves to be known.'

On My Way Home?

One of my favourite songs is Enya's 'On My Way Home' (from her *Paint the Sky with Stars* compilation) in which she sings: 'We have been given some moments from heaven', with the chorus being 'On my way home'. But where is home? For some there is a very strong sense of home in the place they were born, which may be expressed in a sense of rootedness, a specific accent, cultural characteristics and habits, etc. Dr Kwami McKenzie's studies (2007) of second- and third-generation West Indians living in Britain have shown that identity challenges have affected their mental health. Whether we are considering Tariq Modood's classic text (2007) on multiculturalism or smaller-scale studies such as Zobia Arif's (2002), the question of identity is key. Arif, in a survey of young British Asians whose parents moved to Britain from Pakistan, speaks of them as representing 'a generation caught between two cultures'. One young person separated her identity into three:

> 'I have many different identities depending on where I am and what I'm doing. So my religious identity is Muslim, culture is Pakistani, and my national identity is British.'

Perhaps because I was born on the island of Jersey, and still return there when I can, I feel 'at home' on islands. On an island there is a strong connection between the stark boldness of the sea and sky and the ability to cut off from our usual incessant and insistent activity. For some reason Greek islands seem to enfold me in a positive way, perhaps because the relaxed character of the people means that I need to slow down a pace. It is also, as Lawrence Durrell describes it, where 'the blue really begins ... other countries may offer you discoveries in manners or law or landscapes; Greece offers you something harder – the discovery of yourself' ([1945], 1962). Once, on another island, Skiathos, in the Sporades, I was running through a glade of pine trees, filled with the croaking of cicadas, when I arrived at a pristine beach, embraced by limestone headlines. I was amazed to find that I was completely alone and spent a moment in contemplation. During dinner at a *taverna* that evening, I described to the patron my sense of peace and oneness on the deserted beach. 'Ah,' he replied, 'in Greece we have a saying: "the sea, me and God"' (Nicholls & Gilbert, 2002).

For people with a religious faith, the ultimate home may well be the merging of the individual with the cosmic spirit, so that death becomes not a barred and bolted blackened door, but a gateway to a greater sense of unity (Gilbert, 2008) or flowing through a sense of purgation to an afterlife that may be glorious or punitive. Because human love, however deep, is always partial, conditional and tidal, belief in an everlasting, unchanging and unconditionally loving divine entity can be very consoling at a time of physical or mental crisis. The poet Sue Holt (2009) speaks of God 'wrapping sacred arms around' human beings in trouble.

The Wandering Soul

The embryologist Lewis Wolpert is an atheist who uses religious language to describe some of the deepest experiences we have. In his book *Malignant Sadness: The Anatomy of Depression* (2006) he writes:

> If we had a soul – and as a hard-line materialist I do not believe we do – a useful metaphor for depression could be 'soul loss' due to extreme sadness. The body and mind emptied of the soul lose interest in almost everything except themselves. The idea of the wandering soul is widely accepted across numerous cultures and the adjective 'empty' is viewed across most cultures as negative. The metaphor captures the way in which we experience our own existence. Our 'soul' is our inner essence, something distinctly different from the hard material world in which we live. Lose it and we are depressed, cut off, alone. (Wolpert, 2006: 3)

All philosophical and religious traditions speak of a 'spirit' and/or 'soul' (sometimes these have different meanings) as being an essential part of our lives as created and/or evolved beings. The Jewish faith has the concept of an individual soul imbued by God, but also a spirit – *ru'ach* – with its connotations of 'breath' and 'spirit', and its essence being not just life – but invigorated life. During episodes of depression the spirit flags. The Greeks spoke of *pneuma*, which also has meanings around the breath of life and liveliness. *Pneuma* has modern reverberations around breathing and also power, as in 'pneumatic drill'. Ancient Greece had a variety of words to describe both the individual and the cosmic spirit (King, 2009) The philosopher Plato suggested that it was vain indeed to try to cure the body without the mind or the mind without the spirit, and in a warning that echoes down the centuries to mechanistic medicine, he adjured that the part can never be well unless the whole is well.

The *Oxford English Dictionary* defines spirit as a person's 'animating or life-giving force'. For services to neglect that in mental health care is an affront to human dignity, and a gross waste of time and money. We all appear to be wanderers, strangers in a foreign land, trying to connect with ourselves, with other people and with something other than ourselves (see Hay, 2006) – perhaps something cosmic, a personal divine being, or the natural world.

For those born into the Judaeo-Christian tradition there is a profound longing for connection. Psalm 119 says 'My soul is consumed with longing' (v. 20); 'My soul pines away for sorrow' (v. 28); and 'My soul languishes for your salvation' (v. 81). At several stages in their nation's history the Jews were taken into exile, and in Psalm 137 they recall:

> By the waters of Babylon we sat down and wept
> When we remember Zion.

That experience of exile, of wandering in the desert, searching for a lost home or a new one, can provoke a sense of empathy so that God is said to demand justice for the orphan and the widow, and love for strangers: 'You shall love the stranger, for you were strangers in the land of Egypt' (Deuteronomy 10: 18–19) (see Mursell, 2005: 10).

Whether in a religious sense or not, humans always seem to have told stories, and one of the deep frustrations of a mechanistic, reductionist health model (or ill-health model as one distinguished community physician put it) is that we do not have time to tell our stories. We only have to look at the prominence of modern storytellers (J. R. R. Tolkien, J. K. Rowling, Ursula Le Guin, Terry Pratchett, Philip Pullman and others) to appreciate the power of myth. In Le Guin's *The Dispossessed* ([1974] 2002), her protagonist, the physicist Shevek, finds himself the victim of unacknowledged power systems in a society where there are no formal power structures, only influence. He then moves into different societies, experiencing the opportunities and dangers these provide. Eventually, he returns home, with greater experience, but no more formal power than he had before. The final lines in the book are a motif for many of us:

> 'I am ready. I have nothing to pack.' Shevek laughed, a laugh of clear, unmixed happiness. The other man looked at him gravely, as if he was not sure what happiness was, and yet recognised, or perhaps remembered, it from afar ...
>
> 'I will lie down to sleep on an Anarres, tonight,' he [Shevek] thought. 'I will lie down beside Takver. I wish I'd brought the picture, the baby sheep, to give Pilun'.
>
> But he had not brought anything. His hands were empty, as they had always been. (pp. 318–319)

Of Individuals and Tribes

Caroline Myss writes:

> We are all born into a particular tribal culture. Beginning life as part of a tribe, we become connected to our tribal consciousness and collective willpower by absorbing

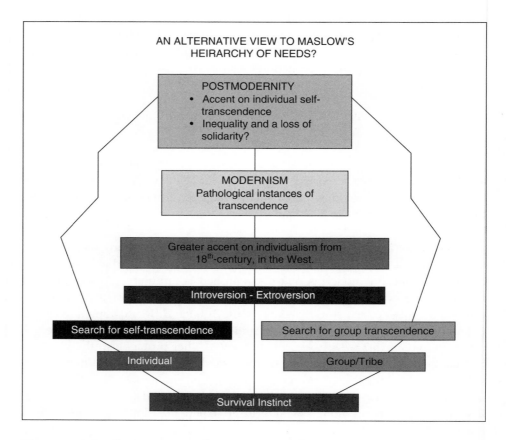

Figure 9.1   An Alternative to Maslow's Hierarchy of Needs

its strengths and weaknesses, beliefs, superstitions and fears. Through our interactions with family and other groups, we learn the power of sharing with other people. We learn how painful it can be to be excluded from a group and its energy. We also learn the power of sharing a moral and ethical code, handed down from generation to generation. (quoted in Aaron, 2008)

Abraham Maslow's well-known 'hierarchy of needs' model (1968) appears to assume that humans only sought physical comfort and security at a particular stage of their development and moved on to self-actualisation only when those needs had been satisfied. My variation on his model (see Figure 9.1) attempts to show humankind seeking transcendence right from the beginning of human development.

Studies in anthropology demonstrate that at least from Neolithic times humans have buried the dead with material goods, presumably to ensure that the departed are provided for in the afterlife. Again returning to my island of Jersey, the

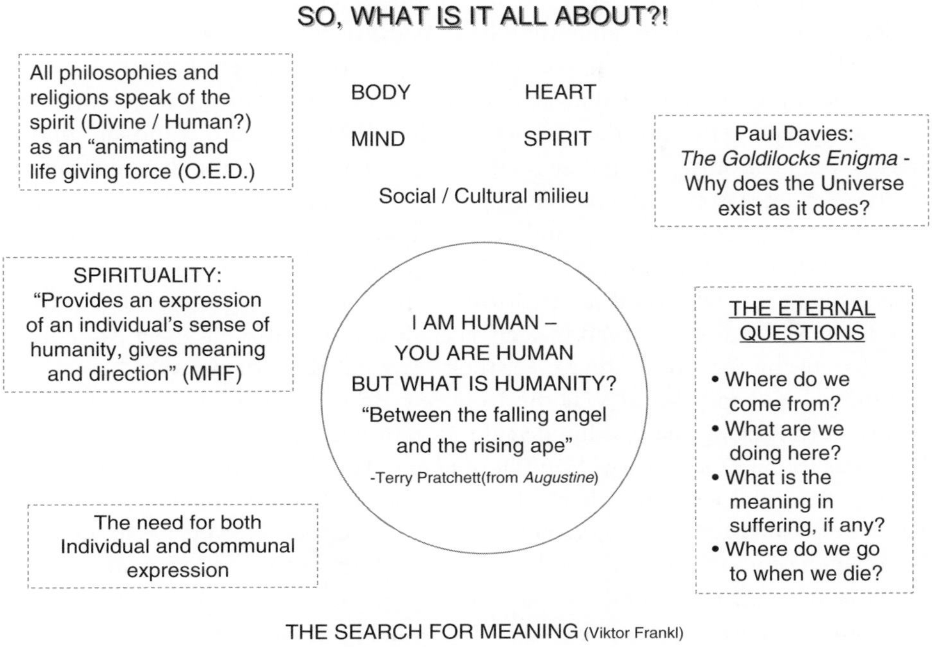

SO, WHAT IS IT ALL ABOUT?!

All philosophies and religions speak of the spirit (Divine / Human?) as an "animating and life giving force (O.E.D.)

BODY   HEART

MIND   SPIRIT

Social / Cultural milieu

Paul Davies:
The Goldilocks Enigma -
Why does the Universe exist as it does?

SPIRITUALITY:
"Provides an expression of an individual's sense of humanity, gives meaning and direction" (MHF)

I AM HUMAN –
YOU ARE HUMAN
BUT WHAT IS HUMANITY?
"Between the falling angel and the rising ape"
-Terry Pratchett(from *Augustine*)

THE ETERNAL
QUESTIONS

• Where do we come from?
• What are we doing here?
• What is the meaning in suffering, if any?
• Where do we go to when we die?

The need for both Individual and communal expression

THE SEARCH FOR MEANING (Viktor Frankl)

Figure 9.2   So, What *is* it All About?

Neolithic site at Hougue Bie demonstrates graphically how, even at a time when existence must have been a daily struggle, they were investing in symbols celebrating the afterlife.

Paul Keedwell (2008) suggests that there is an evolutionary basis for depression, as its prevalence must mean it has some purpose in enabling humans to adapt and survive. I believe that the initial small tribe basis of our society means that identifying and reacting promptly to difference was an essential element of survival. Identifying who was a member of your tribe and who was not was a vital element of safety; and ascertaining a difference and avoiding or attacking it were also a survival mechanism. Today, humans need a sense of solidarity in order to flourish. In a way most of us are Aristotelians, we sense that human flourishing depends on our behaving as civilised citizens (see Figure 9.2). Humans also need to demonstrate individual initiative to create positive change, and in an existential sense we are always alone even when we are breaking bread in companionship with others.

These tensions are played out all the time, and although there is a tendency to speak about religious tribalism, which clearly exists, writers such as Michael Burleigh (2006) and John Gray (2007) point to the secular ideologies of the twentieth century as destructive forces.

Nazi Germany is still a cogent warning of the dangers of pathological solidarity. A people, feeling isolated after the Great War, turned to a demagogic dictator who gave them a clear message of oppression without and betrayal within. There are many layers to be peeled away here in that the Communists were portrayed as an external enemy and the Jews as a distinct enemy within, who were undermining the economy and society by their separateness and capitalist approaches. Going further, however, the perceived purity of the race demanded that Germans with a learning disability, profound physical disabilities or mental illness also had to be murdered in the Holocaust. Peeling away yet another layer, were the Nazis essentially at war with themselves? Most of the leading Nazis were very far from obvious members of an Aryan master race. How much of their anger came from the recognition that they didn't meet their own standards of purity?

After the Second World War the Iron Curtain came down between Western and Eastern Europe and was lifted again. Recent films demonstrate issues around individuality and solidarity. Von Donnersmarck's *The Lives of Others* (2006) describes the sinister atmosphere of surveillance in East Germany. On the other hand, in *Goodbye Lenin* (2003) Wolfgang Becker describes, in ironic form, how the breakdown of a social system can leave some feeling bereft. In a recent description of Poland in 2009, several people who were involved in the overthrow of Communism have expressed concern that Poland has become overly individualistic and consumerist. One suggested that the country lacked 'moral and political order' and that the poor 'have been betrayed'. Another said: 'Solidarity is not just a slogan or the name of an organisation, it can only be something that exists between people. There isn't any real solidarity in Poland any more' (Burke, 2009).

A Pilgrimage of Hope?

If one paradox and tension is between individuality and communality, another is between being static and exodus. Most people don't like change – or at least don't like being changed (!) – which is the experience of many people in organisations. On the other hand, the human race has been continually on the move. It is now recognised that we all came out of Africa at some stage in the very distant past, and this has been beautifully portrayed in the BBC2 series *The Incredible Human Journey* (May–June 2009). All cultures have their stories of intrepid journeys, and one commentator on Homer states: 'The *Iliad* is not so much concerned with what people do, as with the way they do it, above all the way they face suffering and death' (Taplin, 1986).

Many people with mental distress talk about going on a journey; telling stories on that journey; and either holding someone's hope or having that lantern of hope held for them. One might describe it as a pilgrimage. The word 'pilgrim' derives from the Latin *perigrinus*: stranger from foreign parts. This derives from *per* (beyond) and *agre* (field). Mursell (2005) reminds us that when Moses said 'I have been an alien residing in a foreign land' (Exodus 2:22) he used the Hebrew word *ger* (a sojourner or nomad), but whether we have been exiled or not we still often feel strangers in a strange land.

As an islander I often describe myself as being marooned or on a small boat tossed on an angry sea, with no port in sight. I used to live a couple of hundred metres from Corbiere Lighthouse at the southwestern-most tip of Jersey, with its tales of shipwrecks and the heroism of lighthouse keepers going to people's rescue, often at the cost of their own lives. We sometimes don't realise how much of a stranger we are. It was only when I read Brian Sykes' *The Blood of the Isles* (2006) and took a DNA test that I realised that, although my paternal line is Anglo-Saxon, which makes a lot of sense in that Gilbert is a Teutonic, Anglo-Saxon name and I look Anglo-Saxon, my matrilineal DNA goes back to a land between the Tigris and the Euphrates, where my ancestors farmed and then moved along the Mediterranean coast. My maternal grandmother's parents were a Roman Catholic Portuguese man and a French Huguenot woman. My grandmother married a Scots Presbyterian, so within the space of a couple of generations you have a mix of European cultures and religions, with a DNA stretching back to the Middle East. As a Roman Catholic partly descended from a French Huguenot I can see myself in some ways as an asylum seeker from two religious groups.

And as we move on this pilgrimage, is it one of hope – or of perpetual exile?

Tales of Exile

The toughest game of all is against yourself. (BBC1 TV trailer for Wimbledon, 2009)

The author Graham Greene once said that 'childhood was the germ of all mistrust'. I tend to say that I had a very happy childhood on the island of Jersey. What I leave out, unless pushed, is the traumatic experience of going to a prep school in England at the age of eight. It is one of these ironies of life that my father, who was an only child, was sent to a school at an early age because his parents were in India (his father was a doctor in the old Imperial Indian Army). He hadn't enjoyed that experience, but strangely repeated it with me. This is often the case, isn't it, that human beings slip into patterns of behaviour. It's another paradox that these private schools which people paid for their children to go to were staffed with mainly unqualified teachers; they provided food that wasn't fit to be served to animals; they had no heating, so children froze both day and night; and children rarely saw their parents. I do remember some good things about it, strangely enough; the assistant matron was a young German woman, who once told us that when she was a child she took the school bus to school. One day she was late and the bus left without her; it collided with a train on a level crossing and many of her friends were killed. She always felt that God had saved her to do something good with her life, and I remember her being a beacon of kindness in an institution which Dickens would have delighted in describing. There was also a teacher who gave me, with my father, a love of history, and another who first read Tolkien to me, which has remained an abiding love.

But one woman teacher, whose name I vividly remember, took great delight in telling me that I was stupid, over and over again! As we now know with cognitive processes, these messages have a dangerous life of their own. And, under pressure, her voice comes back to haunt me. I know that when this book is published I will look at it and I will raise two fingers to that teacher, but by that gesture does she win or do I?

One of the strange events coming out of those four bleak years is the fact that I am perhaps the only person in the world to have beaten a peer in a boxing match. Alexander, Lord Hesketh, the subsequent owner of the racing car operation which made James Hunt a champion, was a friend of mine, and I beat him over three rounds when we were both nine years old – well it's an achievement of sorts!

At the end of four years my academic standing was appallingly low, and I had to be sent to a crammer in Selsey Bill, Sussex where a combination of edible food, fresh air and sympathetic teaching raised my academic level by about 20 per cent, enough to get me into secondary education.

The Benedictine School of Worth Abbey, Sussex was an overwhelmingly positive experience. The head, Father Dominic Gaisford, was a charismatic figure, who led from the front and created a sympathetic environment where people could build on their innate talents and discover others. I think one of the issues that was relevant to my experience of depression was the fact that I find it very difficult to accept and love myself as a child. This is partly due to the four years being told I was a failure; but also because, although my parents didn't pressure me, I always felt that I didn't live up to their expectations. My parents were both exceptionally good at sport, and I was hopeless. It was only at 15, when I started to play rugby, badminton and especially to run with some degree of energy, if not skill, that I began to gain some self-respect. To be honest I think I have rejected my childhood self. I was delighted, when I started to run competitively, that I became as good, perhaps even a better runner than my father had been.

After school I joined the Army, which was a kind of pilgrimage all of its own; and then from doing a degree in history, I went into social work, where after undertaking generic work, I found myself for six years as Principal Social Worker in one of the old learning disability hospitals. There must be something that attracts me to institutions and although it had a few merits as a service, one of the aspects which will always haunt me is those people who have no written history. Because of the habit of 'swapping' people from one institution to another, some people only had a name and the record of the institution they came from, but no other history whatsoever, except perhaps a date of birth and their religion. For them their pilgrimage was unrecorded. In the pilgrimage of exile and return, what do we do if we have no story to tell?

Into the Crevasse

Hilary Mantel (2004: 6) quotes Margaret Atwood: 'The written word is so much like evidence – like something that can be used against you.' But in Shakespeare's *Macbeth,* Malcolm says to Macduff:

> Ne'er pull your hat upon your brows:
> Give sorrow words. The grief that does not speak
> Whispers the o'erfraught heart and bids it break
>
> (IV, iii)

So sometimes one has to write things down, as well as talking about them, to gain a full perspective. I came into post as a Director of Social Services in the midst of a budget crisis, having to take 10 per cent out of a budget that was already a 'busted flush'. I managed to argue that figure down to 7 per cent, but it was still a massive challenge. I was fortunate that I had a supportive Chair of the Social Services Committee, a very committed and creative staff group and a voluntary sector prepared to work in partnership to try to reshape rather than simply slash services. It may seem an odd thing to say, but when you have good people around you, as I had had in my previous job as Director of Operations in Staffordshire (see Gilbert, 2005: 71–73) crisis work can be much more exhilarating and fulfilling than in times of stability. Having worked through that, though, a few years later when another budget crisis hit unexpectedly, a scapegoat was needed and I was the chosen one!

Hard work and pressure are not a problem for me, but the particular behind-the-scenes backstabbing that I was subjected to triggered the kind of doubts that stemmed back to my childhood at the Dickensian school. Perhaps one of the most difficult things to deal with is the overwhelming sense of personal responsibility that public sector leaders have. I thought it was purely up to me to sort the crisis, even though the systems that had failed were not of my making; in fact that was part of the reason a scapegoat was needed. I slept literally two hours a night, I went into the office when the security guards were still there and the office wasn't properly opened so that I could try to solve the unsolvable. After the crisis, several colleagues at national level asked me why I hadn't asked for help, as they would have supported me. It doesn't seem to have occurred to me at all, because I had to hold the ring and sort things out. Perhaps I was like T. S. Eliot's 'broken king':

> It you came at night like a broken king ...
> It would be the same, when you leave the rough road
> ... And what you thought you came for
> Is only a shell, a husk of meaning
>
> (*Little Gidding*, 1942)

When I eventually went to see my GP, I was already well down the crevasse, yet I had no idea I was there at all. Looking back, I think that the nearest thing to it was something that happened to me when I was in the Army. I was climbing in the Alps, as the middle person of a threesome, when, moving over a ledge, it collapsed, plummeting me earthwards to the extremity of the rope. I can still remember looking down several hundred feet and feeling that this was the end. I was fortunate that my colleagues (both experienced climbers) pulled me back and saved my life. Often now my question to participants in workshops is: 'Who's holding your rope?'

I was very fortunate that the GP I saw was a woman whom I've met on several occasions (one of my friends who suffers from bipolar disorder says that, living in London, she never sees the same GP twice), and her first words were most helpful: 'This is shit!' In some ways these are the most basic, but also the most poetic and powerful words anyone has ever said to me (except 'I love you'). This may seem strange, but 'this' was helpful because she didn't say 'you' are shit, but being cognisant of the severe difficulties both health and social care were in around the county area at the time, she spoke about the situation and helped me see that I didn't need to feel responsible for others' mistakes. The use of the word 'shit' was a great human response to my personal distress. Sometimes the anger of others on our behalf is very cleansing and purifying. My GP was also very skilled in diagnosing what I needed and suggested both sleeping tablets and antidepressants. Like so many professionals I know, I really didn't want to take the antidepressants. I really didn't want to admit that I was ill – I couldn't afford to be depressed – as I had to save the situation, didn't I? I don't know how she did this in the time, but my GP managed to take on board that I had other social supports and allowed me a sense of control in not accepting the antidepressants at the time, even though she felt I needed them (in retrospect I did), but offered me an open door to return. Within six weeks I was back asking for the antidepressants, which I have to say were very helpful. I couldn't have got through the crisis without them.

At this stage I was feeling both anxious and depressed; hyperactive, but beginning to slide further down the crevasse; I had suicidal thoughts, but perhaps was fortunate that my career ambitions have always been much more to do with creating new and innovative ways of working than social status. Being a Director of Social Services had never been a lifetime ambition and therefore losing that status, as I moved within six months to early retirement from local government, was not the end of the line. I was not like the recent example of bankers committing suicide, left without a meaning and purpose in life. On the other hand, I wasn't sure where my path would lead me next.

As an extrovert and somebody who, in terms of the Enneagram (which I find helpful, see Hampson, 2005), majors on achieving things and caring for others, I wasn't sure where I was going. As somebody who lives through connections, I felt strangely disconnected from myself, from other people, from the world around me and from God. I was very much a stranger in a strange land, with no path clear to me. As Eliot puts it:

> The parched eviscerate soil
> gapes at the vanity of toil
> (*Little Gidding*)

I'm a firm believer in people coming into one's life at a particular time for a specific purpose. A new friend came into my life just before the crisis, somebody who worked in the voluntary sector and could see exactly what was happening. As the crisis hit, she took the trouble to recognise that I would be suffering from a crisis of confidence and wrote me a letter:

> Over the next few weeks things that are 'put in writing' are going to be very important to what happens to you, and with you, so here's a few things in writing.
>   You are one of the most supportive and intuitively understanding people I know. You care about people and you care about justice ... Your style is people-centred and you make everyone feel that they matter – whoever they are and whatever their position. It will be hard to hold onto your self-esteem and self-belief. But I'll do all I can to help ... I'm here for you.

In many ways, like my good GP, that was the jolt on the rope, holding me, stopping my downward trajectory into the chasm, the crevasse. I still carry that letter with me, though no longer 'need' it as I did then. It has changed my personal behaviour, because, while I might have been 'people-centred' before, I now say and write things with more emphasis. With people who doubt themselves, I speak with them as though that moment is the last chance we have. I notice that many people, when given a compliment, throw it over their shoulder! Perhaps it is importunate of me, but I repeat the compliment and ask them to look at me while I am giving it. So many giving people give very little to themselves; while the self-centred and selfish ones hog everything.

I was fortunate that during the crisis I had a place of spiritual asylum. I have mentioned the Benedictine school at Worth, and I went back to the monastery, stayed in one of the guest rooms and joined the community as much as I could. They were very warm and welcoming, very affirming and supportive. I felt disconnected from God, and I suppose my belief in God is always somewhat shaky. Perhaps I should thank Richard Dawkins for reinforcing my belief in God, because I sometimes think that it increases just to counteract Dawkins' smug atheism! It is the benefit of ritual that I could go into the abbey church for the regular chanting of the monastic office and simply sit with the monks as they prayed the psalms. I didn't have to do anything; it was their belief that held me up, like being in a salt bath, buoyed up by others' faith. I wrote about this a few years ago, and part of the poem follows:

Years later ...
When the tomb door was shut on me,
So sand silted up my ears,
My eyes, my brain, and my heart.

The crypt sealed with a metal trap door –
Tight! Bolted down.
Then, it was human hands
Reached down to me
And pulled me up.
Because I couldn't hear.
Could bear,
The music,
I sought the comfort
Of my faith family
And listened to the rhythm
The measure of the psalms
The rhyme and rhythm bore me up
Like the waves ... beating, carrying.

The listeners delved,
And dug out the silted, cloying sand,
With their ears and hands,
Listening to the ear of the heart.
They digested the grit for me.
So, another conversion
In conversation,
Communion
In communication.

Flow and ebb, blue on blue,
The restless sea,
The restless heart,
But there is a me, and there is a you.
                    (Coyte et al., 2007: 275–276)

Another vital element on my road to recovery was a friend who had been through a similar experience. He and I used to run together and share common concerns. My running club, of which he was a member, was also a great support. It may seem odd to say so but running in company is very much like praying in community. The rhythm of the movement in company – companionship without the necessity of conversation; the solidarity of a mutual society – is very healing, as well as the physical effects of the endorphins (see Gilbert, 2005).

I also went for counselling on my own initiative, rather than through the NHS. In many ways I found it helpful in looking back at my life to ascertain how the past influences the present. Now, I feel sure that I should have undertaken some cognitive behavioural therapy (CBT) as well as a more psychotherapeutic approach. While I think there is a real danger in seeing psychological therapies as a panacea, as some seem to think, and while they are not necessarily helpful in all cultural circumstances, I think in my case they would have been helpful to change the messages in my head.

Lastly, I was very fortunate to have a number of colleagues show faith in me and invite me to work for them. I was particularly privileged to have Antony Sheehan, who was then setting up the National Institute for Mental Health in England (NIMHE) ask me to take on the lead for social care, which then became the NIMHE/SCIE Fellowship with Professor Nick Gould; and subsequently to take on the lead role on spiritually and mental health, which was a role which has in many ways transformed my life, as it has brought me in touch with so many exceptional and courageous people (see Stickley & Basset, 2008: chapter 28).

One final reflection is that, although I see myself as a supporter of the recovery approach, with major connections between recovery and spirituality, there are always problems with the use of language. Just as with spirituality, people often think that we are really talking about religion, when it is not necessarily so. Our essential life-force may have a religious dimension, but the sense of the transcendent may not involve membership of a religious organisation. The problem with the word 'recovery' is that there is sometimes a pressure to recover! Many people I speak to prefer to use the word 'discovery', with its connotations of a continued journey, a pilgrimage. I kept thinking that I had recovered, only to ponder more deeply and realise that I hadn't. When I started to return to partial employment in the spring of 2001, I thought I was better, but soon realised that I was still very vulnerable and liable to relapse. A real moment of transition from illness to semi-illness to wellness occurred in June 2002. I joined NIMHE colleagues at the launch conference in Newcastle upon Tyne and was struck by my colleague, Tony Russell, remarking that the distinction between severe and mild mental illness was quite often unhelpful, because quite often he felt both – sometimes on the same day! The conference was a very uplifting event, and I took the time afterwards to spend three days on my own visiting the island of Lindisfarne, where St Cuthbert had had his sacred space, and Bamburgh Castle. I recalled my days sitting at the feet of the admirable Maurice Keen, my history tutor at Balliol, talking about the Anglo-Saxons and their struggles with the meaning of life. On the last day I was there I was running along the beach with the castle on my left, the white-tipped waves rolling on my right and Lindisfarne Castle etched on the skyline with a deep-bloodied sunset. In a moment, and I don't think it was especially a religious moment, I felt a sense of transcendence – a deep sense of hope, if not peace; and a beacon of promise for the future.

The Bridge of Love

Only the soul that knows the mighty grief can know the mighty rapture. Sorrow comes to stretch out the spaces in the heart for joy. (Edwin Markham, 1915)

Recognising our common humanity and our uniqueness seems to me to be at the heart of our being (and *doing*) human, our role as citizens and our work in whatever vocation we profess. In his recent Reith Lectures, the philosopher Michael Sandel states that civic virtues are strengthened by use and that we must be careful that we do not descend into a purely market-oriented society in which humans are merely units of consumption (Sandel, 2009).

As a lover of fantasy novels, I am intrigued to note that Terry Pratchett, who has recently done a great service to people with Alzheimer's by talking about his progressive condition, writes about ethical dilemmas of citizenship. Characters such as the monk Brutha, in *Small Gods* (1993) and Watch commander Sam Vimes, are models of integrity in a shifting world. If integrity is about wholeness, it is noticeable that well-known villains, such as Sauron in Tolkien's *Lord of the Rings* and Lord Voldemort in Rowling's *Harry Potter* series, are partly undone by their lack of empathy with others; and also because they have, through a lack of integrity, split their souls into separate component parts to try to make themselves stronger, but this is their weakness. Whereas for T. S. Eliot 'The fire and the rose are one', for those without integrity they are separated.

Over the past few years people have begun to tell their story so that there is the sharing of the fullness of humanity. As Cardinal Basil Hume put it: 'Shared weakness binds more that shared strength' (McAllister, 2009).

It is still sometimes difficult for people in a position of authority to disclose strength through tears, as opposed to the Nazis' rallying cry of 'strength through joy'. Although Winston Churchill, often spoke of 'the black dog' of depression, David Brindle (2008) pointed out recently that while Alastair Campbell should be congratulated for 'coming out about his depression', most politicians are still wary of doing so.

Recently, Ian McPherson, the former director of NIMHE and now head of the new National Health Development Unit, spoke about his episodes of depression and how it allows him a measure of understanding as to what it is to be seen as 'separate' because of mental ill-health (O'Hara, 2009).

I find that as I speak about my own experiences, as I give presentations on spirituality across the country, this seems to open a 'bridge' to those in the room who feel that they can gain increased empathic connection through this disclosure.

Recently, a student social worker wrote to me after I gave a lecture to a new group of social work students:

I just want to say thank you for giving me inspiration to complete my social work course. I came to the opening seminar that you led feeling quite poorly as I was struggling with anxiety and depression. I was wondering how I was able to help people if I was feeling so bad and vulnerable myself. I was doubting myself at a difficult time of my life. What you said in the seminar gave me inspiration and strength.

I saw you as a strong professional figure with passion and dedication to helping people, who most importantly, wasn't afraid to admit that you have experienced such difficult times that each and every one of us do. I was inspired by you and decided to continue with the course. I agree when you said that people like you and me are more connected to experience and have the deeper understanding of the impact that mental health has on us. It opens us spiritually and widens our understanding. (personal communication)

To use religious language we might say, as Paul of Tarsus put it: 'Let us exalt too in our hardships. Understanding that suffering develops perseverance, and perseverance develops a tested character – something that gives us hope. A hope that will not let us down, because the love of God has been pulled into our hearts by the Holy Spirit' (Romans 5:3–5). Or in a secular sense we might identify with Thornton Wilder's journey of a series of disparate characters in *The Bridge of San Luis Rey* (1927), when he writes:

> But soon we will die and all memory … will have left earth, and we ourselves should be loved for a while and forgotten, but the love will have been enough: all those impulses of love return to the love that made them. Even memory is not necessary for love. There is a land of the living and a land of the dead, and the bridge is love. The only survival, the only meaning.

Recently, I sat and listened to a friend and colleague whose mother was dying of cancer. She'd been given six months to live. Some members of her family were pushing her to fight the illness, but her daughter wished to accede to her wishes to let go of life in peace. As she talked, I had tears running down my cheeks. My friend said: 'Thank you for crying for me, because I do not have time to cry now, while I may cry later.' The next day she got her mother into a hospice. Her mother didn't last six months, she died three days later, surrounded by the hospice chaplain and her family.

In society where we are always looking back and looking forward, and find what has been called 'the sacrament of the present moment' so hard to embrace and celebrate, there is a danger that we put off to some nonexistent future what we need to say and do today. As we cross our bridge on the pilgrimage of life, we need to share the laughter, joy, hope – and yes, our tears – because all we have is *now*.

References

Aaron M (2008) Spirituality, the heart of caring. *A Life in the Day*, *12(4)* (November 2008): 23–26

Arif Z (2002) Islam and Identity among British Pakistani Youth. BSc dissertation, Keele University

Brindle D (2008) A positive spin on mental health issues. *Society Guardian* (15 October): 4

Burke J (2009) 'Divided Poland falls out over solidarity', *The Observer* (31 May): 26–27

Burleigh M (2006) *Earthly Powers: Religion and Politics in Europe from the Enlightenment to the Great War*, London: HarperPerennial

Coyte M E, Gilbert P & Nicholls V (Eds.) (2007) *Spirituality, Values and Mental Health: Jewels for the Journey*, London: Jessica Kingsley

Davies P (2006) *The Goldilocks Enigma: Why is the Universe Just Right for Life?* London: Allen Lane

Durrell L ([1945] 1962) *Prospero's Cell: Guide to the Landscape and Manners of the Island of Corfu*, London: Faber and Faber (see Nicholls and Gilbert, 2007).

Faulks S (2005) *Human Traces*. London: Vintage

Gilbert P (2005) *Leadership: Being Effective and Remaining Human*. Lyme Regis: Russell House Publishing

Gilbert P (2005) Keep up your spirits. *Open Mind*, *135* (September/October): 6–8

Gilbert P (2008) *From the Cradle – To Beyond the Grave?* Proceedings of the second National Multifaith Conference, DVD. Stafford: Staffordshire University

Gilbert P (2009) *Being and Doing Human*, SSSMHNHSFT Conference (6 November)

Gilbert P with Bates P, Carr S, Clark M, Gould N & Slay G (2010) *The Value of Everything: Social Work and its Importance in the Field of Mental Health*, second edition. Lyme Regis: Russell House Publishing

Goffman E ([1963] 1990) *Stigma: Notes on the Management of Spoiled Identity*, London: Penguin Books

Gray J (2007) *Black Mass: Apocalyptic Religion and the Death of Utopia*, London: Allen Lane

Hampson M (2005) *Head versus Heart and Our Gut Reactions: The 21st Century Enneagram*. Ropley: O Books

Hay D (2006) *Something There: the Biology of the Human Spirit*. London: Darton, Longman & Todd

Holt S (2009) *Psychotic Interlude*. Brentwood: Chipmunk Publishing

Inge J (2003) *A Christian Theology of Place*. Aldershot: Ashgate

Keedwell P (2008) *How Sadness Survived: The Evolutionary Basis of Depression*. Oxford: Radcliffe Publishing

Kershaw, I. (2008) *Hitler, The Germans, and the Final Solution*, New Haven, CT: Yale University Press

King U (2009) *The Search for Spirituality: Our Global Quest for Meaning and Fulfilment*. Norwich: Canterbury Press

Le Guin U K ([1974] 2002) *The Dispossessed*. London: Millennium Press

McAllister S (2009) A pastoral heart. *The Tablet* (13 June): 8–98

Mantel H (2004) *Giving up the Ghost: A Memoir*. London: HarperPerennial

Markham E (1915) *The Shoes of Happiness and Other Poems*. New York: Doubleday

Maslow A H (1968) *Toward a Psychology of Being*. New York: Von Norstrand

McKenzie K (2007) Being black in Britain is bad for your mental health. *Guardian* (2 April): 32

Modood T. (2007) *Multiculturalism: A Civic Idea*. Cambridge, Polity Press

Mursell G (2005) *Praying in Exile*. London: Darton, Longman & Todd

Myss C (1997) *Anatomy of the Spirit*. New York, Bantam Press

Nicholls V & Gilbert P (2007) The sea, me and God. *Open Mind*, *144* (March/April)

O'Hara M (2009) Voice of experience. *Society Guardian* (24 June): 5

Parkes M & Gilbert P with Deuchar N, Thomas S & Barber J (2010 forthcoming) Gods and Gurdwaras: the spiritual care programme at the Birmingham and Solihull Mental Health Foundation Trust. *Mental Health, Religion and Culture*.

Pratchett T (1993) *Small Gods*. London: Corgi Paperbacks

Sandel M (2009) A new politics of the common good. *Reith Lectures* (30 June)

Stickley T & Basset T (Eds.) (2008) *Learning about Mental Heath Practice*. Chichester: Wiley

Sykes B (2006) *The Blood of the Isles*. London: Bantam Press

Taplin O (1986) Homer. In J Boardman, J Griffin & O Murray (1986) *The Oxford History of the Classical World*. Oxford: Oxford University Press

Wilder T (1927) *The Bridge of San Luis Rey*. New York: HarperPerennial

Wolpert L (2006) *Malignant Sadness: The Anatomy of Depression*, third edition. London: Faber and Faber

I am, can't get over it
The sadness and the loss
The memories that just
Won't budge
How to experience the suffering
Of somebody else
To actually live this way
To give more than you get
To change your own life
By sacrifice
There must be something worthwhile
In all this
I miss my parents even my brother
And sister
I can't get around it
There is so much left to do
I must work hard
Some might think that this activity
Isn't as strenuous
As working as a skilled labourer
And yet. By allowing myself,
David, to turn into something
Or somebody else
It might make a difference
It might have the effect of changing
What I was before I left life behind
And lived off my experiences.

Dave St. Clair, 'Have You Ever Felt Lonely?'

Ian – he rose to the challenge
Seeing me lying there
On the railway line
I didn't realise that he
Must have seen me jump
Off the bridge
Anyway his heroism
As he climbed the
Surrounding fence
I was in so much pain
From fracturing my spine
That my recollections
Vague so seeing a group
Of people watching
I yelled something or other
At them
It was weird
So strange
What I done well it was
Too late to make it right
The deed
By attempting my life
I felt finally
That it was me who made
That decision to kill myself
No one else
Yet having done so now
In recollection I certainly
Wouldn't advise it to anyone.

Dave St. Clair, 'He Saved My Bacon'

10

The Holy Spirit – Healer, Advocate, Guide and Friend

Richard Lilly

When I had my first psychotic interlude in the spring of 1971, I had no idea that it was not just a one-off nervous breakdown, but a chronic illness I was condemned to live with for the rest of my life.

The medicine I was put on, as I was diagnosed as suffering from paranoid schizophrenia, gave me an appalling time. In terms of thinking I could neither remember nor articulate any thoughts. Physically, I was like an old man, even though I was only 24 years old at the time. This experience led me to an initial, but deeply felt hatred of psychiatric drugs.

How my life continued, as a later diagnosed manic depressive, covers nearly 40 years' experience of the mental health circuit. In that time I have learnt about many alternative treatments, but despite using these as complementary, my experience has taught me to stick to the established medicines, even though their effects are not always helpful.

In this chapter I write about my Christian faith which has sustained and nourished me throughout my life. Without my faith I could not have perceived a way to continue to make sense of my life as someone condemned to suffer my illness, together with the drawbacks of treatments that are really in their very early stages, considering all that is yet to be known about the function of that extraordinary organ that controls each human being – the brain.

The Holy Spirit has been many things to me on my life's journey.

In the Old Testament, the Jewish view of the Holy Spirit is that it was the guide to right and wrong. At best it is that which enables one to recognise God. The Holy Spirit inspired the prophets.

With Jesus Christ the Holy Spirit took on a new life. In St John's Gospel, in the Last Supper dialogue, Jesus lays out the basis of this new friend, which he was

Voices of Experience: Narratives of Mental Health Survivors   Edited by Thurstine Basset and Theo Stickley ©2010 John Wiley & Sons, Ltd.

going to send his disciples when he returned to Heaven. Jesus calls the Holy Spirit the 'spirit of truth', 'the teacher in all things', that which would bring to the remembrance of his disciples all that Christ said and taught.

He would be the reproof of sin, as after Christ man had no cloak for his sin; the reproof of righteousness, as Jesus Christ had risen to the right-hand side of God to reign on his throne in Heaven; the reproof of judgment, as the prince of the world was judged.

Different translations give different names to the Holy Spirit. In the New English he is the Advocate. In the King James he is the Comforter and the Councillor. In Barclays (A famous Bible commentator theologian) he is the Helper. The latter is based on the Greek word for the Holy Spirit, *Parakletos* ('answer for a call for help' in translation).

In the history of Christianity the Holy Spirit has picked up numerous descriptive names: guard, guide, stay, provider, intercessor, interpreter, sustenance, adviser.

In the Gospels and Acts the Holy Spirit is responsible for the conception of the Christ Child, the healing strength of the apostles. He is the inheritance of converts who are baptised with the Holy Spirit.

The hymn 'Lead us Heavenly Father, lead us' sums up the Holy Spirit for Christians:

> Spirit of our God descending,
> Fill our hearts with heavenly joy.
> Love with every passion blending,
> Pleasure that can never cloy.
> Thus provided, pardoned, guided,
> Nothing can our peace destroy.

How does one practically interpret such a force? One man put it, 'adequate, accurate, definite information can come from the mind of God to the mind of man', this through the power of the Holy Spirit. He also said: 'When man listens, God speaks. When man obeys, God acts. The result is miracles' – this through the power of the Holy Spirit. At best prayer in silence is a two-way process of us speaking to God and God speaking to us. The best way to remember the thoughts that come in this way through the Holy Spirit is to write them down, making a form of contract.

The Holy Spirit will comment on every detail of our life, however large, however small. He may demand costly decisions in our behaviour: forgiveness, reparation, apology, honesty, a change in relationships. Absolute love, *agape*, the love of God for mankind, and the love of God between human beings, is the guideline.

I have found it of priceless importance, on my many admissions to hospital, to actually think out to the other patients and staff in a time of quiet; seeking the guidance of the Holy Spirit on what to do with my time, as a daily discipline.

I am afraid there is confusion here. The rapid flow of thoughts in hypo-mania makes one think one is inspired. There is no alternative here to the slowing effects of anti-psychotic drugs. I have to admit I suffer from a brain disease which can only be cured in my experience by the control of proteins in the central nervous system, in the higher areas of my brain, the control system, by taking medication.

Being able to distinguish between the speeded-up ideas of my brain when I am hypo-manic and normal thought is something I do in order to know when I require extra medication. I medicate myself through and out of my highs.

The objectivity to do this is guaranteed because I am not alone; the Holy Spirit dwells within me. It is a property of God that he has the humility to tell me when a major tranquilliser is the only thing between me and insanity.

When I am hypo-manic I have an almost constant flow of thoughts running through my head. As I am excited it is very difficult to slow down and distinguish what is worthwhile. Only by being able to relate to people around me and continue to be practical can I remain realistic. Only by taking medication is this possible.

The Holy Spirit is also subject to the illness. I have to trust in the grace of God until I come down, and medicate myself.

In morning prayer the *Te Deum* ends with the lines: 'O God in thee I have trusted. Let me never be confounded.' After mental illness that becomes: 'Though I be confounded. O God may I still trust you.'

There is a story of a man's dream of walking along the seashore with Christ. In his dream the man saw two sets of footprints in the sand. Sometimes these would come to an end and there would only be one. The man said, 'Christ why did you leave me?' Christ answered, 'I did not leave you. Those were the times that I carried you.'

It is worth remembering what Christ said in Luke 4, on his return to his hometown:

> So he came to Nazareth, where he had been brought up, and went to synagogue on the Sabbath day as he regularly did. He stood up to read the lesson and was handed the scroll of the prophet Isaiah. He opened the scroll and found the passage which says,
>
>> The spirit of the Lord is upon me because he has anointed me;
>> He has sent me to announce good news to the poor,
>> To proclaim release for prisoners and recovery of sight for the blind;
>> To let the broken victims go free,
>> To proclaim the year of the Lord's favour.
>
> He rolled up the scroll, gave it back to the attendant, and sat down; and all eyes in the synagogue were fixed on him.

In the twenty-first century it would seem that Christ no longer healed in this way. But it is worth referring to the words of Paul in 2 Corinthians 12:

> and so, to keep me from being unduly elated by the magnificence of such revelations, I was given a sharp physical pain which came as Satan's messenger to bruise me,

this was to save me from being unduly elated. Three times I begged the Lord to rid me of it, but his answer was,

'My grace is all you need; power comes to its full strength in weakness'. I shall therefore prefer to find my joy and pride in the very things that are my weakness; and then the power of Christ will come and rest upon me. Hence I am well content, for Christ's sake, with weakness, contempt, persecution, hardship and frustration; for when I am weak, then I am strong.

As Mother Theresa said, we who suffer are as the Christ Child to be cared for. The Roman Catholics insist on the identification of our suffering with the suffering of Christ on the cross. The Holy Spirit is the keeper in heart, soul, mind and body. He is the healer. He is the friend.

Alone in the dark he lies there and waits
Afraid now he trembles like outside hell's gates
A boy still inside although outside a man
He cries himself to sleep 'Is this part of god's plan?'
This pain that he feels from deep down inside
Wipes the tears from his eye in effort to hide
The walls of his life just keep crashing down
No wonder he's often seen sporting a frown
She enters the room bringing the freshness of joy
As the boy in this man seems quiet and coy
She moves to him swiftly a hurried event
And tells him most gently his problems to vent
The boy and the man start to cry once again
Through emotional turmoil and anger and pain
She kisses him softly and speaks in his ear
That there's no need to worry as she'll always be here
Through the mist of his tears he stares at her eyes
Searching for untruths, deception and lies
His fears are unfounded as he detects nothing there
And pulls her in closer whilst stroking her hair
Their arms lock round each other in the strongest embrace
As she looks to see the smile return to his face
The feelings of distrust all gone, as is the fear
Just because of this special woman and having her near.

Brice Jones, 'Mist of Tears'

11

CAPITAL Writings

CAPITAL (Clients and Professionals in Training and Learning) is a Sussex-based, service user-led organisation founded in 1997.

In this chapter some CAPITAL members relate their narratives of coping, survival, discovery and recovery. The important role of CAPITAL as an organisation is often central to these stories.

Millennium Madness: My Journey through Mania over the Millennium Period

Thomas France

In 1997 I had what is often known as a nervous breakdown or, in the office trade, a 'yuppie' breakdown. In 1997 Tony Blair had just been elected, and now the country was full of enthusiasm and looking forward to the twenty-first century, like a young, bright child. However, this time was not such a rosy picture for me ... the stress of working in the American Express Office with its VDU terminals in upgrade (to Microsoft IBMs with 'Windows' and 'PowerPoint'), along with corporate debt collection, slowly piling pressure on me. My hair started to thin into a balding allotment patch, my home life became more and more strained, not fitting into the family home with mum and dad after the shenanigans of my student lifestyle away and, to top it all, my health started to suffer! I went down with bronchitis and a fever. Going to my doctor for antibiotics, he suggested I might be run down, with stress as a factor, and suggested antidepressants. So I went on Prozac, amitriptyline and temazepam. Bad idea! I rapidly started hallucinating and went a little mad. My teddy bear seemed to be talking to me, nagging

Voices of Experience: Narratives of Mental Health Survivors Edited by Thurstine Basset and Theo Stickley ©2010 John Wiley & Sons, Ltd.

me for not giving him a wash over all these years … nagging me over neglect over these long years of adulthood! My mum found me in the shower, in my clothes, scrubbing my teddy bear – she knew something was up. My thoughts were racing like a Formula 1 car; I started to lose my perception of self or identity, thinking my name as a moniker that I could not live up to. My father had recently had a heart attack and was taking early retirement and he'd decided to chop down the apple tree and replant it with a new one. In the rain, I scrambled into the back garden nude and tried to splice one of the old roots to the new tree, as if I could transfer the sap from one tree to another. I began to see myself as old dead wood – the old tree a reflection of myself. My mother worried, tried to calm me down, but failed. My brother, also at home, could not understand me as I raved. Evil moods took my temper and I'd curse into my pillow at night and insomnia gripped me. I dared not sleep; I started to pray to God. Despite being a theological sceptic as a student, mania made me believe again, making me check out St Peter's Church in Brighton, with more curiosity in the church than my million pound accounts at work! I turned up to the office not in a suit but ragged clothes from my student days, creating a ludicrous image. My bosses told me to take some time off. Soon, psychiatric services were alerted and I was told I was to be put on a section.

The next thing I know I'm being told I have to have an injection – anally administered!! It might not have been so bad if it was a pretty nurse, but it was a bearded guy … still it can't have been too much fun for him either. Actually, Matthew turned out to be a respected member of psychiatric services and has showed an interest in my life since 1997! At the time the drug he injected (500 ml Clopixol) knocked me for six, like a potent opiate. It worked to slow the hyper-manic speed of consciousness and speed of speech that possessed me, but at the expense of leaving me like a George Romero zombie from *Dawn of the Dead* – monosyllabic and deeply depressed. The ward had young women running up and down cutting their wrists and screaming they wanted to die. Upon waking it seemed like being in hell – from executive dreams on the top floor of the Amex office to the bedlam of being in an acute unit. I had little experience of mental health issues and felt it a biological failure to be branded bipolar or manic depressive! I tried to read Marx to pass the time, wondering if capitalism had caused my downfall. The words would swim in front of my face – I couldn't focus or concentrate, my vision had lost its edge! I left the ward and went to the shops. I took an eye test and they said one eye seemed weaker than the other. They prescribed glasses and I bought them. The nurses noticed the new spectacles and told the doctors. They took them off me, saying it was the drugs affecting my vision. I stared at Marx and the page blurred! I picked up a novel (*Treasure Island* by Robert Louis Stephenson) and still the words would not sit still. The Clopixol was pretty powerful. A year after my diagnosis, my psychiatrist was struck off the NHS for wrongful prescription of medications and I still wonder if the drugs I was on were the right prescription. But Matthew says it worked to stop my mania and was necessary at the time. I gradually made friends among the patients and a group of us would make a daily pilgrimage to the hospital fish-tank. I'd help put the daily crossword on a white board every day. This task seemed a burden on the drug-induced fever and I'd be sweating and squinting the whole time I was writing the crossword on the board! Every Sunday I'd go to the hospital chapel and sit with a group of elderly ladies. Embarrassingly, my voice would croak, cracked and dry, the result of having a sore throat from smoking too many fags to pass the time. The old folk seemed fitter and healthier than me in my twenties! I started art therapy and picked up a paintbrush for the first time in nearly ten years. I even helped in the garden – cleaning out an old shed that had gone dusty and was filled with spider's webs. Matthew decided I could become an outpatient and found me a council flat so I could have a new start. Despite being depressed with what I perceived to be a fall from grace, I knew I had to grasp this opportunity to live again by the horns and took the flat on. A new life … a new beginning. But I was to go through a darker spell before recovery!

I had to go to a day hospital for three months. Despite doing pottery and art therapy along with yoga and relaxation therapies I wanted more! I was in denial about my condition and believed I was normal again. I had put on a little weight (from the medication), but other than that I was the same as before and knew I could go back to work! After three months at day hospital I decided to ask for a return to work, my boss agreed, but on a part-time basis. I was to have a weekly consultation with my boss, but was treated much the same as before by the staff. I felt like I was rejuvenated by my time away and after a month I was awarded 'employee of the month' for my return to work from adversity and I banished my breakdown from my mind, like sweeping dirt under the carpet! Soon, I was working full-time again. But when my mind started to daydream I would start to sweat with a paranoia – was everyone treating me with kid gloves, was I just being humoured by the staff, was I being intellectually patted like a poodle? I'd find my temper stretched, cursing under my breath at the smallest mistakes and my karma became more and more negative. I started to worry … was I leading a double life? However hard I tried to banish my time in the psychiatric ward, I couldn't succeed in wiping the time away. The pressure of trying to fit into the image of the professional moneyman was making me crack up. One day the Amex computer network started to play up and I found myself cursing at my terminal, and my boss, worried, suggested I took another break. Slightly bitterly I left the office wondering what had happened to 'employee of the month'. That day the whole Amex network crashed and I felt like a scapegoat … I was the bug on the system or the ghost in the machine! From there my mood worsened.

I tried to keep up links with the day hospital and attended a community centre for people with mental health problems. Just because I knew it must be good to share my experiences with other sufferers (or as they are now known, 'service users') I could not beat my depression. From a degree with honours and aspirations for a 'normal' life with a wife, kids and all the middle-class trappings I knew I was now destined for a different lifestyle. Was I a failure? Lethargy filled my bones and I found myself wiling away time to just be back in bed sleeping, I didn't want to be in the daylight at all! I started wondering what it would be like to take my life! One day I wrote a suicide note for my parents and stuffed it into my sock draw. I wandered the street and ended up at the station. Should I jump in front of the train? I dare not do that as it would emotionally scar the driver – it would not be fair on him. I ended up on the top of a multi-storey car park. I knew someone who had jumped and broken his spine there … maybe I would be more successful if I did it. I sat on the edge with my legs dangling over for what seemed like hours. Only Christ stopped me from dropping there, dare I go to hell as a suicide victim, like a character Beatrice saw in Dante's Inferno? I prayed there was a future for me … that it wasn't always going to be a dark time. An attendant approached me asking if I was all right, an old lady had seen me and had telephoned the council. I said I was a little down but was glad someone cared. He told me not to be stupid and to smoke a fag downstairs. So I did exactly that.

Soon I knew the only way to beat the depression was to be more outgoing, more social. I ripped up the suicide note and vowed never to write another. I smiled that I had turned around and not crossed the thin red line. I had chosen life … not to jump off the the roof, but to climb back down to life. But it was no easy climb down! I knew that in my student days I had dabbled with dope and MDMA / ecstasy and wondered if that was a factor in my breakdown. If I was to start again, maybe I should at least compare these street drugs to NHS prescription drugs. I had been on a few by now (Prozac, temazepam, amitriptyline, haloperidol, procyclidine, Clopixol, Cipramil and latterly, Lustral). I soon found myself spending my Amex health pension on cannabis, speed and MDMA. It surprised me, but NHS drugs were almost stronger than street drugs in terms of effect, but I was now in a throng of more criminal society. Obviously this was an improvement on suicidal depression, but it led into a spiral of self-destructive behaviour. I decided to get pet rats at this time. I had kept a rat at university and now I thought I'd breed them. My flat became a bloc party centre and half the dropouts of Horsham passed through it … I wouldn't have dreamed of living like this a year ago. I decided my life was like a jigsaw, I was breaking up the pieces and a new jigsaw could be started!! I had a new girlfriend, Keeley, and she kept a snake. I used to let her have the baby rats that I bred as food for her snake … it's nature's way. But the relationship didn't work out. We took heroin together … to be honest the clopixol was stronger.

The next day the dealer beat me up. I thought if that's what they mean by smack I'm not going to pay for it. He ransacked my flat with his gang stealing property … golf clubs from my dad, Toby jugs collected from childhood. His girlfriend even stole my teddy bear – that's low! My flat was trashed. I watched the eclipse with a whisky bottle in my hand! When Matthew next saw me for CPN review, I had two black eyes and a broken nose. He said I should move out of town and try to start again. Keeley didn't want to quit the drugs lifestyle and we went our separate ways. A few years later she hanged herself – truly a tragedy. I know why I did what I did at that time, I was letting the sock draw annihilate that letter in a sociological way, but I knew I could never live like that again. I had to live a fresh new life and build a new lifestyle. I ended up in a small village in West Sussex.

When I first moved to the village I had very little property and huge bills and debts. My bed was broken, with only three legs; I had to prop it up with books from uni, sleeping on Chaucer and Shakespeare! Actually, there was a yellow mobile library in the village, which I had used as a boy in my mum's village. I started to read books from there and found that my focus was much improved than a year earlier. My back garden was a slightly magical place. There was a giant oak tree there and it had a preservation order on it (so it's a much valued tree!). My neighbours were elderly and couldn't tend the garden. The grass was long and hundreds of baby oaks had grown knee high from all the acorns that had dropped. The rhododendron at the back was wild and the hedge ragged, rather liked the mini-forest in the back garden and it took me half a year to get round to tending it. I had been doing a conservation course at Tilgate Forest. We had been chopping down dozens of rhododendrons as glade clearance. I realised it was ludicrous to go halfway across Sussex to chop rhodies and not tend my own! Now there are floral borders and a rose garden and pots at the front and the rhododendron (and hedge) is trim and tamed. I built a rockery by the shed door … it's called the Stone Garden. I still only see myself as an amateur gardener, but where once I'd wander into town for a packet of crisps and a fag when at a loose end, now I work the garden! I needed a new pet and a friend passed me a fish-tank – a cold-water tank. Now it's a tropical tank with angel fish and they're a great pet to keep, as they don't need constant attention. Through MIND initially, I started watercolour classes in Horsham. A few years on, I did a course on oils at Northbrook College and have now exhibited in several Sussex towns. What inspired me to take my art seriously was my decision to quit smoking. I went to a quit course at the hospital and whilst there I was like a naughty schoolboy. I kept smoking cigars all the way through the discussion period, but ultimately, by the end of the course, I had stopped and have never smoked anything since. I picked up a paintbrush rather than a cancer stick, and have found art a great therapy. Where once I might sink into an existential angst, now I'll work a blank canvas and put my creative fevers into something with a visual focus, which stops introversion.

It was around the time I quit smoking that I found CAPITAL (Clients and Professionals in Training and Learning). CAPITAL is a charity for mental health service users and I took up the basic training and then the advanced training. Now, having a more mature perspective on coping with mental health issues, on both a personal and sociological perspective, I find the depression seems less inhibiting than before and the suicidal thoughts are locked away. I never know if this is my manic depression conquered or a healthy denial! I hope that this is me beginning to cope with bipolar disorder. I have managed to shift my ambition from money and materialism to a more artistic lifestyle. Recently, I failed an eye test and have a new pair of specs, this time I will have to keep them! I know I may never afford a mansion, but the house of my consciousness and conscience is more important to me than the trappings of middle-class success. I hope in the twenty-first century to be a better citizen than I was in the twentieth. I look forward to a rosier future with the wisdom of the errors of the past. I'm taking an active part in the northern locality CAPITAL group and their move from Crawley to Haywards Heath and hope CAPITAL's future is equally rosy!

A Journey in Time

Timothy Bird

Fear, shame, guilt, disbelief, even horror – these are the thoughts that went through my mind when I found myself on the acute ward of a psychiatric unit. In the next few months I had plenty of time to ponder those thoughts and try to come up with answers which would help me cope with severe depression, but first I needed help in order to believe that there was life after mental illness. Luckily that help was there and gradually self-belief returned. Eventually, I came to understand that once again I would be able to make a contribution to society.

I grew up in a middle-class family with an almost Victorian outlook on life. I do not remember mental health ever been talked about in our family, despite the fact that one of my parents had had a mental health problem when I was very small. To this day I do not know what the problem was and, of those who are still alive, they either won't say or don't know. The only time I can remember mental health being discussed was at school after a report in the local press. Most of what we said had little to do with fact and a great deal to do with vivid imagination, especially when it came to talking about what we thought went on in the county psychiatric hospital. All of this shows a degree of ignorance, which I still find embarrassing and very much regret.

I had a huge amount of excess baggage when I arrived in hospital and some means had to be found to offload it and rebuild my life. The process was to be long, slow and not without hiccoughs. When you have reached rock bottom, it is very difficult to climb back up and one has first to be persuaded that it is possible and that as an individual you can actually achieve it.

The first step on the road to recovery was probably exercise. At first, it was just simple exercises on the ward. This progressed to visits to the gym where I did step-ups, press-ups, used weights and a bicycle machine. I then started playing badminton. I found that, whilst exercising, I concentrated on the activity and stopped beating myself over the head. Medication obviously had its part to play, although it took a long time to sort out the best option. I remember two nurses on the ward. One was absolutely brilliant and made you feel that someone really cared. The other was the exact opposite and yet, in an odd way, played an important role in my recovery. What happened was that this nurse kept on and on at me to go to the local shop with another patient. I was lying on my bed listening to music and I didn't want to go out. In the end I snapped and said, 'P–s off and stop hassling me.' Quite some time later, I realised that I had stood up for myself and I began to believe that maybe there was some sort of future to be had.

In due course I moved from the safe environment of the hospital to a group home and I remember this as being a particularly difficult period. The change was quite dramatic. One day all decisions were made for me, the next I had to decide everything for myself. I was supported by a community psychiatric nurse, a project worker and various friends, who were a great help. Leaving hospital after a long stay is difficult under any circumstances, but if the stay in hospital is for mental health reasons it is doubly traumatic. However, I was able to cope, albeit with ups and downs. I knew I needed to keep myself reasonably occupied. During the working week, I attended a day hospital or other day centres, but the weekends were difficult. I eventually joined a restoration and conservation group and I still belong to this group. There were a few setbacks caused by people who made snide comments about weirdoes who shouldn't be allowed near the public. I refused to be put off by these people, gritted my teeth and stuck it out.

Stigma is never far away and is largely caused by fear, ignorance and an institutionalised perception of mental health. At about the same time I joined the CAPITAL project trust to take part in their training programme and to participate in their activities. I continue to take part in the activities and to this day I tell people that they have been, and still are, hugely important to my stability.

My ability to cope slowly improved and, in due course, I was offered a move to a flat. Again, there was trepidation, but I chose to accept. The thought of having my own place and greater independence was too good an opportunity to miss. The downside was that it could feel very lonely. Living as a single person in the community can leave one very isolated and isolation can bring real setbacks. However, I have made a list of the signs that act as triggers to a potential breakdown, and I have a group of people around me who also recognise the signs. This is very important as I tend not to ask for help, but try to deal with the situation on my own, which is not a wise move – but that's the way I am.

I continue to live on my own. I take my medication because I know things go wrong if I don't. I keep myself occupied and try to keep a balance between doing too much and doing nothing. The need to keep to a middle course is of paramount importance. One other thing I have found is that perceived stressful events are often easier to cope with than I first imagined. I am now a pensioner, but I will continue to do what I can when I can and for as long as I can.

Finally, my motto: It's my life, my strategy for coping and I want my say, there is life after mental illness.

Healing through Mental Health

Richard Love

I am currently diagnosed paranoid schizophrenic. Having been discharged from a psychiatric hospital in May 2004, I am taking clozapine 300 mg (once a day) for this condition.

I am happy, healthy, proactive and positive in the community. I live alone – I tell a lie, I have an adorable pet bird named Bobby, who is free to fly where he likes within the confines of my one-bedroom flat – as a private tenant in a very pleasant estate which looks rather like a holiday retreat on the South Coast of Bognor Regis.

I am at Chichester College learning computer skills and literacy (spelling, punctuation and grammar). I am also a member of a local outreach charity named CAPITAL. Fundamentally, CAPITAL's mission is to raise awareness of mental health issues in the community.

This is very noble and bold mission that I feel CAPITAL has embraced for its members and everyone who is willing to listen. Statistics show that one in four people will be touched by or suffer from mental health issues or will know someone who will be, such as a friend or family member.

I was first diagnosed with mental health problems in 1995 and subsequently went through various institutions (open wards, locked wards, secure wards, prison) because of my addiction to alcohol and illicit drugs. As a result I attended 'rehab' three times. So far I have been sober and teetotal for almost three years and 'clean' for almost five. Suffice it to say, it took almost ten years to break free to the freedom and peace I feel today.

I am in a long-term relationship with my girlfriend who, although she has never had an admission, was once referred to a day hospital by her GP. My girlfriend is, I feel, one of the main reasons I have done so well since moving to independent living in the community as a 'normal' person living a 'normal' life.

So for me, I have a reverence for the incredible resources of the human spirit to battle through adversity to reach a place of calm, clarity and peace of mind. I could never have reached such a place without an overwhelming purpose to achieve my dreams and goals, not least my faith as a Christian.

I have read countless books and am always motivated to achieve my short-term and long-term goals. Since my last discharge from hospital, I have been employed on two occasions and have good references as a result.

I had no desire or inclination to pick up a book during my most difficult experiences pertaining to my three admissions in a medium secure unit, purely because my frame of mind was in such a sorry state. It was once said, 'Those who sow the wind reap the whirlwind' – or more commonly 'what goes around comes around'. A friend recently said, referring to his mental torment with no focus, 'I was deaf, dumb and blind'. Now we know our sense of peace is our surest guide to what works for us to be safe. A saint was quoted, 'Never be in a hurry ... do everything quietly and in a calm spirit.'

Psychiatric services, I feel, are there in their various guises to help the patients. In my opinion the services in their various forms are there to provide therapy to allow patients with mental health issues to break through their early life-conditioning which has dictated their life path, and to allow them to develop their own personality, beliefs and values. We don't know we've been in prison until we've broken out, though perhaps not as violently, metaphorically or dramatically – thank goodness.

Survival and Mental Health

Kay Phillpot

Coping and resilience

As a survivor of bipolar, I feel the turning point came in my life when I was actually diagnosed with the condition and started to pursue finding out as much as I could about the disorder. Although I have suffered on and off for nearly 35 years, I was only diagnosed five years ago and since then I have had more explained to me by my clinicians and have read avidly about my condition.

I realise my stable condition is also due to the correct balance in my medication and having an excellent CPN who is the link worker in my GP's surgery. Over the years both medication and supervision in the community has improved so much. For this I am eternally grateful.

I know I have to avoid stress in my life, but I have now learnt my own coping mechanisms, which have made me resilient to my condition by adopting my strategies for living.

Self-management and self-help

I have found my strategies for living help me to manage my day-to-day living and therefore help me to function as a member of my family and of society and to build up a meaningful life full of purpose, which is supported by a strong Christian faith.

By reading about bipolar in *Pendulum* magazine where others' experience of the illness is illustrated, I have learnt more how to cope with my condition. I have realised the importance of a routine and of having structure to my week to keep me well. Having had to retire from full-time teaching 14 years ago, I found it very difficult facing a 24/7 situation.

Voluntary work in a charity shop has played a large part in developing my routine and feeling that I am contributing to the community.

I realise too the importance of a regular good sleep pattern. I ensure regular habits – for example, getting up at the same time aids recovery, although I am only too aware of those horrible lethargic mornings when getting up and preparing for the day seems a real effort. However, I now know that once I have achieved these basic things of getting ready, I will feel much better and ready for the day. It is much easier to get up when you have something meaningful to get up for. I am too ashamed to think of the three months I stayed in bed when I first retired.

Apart from getting up and being taken to see my psychiatrist whom I didn't feel at all at ease with, I achieved nothing. I had no CPN at that time.

I realise the importance of eating the correct balance of nutrients as I attended a course on 'Food and Mood' – they are related for good mental wellbeing. I also find taking supplements of Omega fish oils and a selection of seeds and wholegrain cereals a good boost to the day, followed by my medication. My other medication I take before I go to sleep at a regular time. Thus during the day I am not constantly thinking about it and I can get on with my life.

I am aware of the importance of exercise and find this difficult as I have never really enjoyed it, but I am trying to build one session of aerobics into my week and walk as much as I can. I know this will help my serotonin levels as well as helping with my weight. I am aware that too much sugar is bad for good mental wellbeing and do my best to keep this to a minimum.

Discovery and recovery

Before joining CAPITAL, I was completely unaware of how I could find or discover more about my condition and had no idea of the meaning of 'recovery' in my life. I think that discovery leads to recovery; they are both a process and a journey maintaining good mental wellbeing. Sometimes one feels one is winning more than others but the important thing is not to give up – to hang in there even when things get tough and a relapse may be on its way. It always passes, and it is here again that I find my own coping mechanisms help me through, as well as offering hope for the future. I find listening to music very relaxing and the radio can distract me from thinking about myself.

I love meeting friends for a coffee and a chat and, of course, find the fellowship of my church and attending services and home group a great help.

Speaking out and combating discrimination

First and foremost, let me say why I joined CAPITAL and why I was attracted to the organisation. Their logo is to break down stigma and to build up respect. I was feeling in need of both those aspirations at the time. I was completely unaware of the service user movement and that the voices and ideas of service users could be worth anything. I realise now I am in the position to speak out as someone with direct experience and am an 'expert patient'. This at once gave me the confidence to get involved. I have now got involved with committee work, which I am really enjoying.

I know what it is like to be a patient on an acute ward for long stays. Thank God, now the stays are short and there is much more help available in the community. I know what it is like when you are discharged from hospital with no support. That does not happen these days.

It is a battle and we service users or clients must speak out and combat discrimination against us. Thank God for the service user movement where so many organisations such as CAPITAL are helping to break down barriers and stigma and build up respect for those of us who want to contribute to society and make it a better place for anyone who may be in a position sometime to suffer mental illness through no fault of their own. May these organisations long continue.

The Effects of a Lump in the Head

Howard Pearce

It was 1975 when I first suffered a bout of depression. In fact, that first experience of depression was the worst I have ever suffered. I went down further than at any time since. My health, my marriage, even my life were all put at risk, but fortunately I managed to survive it. Looking back I call it depression, but at the time I did not realise that it was depression; nor did my family. I just knew that I was desperately unhappy and that I was not coping with life at all well. So I never received any medical treatment or any other kind of support that might have helped me to recover sooner.

Eventually, I did recover but there were further periods of depression over the years. None of them was as bad as that first time. However, now I consulted my GP and was prescribed antidepressants. They helped, up to a point.

In the early 1990s the depression came once again and this time it became a more or less permanent feature of my life. I read books on depression, but none of them helped me to understand why I was depressed. I saw psychiatrists and counsellors (some better than others) trying to find out the cause of my depression, hoping that once I knew the cause, I could perhaps do something about it and work towards a cure.

Then in 1996 the cause was finally discovered. Not problems from childhood, not a result of life events, nothing psychological at all. I was suffering from a benign brain tumour of the pituitary gland which had caused some minor brain damage and messed up my hormone levels. Soon I was taking replacement hormones and other medication and the doctors told me that soon I would feel much better. Unfortunately, the hormone treatment made little difference to my state of health.

Knowing the reason for my depression did help in some ways. My family became more supportive and stopped telling me to pull myself together. Having a rare illness, I became an interesting patient for the doctors instead of just being another patient wanting a repeat prescription of antidepressants. Knowing about the tumour and its effects also helped me to understand things that happened in my life many years ago. Looking back, I suspect that the tumour has probably been there since I was a child, growing very slowly and gradually having an increasing effect on my life.

It also helps when someone asks me why I am not working. First, I tell them that I have a brain tumour and that immediately makes them sympathetic. If I then tell them that it gives me mental health problems, they are usually still sympathetic. It is very different from the usual negative reaction when someone learns that you have mental health problems.

It would be nice to be able to compare notes with someone else who has my pituitary condition. However, it is a rare illness, and even then it is unusual for it to cause significant mental health problems. I have never yet met another person with similar problems. It happens to be more common in women than in men, but the symptoms are different because sex hormones are involved.

Until 1997 I had a high-powered job as a professional engineer. During my last year or so working, I found that it all became too difficult for me. My performance suffered and it became clear that I would not be able to continue to work for much longer. Eventually, my boss told me to go home and not come back until I was better.

My first reaction to hearing this was a mixture of disappointment and relief – disappointment that I was no longer able to do my job; relief that I no longer had to struggle and fail at work every day. A few weeks later the disappointment had gone and all I felt was relief.

When I first left work I would sit around for most of the day and do very little. Every day I tried to set myself the target of doing six small tasks, such as walking to the letterbox round the corner or sweeping the kitchen floor. Often I did not get many of them done.

Things are very different now. I am an adviser at a Citizens' Advice Bureau one day a week, chairman of the local branch of the Pituitary Foundation and I have completed a psychology degree at the Open University. I have many pen-friends, I write music, I am working on writing a novel. In 2007 I started my first paid job in ten years, working part-time, eight hours a week. Maybe I will be well enough soon to look for full-time work once again. In addition, there are the regular tasks of running a home and being a husband, father and grandfather. Nowadays I have to set limits on how much I do, because there are only 24 hours in a day.

One thing I was able to do in 1997 was to become a volunteer adviser at the local Citizens' Advice Bureau, something I had wanted to do for years. Soon I was advising all kinds of people on a variety of problems, one day a week. This has done wonders for my social skills, self-confidence and ability to relate to people. Now, at Citizens' Advice, I mainly specialise in helping people to fill in big forms – benefits, divorce, bankruptcy, and so on. My appointments are often fully booked three or four weeks in advance.

In 2001, there was a training morning on mental health awareness for advisers at Citizens' Advice. I went along and I was most impressed by the training by two people from the West Sussex mental health charity CAPITAL. Afterwards I spoke to one of the trainers and asked if I could join the organisation. It was too late for me to start that year and so it was not until ten months later when I went to the

2002 taster day. I decided to join and to attend the monthly training sessions for new members.

I enjoyed the training, both from what I learned and because I met some great people. Anne was keen for us to start working for CAPITAL as soon as possible. Every month at the training day she went through the diary of events and invited us to the interesting ones. Before long I was helping with CAPITAL's finance. Then about six months into my training I was co-opted as a trustee and became CAPITAL treasurer. I became a proper trustee when I was voted in at the 2003 AGM. I think that was also the first time that I had to stand up in front of a big CAPITAL meeting and make a speech, giving the treasurer's report.

I have now been CAPITAL treasurer for about six years. People assume that I have a background in finance. In fact, I only learned about financial matters as I went along. In the early days we also had support from one of the Trust account-ants, and she helped me to develop my ideas and expertise. I must be doing something right, because at the February trustee meetings, after the new trustees have been voted in at the AGM, we all have to vote for who we want to be chair, vice-chair and treasurer. Sometimes we have two or more people who want to be chair or vice-chair. So far nobody else has wanted to be treasurer. But I keep hoping!

During my time at CAPITAL I have been involved in many projects, as well as dealing with finance. One of the first was the New Hope project. This was a series of training sessions for people on the wards at a mental health unit in Chichester and from a mental health day centre at Bosham. The final week involved the course participants being interviewed in front of a big audience. The audience included staff from both places, including psychiatrists, parents and partners, leaders from day centres and others. It went really well, and everyone spoke well – very brave of them. I think it was quite brave of my colleague and I, as the trainers, too.

Since then I have been involved in various projects and have met a lot of people. Some projects have involved co-operation with other service user groups, for example, the leadership training course in 2004 with people from across the south-east. There was also the Surrey and Sussex service user collaboration, SUSSED. Now I am working with groups from across Sussex in the Sussex Recovery Alliance and in Sussex Peer Approach. Through this I have developed some valued friendships.

My voluntary work, especially at CAPITAL and Citizens' Advice, has helped me to develop and use new skills, such as those needed to be a representative, for interviewing, evaluation of services, leadership, social skills, relating to people and much more. CAPITAL has also helped me to develop the financial skills needed as treasurer. In addition, my self-confidence has improved a lot. To some extent, just attending training and meetings has helped me to develop. I could have enjoyed the social contact, but then have sat back, attending meetings and enjoy-ing the free lunch, and then gone home again. However, instead of sitting back I volunteered for a number of tasks. I have gained so much from being active in CAPITAL and Citizens' Advice, for example accepting the responsibility of representing CAPITAL in meetings with the NHS Trust and other organisations. Getting involved and doing things has really helped me to grow and develop.

It has been a very long process and I have not yet reached the conclusion. I know that there may be setbacks along the way, but I have the hope that I will continue to progress in the future.

More than any number of consultations with doctors, psychiatrists and psychologists, or taking antidepressants, replacement hormones and other tablets, I have found that the best medicine is to get active, making a useful contribution to society. This is what has really helped my recovery to the state where I am now able to contemplate working full-time again.

A Mouse's Tale

Clare Ockwell

People like me are the natural mice, the quiet ones who end up with mental health problems after being trodden on too many times. It is never easy for us to stand up for ourselves, if perhaps a little easier to stand up for others.

My first experiences of what might be called user involvement came from my natural mousiness. I said yes when I was asked to attend meetings, simply because I lacked the courage to say no. So it was that in the mid-1990s I embarked on a career as a tick-box service user. Services were being told they must involve people, but were generally far too institutionalised to want to do so properly. That was where the mice came in. We were fairly clean, presentable people who could be easily persuaded to come to sit at the table, but most importantly we were quiet. We could be trusted just to sit there so that the box could be ticked and the boat left un-rocked.

It was a similar story when a drop-in centre manager and a social services trainer approached me about talking to care workers as part of their training. Despite the terror that swept over me, 'no' was simply not in my vocabulary. Besides, there was the niggling thought that if we didn't tell people what it was like to experience mental distress, then no one would. All I could do was tell a brief life-story and let people ask questions, but it seemed to work, even if it left me feeling awful.

In hindsight, those ordeals were probably the first step. Recovery is not an easy process. They certainly made me more willing to sign up for the Users as Trainers project (soon to be renamed CAPITAL) when it began in 1997. I'll never forget that first meeting, sitting on the end of the back row by the door, ready to leave when it all got too much … but somehow that never quite happened.

Within weeks the opportunities started to arise, we put together a handout and trained post-qualifying social workers. We spoke to our local mental health trust. It was exciting but also very scary. Most of us were unfamiliar with the idea of empowerment and were as yet uncertain whether we really wanted to be empowered.

Nothing happened overnight but slowly we were changing … I was changing. As a group we were growing in confidence, a confidence that could be 'borrowed'. If the group believed someone could do something, then it was so much easier to believe it for oneself. Borrowed confidence, coupled with practical support, were the making of me. Within the next year, I was regularly going out to assist in training approved social workers, something I was initially volunteered for, but also something that took a little help from my friends to achieve.

Travelling was my Achilles' heel. Even getting out of the front door alone was too much, let alone travelling 30 miles to Brighton University to teach. So other CAPITAL members became my 'minders' for the day. This worked for some time, until I missed my companion one day and found myself alone on an already moving train. Forced to choose between getting myself home or continuing my journey, I carried on and arrived an hour later a gibbering wreck, but picked myself up and carried on with the session.

Being involved felt good, but to do so effectively living in West Sussex meant that travelling was essential. Cognitive behavioural therapy with a psychologist had previously failed even to get me to walk down my road alone. However with the motivation to get to particular places and the feelings of support from other CAPITAL members, gradually my confidence grew so that I could make increasingly complicated journeys alone.

Within two or three years, travelling had ceased to be a problem. Something else was happening too, the mouse was finding her squeak. It was not enough simply to tell a story, to be a trainer or even to be grateful that someone wanted our opinions. Effective involvement demands that we stand up and be counted. We have to challenge when things are not being done in ways that help us as a group. This took me way out of my comfort zone, but became an unavoidable responsibility when I joined the CAPITAL staff team in 2003.

Taking on a leadership role carries more responsibilities and would never have been something I would have chosen for myself, but is something that I have found myself increasingly obliged to do. Even now, I would love to be able to hide in my hole and leave this to other people who are braver than me, as I would have always done in my former life. However, it matters too much, so I have to feign a confidence that I still don't feel and hurl myself into the fray.

This is where the term recovery falls down. It is really neither about necessarily feeling better nor about getting back to where you started, but instead about discovering what you *can do* and the strengths you were unaware of having. It is not a comfortable ride; the external mask often hides huge difficulty within. It can feel more like 'Carry on Crying' than a recovery journey, but it is truly a voyage of discovery.

CAPITAL has now existed for 13 years and in all that time it has been an invaluable network of peer support for me. Without it many people would be far less recovered than they are today. When we started nobody talked about peer support or recovery; indeed, a very well-intentioned mental health professional told me not to expect ever to work again. Today, no service would think of not highlighting recovery-focused working and the value of peer support. It seems ironic that it is in this climate that CAPITAL faces its greatest risk of ceasing to exist. At the time of writing, we have no guarantees beyond the next nine months and a clear message from commissioners that we must change or die. Inevitably, our role must occasionally be to deliver messages to both commissioners and providers that they would perhaps rather not hear. Sometimes we become 'the mouse that roars'. However, we are not opposed to change and, of course, can always improve on what we do. Maybe organisations have to recover too. I hope for the sake of everyone's wellbeing that we can.

My first thought in characterising myself as a mouse was something on the lines of Robert Burns' 'Wee, sleekit, cow'rin', tim'rous beastie – O what a panic's in thy breastie!' However, mice in literature are not always cringing and powerless. Aesop's mouse saved the lion, while C. S. Lewis paints the character of the fearless Reepicheep at the head of an army of mice. Maybe that is where my journey will take me – who knows? At times it has been a precarious ride, holding on by my fingertips to any ability to function, most of the time pushing myself miles beyond my comfort zone and frequently having to scrape myself off the floor. *But* I have surprised myself with what I can achieve and will not give anything up without a fight. Just remember that, although in the course of events he may get knocked around, Jerry nearly always gets the better of Tom.

A Recovery Marathon

Jude Smith

Life is often a mix of ups and downs. I had a good education and achieved a collection of 'O' levels and 'A' levels. It was after this that life became rather difficult. It took a long time until I got my degree, a BA Hons. in Design. Considering what I was up against, it was a real achievement.

The problem

In 1995 I had an episode of bipolar with a serious high followed by a devastating depression. I was told by a kind GP that I had a 'manic depressive illness' and that I should see a psychiatrist at the local hospital. Whilst I was pleased to receive a diagnosis, some explanation about what had been going on, the news was devastating. It seemed that this was the end, there was no hope. All the problems I'd had in the past weren't one-offs, I had an illness that I was stuck with for life, and the suffering I'd been through was likely to be repeated! I didn't like the term anyway, who wants to be known as a 'manic depressive'? I much prefer the current term 'bipolar disorder', if a description needs to be used. There was no mention of recovery; perhaps conventional wisdom didn't believe such a thing to be possible.

Treatment wasn't all that it was cracked up to be; in fact, it became horrendous. On 7 June 1999 I experienced the start of an adverse drug reaction (ADR for short). I was prescribed an SSRI (selective serotonin reuptake inhibitor) and my life changed forever. I had all sorts of strange reactions: I couldn't feel emotions as I used to and was unable to sleep, something I had been very good at! One pupil became significantly bigger than the other and I became agitated. My memory went, and all I could say about anything I had to do was 'I can't'. So began a most horrible state of affairs for me which was later described as 'serotonergic poisoning'. I reacted badly to one drug after another, my teeth started to 'chomp' automatically and I was incredibly negative. I felt quite demented really, and suffered indescribable hell.

At the end of the reaction in April 2001, I found myself in a terrible state, suffering from oral facial dyskinesia due to damage to the basal ganglia. I was suffering from involuntary chewing motions which meant that I had strange electrical feelings in my teeth and my mouth tugged upwards on the left-hand side. It looked as though I had a permanent slight smile. This pain in itself made me feel terrible. There were lots of other problems too. 'I feel like I have had a stroke,' I said in an attempt to explain how difficult things were.

Words from the song 'No Reason to Cry' by Oyster Band resonate strongly: 'Whatever you are looking for, I wouldn't start from here.'

Recovery

I now had an immense distrust of the medical profession and of medication in general. However, there was one health professional who had come into my life a month or so before the end of the reaction and so knew what had been going on. She was a clinical psychologist, called Vicky, to whom I had been referred for a course of therapy. I knew that she wouldn't force medication on me, and on this basis, I could trust her. This relationship became the backbone of my recovery.

One day she said, 'I will accept any written work or items that you want to share with me.' This started a process on a magnitude that she can't have anticipated! It was like a spring that started with a trickle and became a river. Most of the writings took the form of letters to Vicky.

Throughout that period I wrote about how I felt, how I was trying to cope with daily life and also little stories and drawings to illustrate what had happened to me. I had been traumatised by all that I'd been through and needed to reconnect with my past. I wrote compulsively and also took cuttings from newspapers of anything I felt to be relevant, many of which were on the theme of recovering from various things and about innovative approaches. One major theme I had was that 'one size does *not* fit all' and that treatments should be tailored to individuals. Looking back at these files, the contents are very interesting! Other contributing factors to my recovery include going to classes organised by MIND's learning initiatives programme. These were art, creative writing and Tai Chi. I also got back to my voluntary work with fair-trade at the local Oxfam Shop.

I wrote some relaxations, which Vicky read and I recorded, and I listened to them every night in order to get to sleep. Because of memory impairment, I couldn't remember what came next and so I didn't tire of them! Here is one of them:

A relaxation to send you off to sleep

Listen to the sound of your breathing
and quieten your thoughts.
If something is worrying you
quieten the worry, let it go away
and as you sleep you will find
the answers to your worries.
As you leave your worries behind
you feel peaceful
safe and comfortable
Listen to the sound of your breathing
and the ticking of the clock
the clock sounds quieter and quieter
and you find you are drifting off to sleep.
You enjoy sleeping
you like to go to bed to sleep
Gradually you sleep deeper and deeper
and for longer
right through to waking up time.
Imagine yourself
sleeping longer and longer
Your mind and body sleep together ...
Consciousness comes when it is time to wake up
Your body and thoughts are unconscious
until it is time to wake up.
Now hear some music playing in the background
before it has ended
set sail on your journey into sleep.

I watched the *Panorama* documentary 'The Secrets of Seroxat' and looked on the website and found a long list of comments from people who had taken this medication. Most comments were negative, but not all. Some people do find it helpful. Those who had had problems with it had become suicidal or homicidal (some had carried out their intentions). Others had become addicted to it and could not come off it, experiencing all kinds of horrible symptoms such as feelings of electric shocks if they tried. I added a comment of my own about my experiences. There was a link to a charity called APRIL (Adverse Psychiatric Reactions Information Link), founded by Millie Kieve after her daughter died from an adverse psychiatric reaction to an ordinary pharmaceutical drug. The website (www.april.org.uk) warns of the potential hazards of a variety of drugs to show that medicines can be harmful as well as helpful. APRIL also campaigns for better training for doctors so that they can recognise ADRs. I decided to do some fundraising for this charity and organised a sponsored walk.

On my journey to get better and find treatment that suited me, I read about the Pfeiffer Center in New York state, USA where people with conditions such as schizophrenia and bipolar disorder had been tested for nutrient deficiency and been put on nutritional programmes to rectify these imbalances. Vitamins were used in much the way that you would feed a plant to make it healthy and so protect it from disease. Omega 3 oils are also important in enhancing brain function. I was interested, but could not contemplate going abroad. Then I heard that Patrick Holford, a psychologist, had gone to the Center, trained in this field and then opened the 'Brain Bio Centre' in London. The aim is to get people well enough to start earning again. The treatment does not set itself up as an alternative to psychiatric medicine, but rather runs along side conventional medicine. With increased health the need for some medication is reduced.

In 2004 I visited the Brain Bio Centre and consulted a nutritionist, Lorraine Perreta. The nutritional approach involves avoiding unhelpful foods, having a correct diet and taking a variety of vitamins minerals and Omega 3 oils. I felt tangible benefits two weeks into starting the programme and I experienced a gradual improvement in how I felt. I have been taking supplements ever since, alongside a prescribed mood stabiliser, lamotrigine. I feel that while I take the supplements and follow the programme, the risk of having a relapse is significantly reduced. I have stopped worrying and continually thinking about 'the illness' as I used to. I have had the confidence to re-enter community life. My hope is that this kind of treatment will become mainstream and will therefore be available to everyone, whatever their financial situation. Medication is not a cheap option for the NHS, nor is other conventional treatment and hospitalisation. The nutritional approach makes financial sense if it keeps people well.

At the same time I also joined CAPITAL which has the slogan 'Equality and Respect IN, Prejudice OUT'. I have been involved in working alongside professionals in the mental health system in order to improve the healthcare that is on offer and put the patient's point of view. Recently, I have been looking at issues surrounding older people's mental healthcare.

My recovery process has been a slow one. It took over six years for the mouth pain to be consistently in remission, though the damage is such that it will never feel 'normal'. Vicky said that it was remarkable and that if she had been a writer she would have written a book about me!

This is a poem I wrote that was inspired by the Commonwealth Games when they were held in Manchester. It seems appropriate:

The Determination of Athletes

I am going to win through
I am going to find my way
I'm some kind of an athlete too,
even if my race is not obvious to most.
They can fight
so can I
they train hard
so shall I.
My race doesn't bring glory
but it does take courage
as much courage as they've got
and I've got it
especially when I can't feel it
when I'm protesting
and crying
I'm not weak
I'm just expressing the pain
like they do.
I'm going to stop worrying
about my performance
and get into the swing
and move on freely, easily
like they do
Quietness will interrupt
those busy repetitive thoughts
and I'll be confident
stop chafing at my imperfection
and move on
into the new and the better ...
I'm going to win through.

Now I live carefully, try to keep everything balanced and am generally happier. I still am aware of neurological damage, as anyone who has had an accident, for example, would be. Bipolar doesn't go away, but it can be managed. We know that lots of different things keep us well. I believe that nutritional medicine should be taken seriously and made available to people who cannot afford to pay for supplements.

She struggles through every day evasions,
Sweats through treacle nights,
Hot flushing through a few unhallowed years,
Of spirit somersaulting should-have-beens,
Looking for the Genuine Life of the Soul,
Through the thick fluxing fibres of 'is and seems',
Aiming to be so spiritual, so God-whole,
With scented candles, pot-pourri and essential oils,
With the spring trap strategies that support
The ever precarious present in all
It's studied confusing nicely nicely nought.

Martin Snape, 'Nicely Nicely Nought'

Your unbecome self taps yer foot,
Twiddles yer thumbs,
Catches her eye – but refuses to stare,
It watches reflected reactions,
Senses with unaccustomed smells,
And does another weight of unyouthful things,
In apparently pointless fidgets,
It deviously dodges around in dreams,
Bugs you mercilessly from behind the bathroom mirror,
Just always outside your grasp, grimaces and grins,
In painful feeling parodies of personality,
It cogitates you cunningly,
To the edge of unknown exasperations.

Then in some small domestic mistake,
It suddenly shoots screaming into your static life, a mean curve-ball,
Of meanings you always found muffled,
And actions you've swerved as – Not You.
The funny thing is:
You want to weigh into this diatribe,
And the words you say,
Are the words you've always wanted to say,
But never dared – Till you found yerself shouting 'em.
Then discover you are, who you are now,
And maybe the future promises some flavour,
And the days'll feel more easy-fit.

Martin Snape, 'Feel Easy-Fit'

12

The Value of Self-Help/Peer Support

Caroline Bell, Sarah Collis and Joan Cook

Self-Help

Self-help can save you, self-help can soothe
By offering a safe place to gently remove
Those thoughts that go unsaid so often for years
Locked up in frustration anger and fear
Who will accept me if they know I'm flawed?
Will all conversation leave me ignored?
So often we need to relate to a friend
Who will listen and empathise
And help us to mend

Jean Cave, Nottingham Bipolar MDF Group

Self Help Nottingham is a development agency operating across Nottinghamshire, supporting and providing information about self-help/peer support groups which are formed around a very broad range of health and social issues. With 26 years' experience, the organisation is a unique resource of knowledge and skills about how to establish and sustain diverse self-help groups. The team has specialist skills in supporting individuals, groups and local health professionals to ensure that their involvement in self-help groups is grounded in best practice. The organisation began life as 'The Self Help Team', and the terms 'self-help' and 'self-help groups' are perhaps more widely understood and identified with in Nottingham than elsewhere. We recognise that the term 'peer support' is increasingly used and that there is risk of the term 'self-help' being confused with the vast and expanding body of self-help and personal growth publications (Cadwalladr, 2009). The authors therefore refer to both 'peer support' and 'self-help' in this chapter, while group member contributors mainly use the term 'self-help'.

Voices of Experience: Narratives of Mental Health Survivors Edited by Thurstine Basset and Theo Stickley ©2010 John Wiley & Sons, Ltd.

Self-help/peer support groups bring together people who share common experiences, situations or problems. They are run by and for their members and their activities, aims and direction are determined by the participants in the group. Groups are often small, allowing close relationships to form through sharing experiences, information and support.

While professionally-led support groups share some of these characteristics, there is a fundamental difference: self-help groups are defined, run and controlled by their members. Having said this, there is a range of shading on both sides of this line, with some self-help groups regularly or occasionally welcoming professionals as speakers, sign-posters, advocates and supporters, and some groups explicitly excluding professional involvement.

The core activity of self-help groups is mutual support. Deep connections are made when members identify with the experiences, emotions and reactions of fellow members. Participants benefit from helping each other and by pooling coping strategies, sharing information and drawing on the collective wisdom of the group. Self-help/peer support groups develop as a result of need and when that need has been met, the group may decide to close.

This chapter brings together group members' accounts of what their self-help group has meant to them, related in letters written to Self Help Nottingham in spring 2009. The letters (including the poem) and a subsequent group meeting contributed themes, information and quotations for this chapter, with 12 members of five groups contributing. All quotations in the chapter are from group members' letters and the group discussion, unless otherwise stated. The contributors and authors hope that this will add to the understanding of how and why self-help works, assist others who may seek to set up or join mental health self-help groups, and inform professionals.

The Value of Self-Help

Hope and inspiration play a significant role in many self-help groups. Newcomers to a group gain inspiration from the way longstanding members have managed their situation or overcome obstacles. From addiction groups through to bereavement groups, people who have survived and thrived stay on to maintain their gains and bring hope to new members. Whilst hope may be a powerful force in some peer support groups, it is less easy to understand its role and source in groups where health fluctuates and outcomes are uncertain.

'2002 I was diagnosed with bipolar. My world fell apart; I didn't know what to do.'

'In a bad bout of depression – group really helps to deal with the unpredictability, AND the long-term nature.'

The letters tell their own story, they are uplifting and positive, shot through with a rich seam of hope and inspiration: inspiration drawn from the way other members live their lives, their achievements, the strengths they call upon and the attitudes they adopt – their outlook, insights, their understanding. The letters exude warmth, respect and acceptance; they describe life-enhancing friendships, relationships of trust and sincerity and life-affirming interactions. One person's success ripples through the group and can be shared by everyone.

> 'I have complete admiration for other members. Its like you want to cheer each other on.'

Describing her group one member said it was 'the single most important thing, the most significant thing', and another explained how 'mental health felt like a life sentence before finding the group'.

Hope comes in many guises and for some the prospect of a member moving on to paid employment is a real cause for celebration. Recognition that the group may have played a part in that success is modestly acknowledged and clearly means a lot to the group.

> 'Another woman returned to work after being unemployed for four years. I like to think that the group helped raise her self esteem and confidence.'

A women's group described a similar success: their secretary, who produced the group's poster, constitution and paperwork, went on to find permanent employment in the voluntary sector. Her new work schedule made it impossible for her to continue to attend the weekly, daytime group meetings. The group felt her success instilled hope in the members; it was proof that an individual with a history of mental ill-health could secure and hold down a job. Her continued association with the group, keeping in contact and joining them for evening social events, was seen as a further endorsement of the group's value and worth.

The letters bring to the fore the respect and admiration members have for one another and the tremendous benefits members accrue from making and maintaining friendships within the group.

> 'Listeners group has been part of my life for a long time now and I am glad and privileged to have met the people from the group.'

The value of having friends is a recurring theme, an almost humbling and unexpected outcome of their membership. The relationships described are both sustained and sustaining. Members value having people who understand, who don't judge and who empathise.

> 'I think that self-help groups enable you to speak out about very personal issues that would otherwise stay painfully hidden.'

Equally, members valued having people to socialise with, to join at the pub, meet for a meal or to go on holiday with, people to laugh with and friends to grow old with.

'Nice to think we'll be older together.'

'If I turn up when I haven't been to a meeting for a while I get the feeling everyone is really pleased to see me, and genuinely bothered about how I am.'

'I find Listener members really supportive. It was such a relief to talk to the other members of the group last night.' [after visiting a seriously ill relative]

Although building social relationships of trust and mutual respect is not exclusive to mental health groups, it appears particularly marked in such groups and is mentioned repeatedly as a profoundly important aspect of self-help. One woman described how, before coming to the group, the only people close to her were her family. She had no friends: 'Making friends here was like being re-born, a salvation.' The group talked of the stigma and taboos around mental health and past difficulties of making and maintaining friendships. A member from another group endorsed this viewpoint: 'Relationships and friendships when you self-harm are fraught with peril.'

The importance of being able to discuss mental health problems as an ordinary part of conversation could seem almost too obvious to write about, without realising how rare and difficult this is:

'It may seem surprising to outsiders that this need for mutual support is so hard to satisfy but mental health is not widely understood and there is little appreciation of the special social and personal difficulties to which it gives rise.'

'Mental health is very hard to talk about.'

Time and again people talked about the difficulties and minefields involved in various types of social contacts, including the potential sources of support. Group members described fears and actual examples of rejection:

'I have been threatened with withdrawal of friendship if I ever self-harmed again by one "so-called" friend.'

'You can't really talk to people who haven't been through it. They're judgemental, or they can get funny ideas about you.'

'People see you as a danger to them (totally untrue) or just cannot understand why you hurt yourself, which I can understand!'

'I still have to keep that part of me hidden from general "consumption" of even close friends for fear of reactions of rejection.'

'Still lots of prejudice.'

'So much discrimination still.'

Needing to tell lies, or not feeling able to be open, was a difficultly regularly experienced in casual social settings, including answering or trying to avoid questions in encounters with former colleagues, acquaintances, taxi drivers and conversations with hairdressers. Cruel personal remarks were also experienced, such as a man in the shop queue saying, 'Haven't you killed yourself yet?' Group members helped each other with coping strategies and tactics:

'Not working today then? No, it's my day off.'

'I'd tend to say I suffer from depression, rather than e.g. schizophrenia – more acceptance and understanding about depression now.'

The sense of having to hide and tell lies was experienced both as a constant ('Spent so many years feeling you can't be open with people') and periodically ('Self-harm is by necessity fraught with lies of how you injured yourself') over long periods of time.

Another set of barriers was concern about worrying and burdening other people, particularly family, and the inability or refusal of the family to accept and discuss mental health issues. In contrast, some examples also emphasised the relief at being able to speak freely and share in a group:

'The family is worried all the time, so reluctant to speak to them about it.'

'Can bring things to the group you might not want to burden the family with.'

'It helped my children so much, too – they had been carrying me, but I couldn't worry them more than they were worried already.'

'My parents have seen the scars but choose to ignore mentioning them!'

'I couldn't tell my mum everything – but it's a big pressure to keep it all to yourself.'

'Because it's shared in a group, the burden is shared – you let your tension go, but into the group, not just to one person.'

There were also some issues with specific health professionals:

'Psychiatrists? Well I don't know. They're people, and so they ought to help, and some are very supportive ... The problem is partly that they tend to drug you and that's not going to cure anything and partly that they seem to feel that they have to keep their distance where as it's closeness that's actually needed.'

The importance of normality, and groups' contribution to developing a sense of ordinariness, emerged strongly from the letters. This theme was raised in describing group activities, personal acceptance and ease of discussion of mental health issues, and the ability to have rounded relationships and a wide range of conversations on all subjects:

'We aim to be "normal" with each other.'

'The activities we share, whether it be a cup of coffee or a trip to the theatre, give us back some sense of belonging and normality in what frankly, is a very difficult life.'

Group activities themselves were often described as 'normal' and setting up a framework for ordinary social activities. The heart of most groups' activity is a weekly meeting, whether in rooms in community centres and church buildings, or public venues such as a pub or a coffee shop. None of the groups who responded meet in health service premises, although at least one had done so earlier in its history. Although the group that meets in a coffee shop initially met there because of lack of funding for room hire, group members recognised the venue as a normalising thing in itself. However, this meeting place does impose other limitations such as on the group's size:

'... so the group's too big if everyone comes on the same day – then we take up most of the space in the café, and need two tables. Then it gets uncomfortable, and it's not confidential if there's more than six.'

Open attitudes in venues such as pubs and the absence of financial or social pressure are clearly important:

'There is no expectation from the management that we will buy alcohol, or, indeed, anything. I usually have a cup of coffee.'

Other activities reported by groups were going for a meal or listening to a band, meeting up for Sunday lunch, going to the cinema, day trips to the coast, walks in the park, camping weekends, pot luck suppers, filming an educational video and activities for religious or cultural occasions such as Christmas. Activities are decided and arranged by group members, and it was important that 'there is absolutely no pressure to attend any of these'.

Being part of the group can be described as the antidote to isolation ('mental health felt like a life sentence before finding the group'); one person noted that attending the group 'was the first time I had met other people who heard voices other than on hospital wards'.

The 'mutually supportive philosophy' promoted by groups, meets the need 'to be with people who understand, who accept and who do not ask intrusive or ignorant questions'. The sense and practice of acceptance was felt immediately by a new member:

'What impressed me was the acceptance I received. No-one asked anything about my symptoms or history – which was a relief to me.'

Groups were described as offering a safe place 'to gently remove those thoughts that go unsaid so often for years' and to 'enable you to speak out about very personal issues that would otherwise stay painfully hidden.'

'I think it is good to have places to go with people who are in the same way and they got someone to talk to who is understanding, which is good.'

With this acceptance and openness, away from the strain of trying to carry on regardless and 'act normal', conversation about mental health problems and issues can be ordinary, integrated with conversation about anything and everything else, and neither compulsory nor avoided. Speaking about mental health experiences has parallels with group therapy, where there is much written about the role of disclosure in creating universality. However, in self-help groups the necessity to disclose is neither desired nor proscribed as a means to enabling people to understand that they are not alone – it just happens!

> 'We do not always talk of our self-harm but we know we can if we need to.'

> 'We talk about anything and everything – not just mental health or dealing with hearing voices, but also life, politics and everything.'

> 'We can talk about family, what's on TV, *Eastenders*, and about mental health.'

> 'We also discussed breast cancer, the European elections, holidays and how we were all getting on at the moment.'

> 'We can have normal conversation – and then a bit of awful-ising as well!'

One of the main things that constantly appears in describing the value of being part of a self-help/peer support group is the realisation that you are not alone. Prior to joining a group many people tell us that they truly believed that there was no one else who felt the way they did or who faced the same challenges:

> 'I felt very isolated because I thought I was alone on two fronts! One I self harmed, two I was gay!'

One group identified 'lots of different cut-offs, things that all add up to isolation', including the isolation of living in a small flat and of not going out or answering the phone because of being in debt – also spelling out how debt and unemployment were often aspects of mental ill health. Trapped in a world of individual pain and distress, members express the 'freedom' they felt on finding out that there are people just like them who are 'in the same boat'. In one of the key pieces of literature on self-help and mutual aid, Thomasina Jo Borkman (1999) includes the following quote from Wally, a mid-forties self-help group member facing divorce:

> 'The group was the rope thrown to a floundering swimmer – I grabbed it. At the first meeting people, suffering pain like I was, were there. I was not alone. That realisation that there were people with faces and names floundering just like me was enough.'

It is not uncommon for people first attending a peer support group to fear that it will be like going to a 'group therapy' session. They take a step into the unknown and at a good degree of personal risk.

> 'I think that self-help groups enable you to speak out about very personal issues that would otherwise stay painfully hidden. I remember at one meeting revealing the content of some of my thoughts/delusions and half expecting some people to leave the building!'

When group members do choose to share their experiences, their disclosure is commonly greeted with both the empathy of others who 'get it' because they have experienced something similar and the realisation that they have something valuable to offer:

'Being fellow sufferers bonds us.'

'It was a great relief to meet other people who had been through what I had been through.'

'We've all been through it – you can't really talk to people who haven't been through it.'

'For the first time I saw myself in someone else, listening to them talk I knew I had been there too, I knew how they felt and was so excited knowing that I wasn't the only one.'

The opportunity to help others, and the recognition that this in turn helps oneself, is picked up and explored in most, if not all, the letters.

'I mean you are helped just by helping – if I help one person with my groups its worth every month I run it.'

'It was after I'd been with the group for a while I realised that I was actually offering support to someone else.'

This powerful mix of acceptance and mutual support provides an environment in which there are no fixed 'roles' – the helped becomes the helper and the desire to reciprocate is valued and celebrated.

'Throughout the years the group has been a haven and I have gone for long periods without self harming when I have lent my support to others and seen them flourish.'

The reciprocal nature of self-help groups is well documented, but it is clear from the comments that the ability to help someone else not only cements the communal nature of the group, growing friendships and lasting relationships, but it also directly affects an individual's self esteem and feelings of self-worth.

'I guess it [helping people] increases your self worth and something that can do that is the finest medicine you can get … and it had no side effects. Wow!'

'I think it's difficult to put into a few words because self-help also involves helping others which usually gives you a good return.'

Over and above providing support, companionship and hope, these groups have found new and inventive ways to meet members' needs and aspirations. Between them they have produced a professional video, set up a book group, contributed to consultation events and developed a walking group. They have written and published books (Shaw & Thomas, 2009), organised camping trips, held awareness-raising seminars, made successful grant applications and even tried their hand at renting an allotment.

Group members' quotations give incisive descriptions of the value of self-help/ peer support groups – hope and inspiration, sharing of experiences and activities, and the experience, confidence and self-esteem gained from taking practical roles in groups. Peer support was sometimes compared favourably to treatment, particularly as it has no side-effects, and for one group member was 'the most significant thing'. Self-help groups counter isolation through the realisation that they are not alone, and through the physical presence and activities of the group. Groups can create spaces where there is understanding, acceptance and ordinariness, away from the range of difficulties often encountered in discussing mental distress with family and friends, and where mental health can be part of normal discussions about anything and everything. Genuine empathy and friendship can be built up, without stigma and taboo, and with the realisation that being able to offer empathy to others is valuable in itself. Mutual support enables group members both to be helped and to help others, and to adjust these roles through fluctuations in health.

We would like to finish by thanking everybody who wrote letters and took part in discussions, and by including a final quote which puts the value of self-help/ peer support into a full life context:

> 'One needs, it seems to me, to explore how you can best optimize your quality of life both on your own and with others and in my experience it is others, that help most.'

Contributors

Angie Smith, Cutting Back
Anthony Gariff, Rushcliffe Mental Health Support Group
Carlton and Gedling Women's Group
Jean Cave, Nottingham Bipolar MDF Group
Liz, Cutting Back
Peter, Nottingham Bipolar MDF Group
Sandra Coates, Two Sides Self Help Group
Members of the Listeners (Hearing Voices Group) and Two Sides Self Help Group

References

Cadwalladr C (2009) Welcome to the bright new world of positive living. *The Observer* (11 October)

Borkman T J (1999) *Understanding Self-Help/Mutual Aid – Experiential Learning in the Commons*. New Brunswick, NJ: Rutgers University Press

Shaw B. & Thomas H. (Eds.) (2009) *Rushcliffe Mental Health Support Group: Discovering Recovery from Mental Health Distress*. Woodstock: Writersworld

The colours of Siam
There has never been a clear
From my eyes
A blur a lazy writer
Revealing the truth
What are you.

Causing to happen in
My head
Pain and yet that
Was what I couldn't
Anticipate
Something left over
From words on a piece
Of paper
Pouring thru the imaginary
Poetry
Some going back and forth
Reading in fact the historical
Facts that as of yet
I have not understood
Dig up the categories and concepts
Make them fit into a paperback book
Update the decades
Make the fifties come alive
Do a spell check
Deconstruction
Reinterpret the place of each word
In the sentences translating
That of which we do not speak
Not knowing the language
And the culture we find ourselves in.

Dave St. Clair, 'The Clear Sky'

13

A Recovery Approach in Mental Health Services: Transformation, Tokenism or Tyranny?

Premila Trivedi

Question: Name something that originated from and was developed by mental health service user/survivors ... and was subsequently taken up by mental health services, redefined and re-structured to meet *their* needs rather than those of their service users?

What did you answer? User involvement? Self-management? User empowerment? Recovery? All fit the bill admirably. So what happens when our concepts get taken up by mental health services, which then proudly lauds them (and itself for taking them on) but at the same time seems unable to implement them in authentic ways? In Table 13.1, I have laid out a flowchart of how service user concepts may become distorted when taken on board by mainstream mental health services.

As a Black service user who has tried for many years to work with 'the system' (Trivedi, 2008) I have often struggled with this question, most recently in relation to the concept of personal recovery, born out of service user/survivors experiences, anger, hope, creativity, intellect and wisdom (Repper & Perkins, 2003) but increasingly appropriated and adapted by the mental health system in order to fit in with their pre-existing structures and already established service-led quality standards (Shepherd et al., 2008; Future Vision Coalition, 2009).

In this chapter, I discuss some aspects of this worrying trend. This will be neither an academic discussion nor an evidence-based treatise, nor even perhaps a well-informed argument, but just me trying to make some sense of two of the many confusing experiences I have had over the last couple of years in my encounters with the recovery approach. My aim here is certainly not to knock sincere and well-intentioned proponents of recovery (both service users and mental health

Voices of Experience: Narratives of Mental Health Survivors   Edited by Thurstine Basset and Theo Stickley ©2010 John Wiley & Sons, Ltd.

```
┌─────────────────────────────────────┐
│  Concept from service users born out of │
│  their experience, intellect, awareness, │
│  anger, creativity and hope          │
└─────────────────────────────────────┘
                  │
                  ▼
        ┌─────────────────────────────────────┐
        │  Raised awareness of concept, through │
        │  service user campaigning, writing,   │
        │  teaching                             │
        └─────────────────────────────────────┘
                        │
                        ▼
        ┌─────────────────────────────────────┐
        │  Interest in concept from statutory   │
        │  services, for economic, political ethical │
        │  reasons                              │
        └─────────────────────────────────────┘
                        │
                        ▼
        ┌─────────────────────────────────────┐
        │  Pronouncements of value of concept by │
        │  statutory services – often with great │
        │  fervour                              │
        └─────────────────────────────────────┘
                        │
                        ▼
    ┌─────────────────────────────────────────┐
    │  Policies re adapted concept, with        │
    │  service-led key performance indicators,  │
    │  outcomes, etc.                           │
    └─────────────────────────────────────────┘
                        │
                        ▼
    ┌───────────────────────────────────────────┐
    │  Implementation of concept by statutory     │
    │  services – but in ways that fit in with    │
    │  organizational structures and preserve     │
    │  institutional power relations, oppressions │
    └───────────────────────────────────────────┘
                        │
                        ▼
    ┌─────────────────────────────────────────┐
    │  Pressure on service users to comply with │
    │  new, reworked concept                    │
    └─────────────────────────────────────────┘
```

Table 13.1 Flowchart to show how service user concepts may become distorted when they come into contact with mental health services

workers) who are working tirelessly to bring a more human, holistic and hopeful approach to care, but rather to consider why concepts such as recovery, which have such tremendous potential to be transformative, too often end up being either tokenistic or tyrannical when taken up by mental health systems.

The Emperor's New Clothes

As a service user, in the early days I felt both excited and hopeful about the way in which government departments, mental health organisations and services in the UK were hailing recovery as the new way forward in care. However, my lived experiences over the last couple of years have caused me to seriously question whether recovery can ever retain its authenticity when it is translated and structured into a recovery model/approach/paradigm by mental health systems. For example, I have come across systems and organisations that claimed that recovery is about:

- A social not scientific concept – but they then started looking for proof of its efficacy using standard scientific methodology and even randomised control trials!
- Individualised, personal journeys – but they then set up structured models and approaches with clearly defined stages and standardised outcome measures!
- Hope – but they then skipped over exactly how hope can be generated and self-actualisation achieved when basic needs such as decent housing and enough money to live on are still not being not being met!
- Challenging the stigma and discrimination against those with a mental illness diagnosis – but they then paid lip service to other oppressions, such as institutionalised racism (both within society and services) which may have had a much more profound effect on someone's mental health!
- Social inclusion – but they then focused on getting individuals back into the mainstream (i.e. work) and did very little (if anything) to tackle the structural social inequalities which will continue to result in large numbers of people being denied access to opportunities, resources and economic and political power on the grounds of their race, class, gender, sexual orientation, etc.

Mad or what? Certainly it seems very worrying that such huge contradictions are not being discussed more openly within the mad fervour (? hypo-mania) currently surrounding recovery within mental health services. To me it seems a bit like the Emperor's new clothes, where everyone gets very excited and hails the new clothes (the new recovery approach) as indicative of a radical and positive shift while all the time knowing that the power base and control remain very firmly embedded within the corpulent body of the Emperor (mental health services) and any shift can only happen on his terms. Even if people wanted to, they could not do anything except be positive because if they did express doubts it would not only undermine the authentic concept of recovery, but also their personal investment and position in relation to it (Baker, 2000).

However, two years ago, Social Perspectives Network held a study day entitled 'Whose Recovery is it Anyway?' (SPN, 2007) which did enable service users and others to express their doubts about the Emperor's new clothes. It was a buzzing, vibrant and sometimes painfully raw day. I gave a presentation, using my personal experience to raise some fundamental questions about the ways in which some mental health services implement a recovery approach (see Table 13.2).

In particular, I was concerned with how the mainstream recovery agenda related (or not) to those service users from Black and Minority Ethnic (BME) communities, an area of particular concern since there is such a massive over-representation of certain BME communities within mental health services, particularly at the 'hard end' (Fernando & Keating, 2008). Whether the concept of

Table 13.2   Crucial questions about recovery and the mental health system

1. What precisely is the role of mental health services in recovery? Can they recognise which areas of recovery they have expertise in and can make a useful contribution, and which areas they should not get involved with but enable others with more relevant expertise (particularly service users and community organisations) to have control of.

2. How can the mental health system (which is directed by the Department of Health and works according to central government guidelines using highly standardised systems to achieve service-determined outcomes under the strictures of clinical governance) take on a recovery approach, which is essentially about personal, individualised and very diverse journeys of recovery?

3. How does a mental health system, which claims to be based on service user control and empowerment, also respond to other pressures – for example, the focus on public safety, risk, the Mental Health Act, practitioners and pharmaceutical companies who believe medication to be the first-line treatment for mental distress?

4. Does the mental health system really value individual journeys of recovery as defined by users themselves, or is recovery still defined according to service-determined outcomes (e.g. how many go on to employment, independent living, referred back to GP)?

5. How does the system (which has traditionally disempowered, coerced and excluded people with mental health problems from society) now gain the trust and confidence of users (particularly those from discriminated against communities who often fare worst in services) and prove they are now committed to empowering, giving control to and socially including service users?

6. Is the system able to address issues of power or is it interpreting recovery in a way that enables it to retain power, authority and access to resources? Can the system work towards and practically enable a shift of power from itself to other social agencies, in particular to service users?

7. Is the system prepared to shift its focus radically and prioritise the infrastructure, resources and support necessary to implement a recovery approach over traditional priorities?

personal recovery (derived almost entirely from White service users) is applicable to them is still a matter of conjecture.

Black Service Users – Personal Recovery or Liberation?

Some focus group studies have suggested that Black service users may have very similar notions of recovery to White service users, though it is not always clear exactly if and how difficult issues like racism and internalised oppression which are known to impact heavily on mental health were raised. In my experience, Black users often discuss recovery in broad contexts which invariably include a lifetime of personal and institutionalised racism and the limitations and disadvantage that this has imposed on them in terms of education, work, access to economic and other resources and forced them into spirals of oppression from which it can be almost impossible to escape (Trivedi, 2002). Recovery for BME service users often therefore involves finding a way of overcoming social and political factors as well as personal mental health-related issues that White service users may be concerned about (Fernando, 2008; Griffiths, 2008). In discussing this, Suman Fernando, a Black radical psychiatrist, has queried the use of the word 'recovery', suggesting it may be far too mild to encompass a Black person's personal, social and political journey towards a fulfilling life in a society still riddled with institutionalised racism and exclusion for those regarded as 'other'. Instead, he proposes the word 'liberation' as being more applicable (Fernando, 2008).

Fernando also discusses how focusing on personal, individualised journeys may not resonate with people from non-Western cultures where communality and interdependence (rather than individuality and independence) are emphasised and aspired to. He poignantly illustrates this when he states:

> In the world of twenty-first century Britain, the reality for many black service users is being stuck in the system with heavy diagnoses and 'sectioning' as dangerous people; their journey from darkness into light (as the recovery approach envisages), if it ever takes place, entails circumventing or overcoming many barriers of a social and political nature where family, religion and community are important.

Furthermore, he raises the point that even in focusing on the individual, the current discourse seems to see recovery in reductionist, scientific ways, i.e. in terms of different and separate aspects of the self (e.g. personal psyche, social networks, status, role status) rather than as an integrated whole, something which again may not resonate with people from cultures where there is no such clear divide between body, mind and soul. Finally, Fernando concludes that unless the current recovery discourse is changed substantially, it may well marginalise BME service users and impose on them service defined identities rather than their own (Trivedi, 2004). Which takes me on to one of my lived experiences.

A Warning Note about 'Lived Experience'

Lived experience is another concept currently lauded by mental health services – in my experience until it becomes unacceptable and is then dismissed as biased, subjective and born out of bitterness rather than factual accuracy! But narratives, by definition, can only be written from one perspective using information available to the writer. For the narratives of lived experience included in this chapter, it was virtually impossible to obtain any information on the mental health system's perspective of the situations so they are, by necessity, one-sided and subjective.

A Tale of Marginalisation and Tokenism

Recently, I was invited to be a member of a service user/carer advisory group to a huge national research project on recovery. Keen to be involved in such an influential project, I eagerly read through the project proposal but was completely shocked when I came across the following under the section 'Risk Management':

> This is a challenging programme, so we have a number of approaches to maximising the likelihood of success:
> To reduce complexity, some important aspects, including BME and carer perspectives, will not be addressed.

My initial response was incredulity. How could such a major project say they would not address BME perspectives when in many urban areas more than 50 per cent of service users are from BME communities and fare so badly within services (Fernando & Keating, 2008)? How could a project which hailed inclusion as a key tenet purposely exclude the perspectives of people whose whole life experience has often been one of exclusion? How had the statement passed the scrutiny of project collaborators and workers, ethics committees and service user researchers who I assume must have gone through the project proposal with a fine tooth comb? How did we, as BME service users, once more end up at the bottom of the pile, as people not worthy of having our very real issues addressed but rather as barriers to success, adding unwelcome complexity to (what is often viewed as) the nice, White, middle-class notion of recovery? Was this due to individuals who are purposely trying to marginalise us, or more to do with the mental health systems/organisations within which they work? I knew those involved in the project were basically sound people whom I liked and respected, so initially I accepted the explanation that the statement about BME perspectives had to be included as part of standard procedure, research methodology, technical necessity dictated by the systems of funders, research bodies, services, and so on. But then I got caught up in a maelstrom of feelings at what to me seemed to be exclusion, marginalisation of our issues and clear institutionalised racism.

In anger, I wrote to those involved in the project, very clearly expressing my distress. The result was an immediate and thoughtful response from many of the service users involved (most of whom I had not known previously) but, with one exception, absolute silence from the professionals (several of whom I knew and I thought respected me from previous user involvement work I had done in the Trust). To me that was like annihilation – an almost total blanking of my distress by people who were busy telling the rest of the world how to understand, make sense of and work with distress and move towards recovery. The outcome was that, like many before me who have been disturbed by user involvement work, I retreated into the safety of my bunker trying to fight off the experience of being made invisible and consequent overwhelming feelings of rejection, self-hatred, guilt and a longing to really disappear from the world. Of course, my (?over-) reaction was more to do with my past than the present, but nevertheless it reminded me of how close to the edge we are even when we think we are well sussed and recovered.

Eventually, I got myself under control and started venturing out from my bunker. Catching up with e-mails, I found two from the Recovery research project, one stating that there was still a place for me on the Advisory Group if I wished to attend and one offering me a meeting to talk about my concerns with the chair of the Group. Scared of getting myself into a state again I declined both and tried to forget about the whole thing. Then, several months later, I met one of the main people in the Project at a meeting and he told me that my input about BME issues had had a significant effect on the Project and there would now be a PhD student looking at BME issues! I wasn't sure whether to laugh or cry at what to me was a very tokenistic response to a major concern, but tried instead to be polite and grateful, just as a good service user should be. But then that night, angry with myself for being so compliant, I got thoroughly confused trying to work out what was going on. I could not honestly believe that the professionals involved in the whole fiasco were bad people trying to deny us BME service users our identity and our issues, so the only conclusion I could draw was that there must be something very powerful going on which was maybe not so much about individuals but more worryingly about systems, power relations and the structuring of institutionalised oppressions within the systems in order to maintain the established power relations and preserve the status quo.

Which brings me to the second lived experience re recovery and mental health services that I would like to relate.

A Tale of Tyranny

Ashwin is a 61-year-old Asian male service user who was diagnosed with schizo-phrenia at the age of 18 and has lived in a culturally appropriate group home for the last 19 years. Apart from monitoring his medication, mental health services have played little active part in Ashwin's day-to-day life for the last few years and he is on his own path to recovery, with establishment of meaningful social rela-tionships, increasing involvement in mainstream leisure and community activities and early intervention by staff in the group home who recognise his relapse indi-cators and how best to respond quickly and effectively.

The local mental health services then adopt a 'recovery approach', review all residential placements and decide Ashwin has been in his group home long enough and needs to move on to next step of recovery – independent living. When Ashwin is informed (out of the blue and without any lead-in) he becomes very distressed as he sees his established security being taken away from him. Staff from the Recovery team talk purposely of recovery and Ashwin's best interests, but fail to make any real connection with him or understand his distress at his sudden change in prognosis and the focus on him 'moving on'.

The situation turns acrimonious. The Recovery team insist on the need for Ashwin to move on since he has had no hospital admissions for several years and needs to become more independent. Staff from the group home stress Ashwin has made (and is making) good progress from the stable base of the group home. Ashwin's family express their concern at Ashwin being suddenly disrupted and try to introduce a broader, family and cultural context so that Ashwin's needs are assessed in these terms and not simply in terms of Eurocentric norms and values. Ashwin himself withdraws, intermittently showing his distress in displays of anger and aggression.

The Recovery team attempt to meet Ashwin on his own but, terrified of being moved, he refuses to attend any appointments.

Persuaded by his family, he does eventually agree to meet a worker from the Recovery team but after three or four meetings complains to his family that he is feeling bullied because the conversation always focuses on him moving out of the group home, in spite of the fact that he has clearly and repeatedly said he does not wish to. Suddenly, an Independent Mental Capacity Worker (IMCA) is brought in (without the knowledge of the family) to assess Ashwin's capacity and con-cludes that Ashwin has capacity but doesn't know how to use it! Presumably, he will when he agrees with the Recovery team! The situation then gets stuck, with Ashwin's previous recovery journey being disrupted as he lives in a constant state of anxiety that any moment he will be 'moved on'. Attempts by the family to clarify the situation are unsuccessful.

A stable situation for one service user is completely disrupted with the arrival of the Recovery team. So what on earth was going on to make the situation go

so disastrously wrong? In spite of all the trauma caused (and as in my first narrative), I really do not believe the staff involved with Ashwin were bad people. I'm
sure they were all well-meaning and would claim to have Ashwin's best interests
at heart, but something was obviously going on that turned the approach of individuals within the Recovery team from one of potential transformation to one of
tyranny and coercion when their unilateral plan was not complied with. So if it
was not the individuals themselves, we once again come back to 'the system'.

Systems, Organisations and Power

Many of us (as I have done above) talk about systems and organisations as tangible objects which have a separate existence from the individuals who comprise
them. But Ralph Stacey (2005), using group analytic concepts, describes organisations as being derived from the individuals within them; communicative interactions and relationships between those individuals forming patterns of activity,
which create the experience of organisation. Relationships, by their very nature,
inevitably have power structured into them and so power relations become
established within the organisation, sustaining a version of reality in which certain
identities and differences are privileged and accorded higher status within the
system while others are subjugated into lower positions according to their degree
of 'otherness' (Dalal, 2003). At the same time, specific beliefs, values and norms
evolve within the organisation which individuals are compelled to conform to
if they are to be included within the organisation. Furthermore, they must be
seen to do this and participate in the organisation's dominant discourse, the
ideology it reflects, the power relations it sustains and the patterns of inclusion
and exclusion it upholds if they are to continue to be part of the organisation.
Once this pattern is established, ideology does the work of sustaining the power
relationships within the organisation by convincing all that this is the natural
order of the world (Dalal, 2003).

Following this line of thinking, we can see, for example, that in mental health
services, systems have evolved to focus on public safety and control, minimising
risk, compliance with medication, scientific, evidence-based treatments, quality
assurance and clinical governance and staff must comply with this if they are to
remain and be valued within the organisation. However, individual staff may
also have their own important values such as patient safety, positive risk-taking,
individuality, empowerment, personalisation and recovery, and these may clash
with the organisation's dominant values and cause inevitable and sometimes
unbearable conflict for those who hold alternative values (Stacey, 2005). In order
to remain true to themselves (and also credible to service users and their families
who will benefit from these values) they must be seen to uphold their own
values while still complying with the dominant values of the organisation. If

these values can then, through iterative interactions, become functional while still upholding the dominant values, then the latter may eventually diminish in importance. But this will depend on the power relations within the organisation and the way in which these enable or constrain functionalisation of alternative values (Stacey, 2005).

Making Sense of Lived Experience – or Not

Maybe this can help me make some sense of the two lived experiences of recovery I have described in this chapter.

In my first example, it could be that the Research team were starting with values allied to a recovery approach but within the power relations and constraints of the Research Institution and its allied bodies were compelled to comply with their more dominant values – in this case scientific reductionism, rigid methodologies, objectivity and proving hypotheses through maximising chances of 'success'. Sure they displayed their recovery-focused values too by setting up the project in the first place and by having a service user advisory group. But it seems to me that their inability (or unwillingness) to carry through their recovery-focused values in their dealings with me not only alienated me but missed an important opportunity to 'functionalise' these values and exposed flaws in their commitment.

In the second narrative, it may have been that the Recovery team too were starting with values allied to a recovery approach but within the power relations and constraints of the system were compelled to comply with more dominant values, such as financial pressures to move people out of high-cost supported housing into less expensive accommodation. By insisting that Ashwin's proposed move was nothing to do with saving money and only to do with his best interests, and by transferring the pressure put on them into pressure on Ashwin, the Recovery team failed completely to communicate meaningfully with him and his family and made a mockery of the principles of the recovery approach they were claiming to be advocating.

Conclusion

I'm not sure where any of that leaves me. The concept of personal recovery in mental health is self-evidently a 'good thing' and to knock it would be tantamount to heresy, but it certainly needs to be broadened out to take into account the different perspectives and experiences of those who are involved with services, particularly those from seldom heard and marginalised groups. The focus on individualised personal recovery also needs to be broadened, since for many, recovery is not just a personal journey but also a social and political one. Finally, much more attention needs to be paid to the ways in which systems and the individuals who comprise them operate, the ways in which power and authority operate within those systems and the glaring contradictions which seem destined to disable any meaningful progressive move towards improving services for *all* service users. If mental health services could take recovery on in authentic ways, it would undoubtedly be hugely beneficial to users of services, but at the present time I fear that rather than being transformative, it could very easily end up being tokenistic at best and tyrannical at worst.

Throughout this chapter I have made a very conscious effort not to apportion blame directly to any of the individuals involved in my examples of lived experience and to give them the benefit of the doubt that they are all committed to the principles of recovery. I suspect I too am (for whatever reason) compelled to see the Emperor's new clothes and maybe am doing my best to ignore the painful reality that the problems with the Recovery approach may simply come down to the fact that:

> Despite the new discourse of listening to users' views, a tension remains because of privately held and so undisclosed professional assumptions about patient irrationality. This implies that private pessimism might co-exist with optimistic public rhetoric in professional mental health work. (Pilgrim, 2008)

References

Baker P (2000) Schizophrenia and the Emperor's (not so) new clothes. *Asylum, 12*: 8–9

Dalal F (2003) *Race, Colour and the Process of Racialization: New Perspectives from Group Analysis, Psychoanalysis and Sociology.* Hove: Brunner Routledge

Fernando S (2008) We shall overcome. *Openmind, 149*: 25

Fernando S & Keating F (2008) *Mental Health in a Multi-Ethnic Society.* Abingdon: Routledge

Future Vision Coalition (2009) *A Future Vision for Mental Health.* London: NHS Confederation

Griffiths R (2008) The bigger picture. *MH Today* (February): 22

Mental Health Providers Forum (2009) *The Recovery Star Model and Culturally Competency.* BAME Pilot Report

Pilgrim D (2008) 'Recovery' and current mental health policy. *Chronic Illness, 4*, 295–304

Repper J & Perkins R (2003) *Social Inclusion & Recovery: A Model for Mental Health Practice.* London: Baillière Tindall

Shepherd G, Boardman J & Slade M (2008) *Making Recovery a Reality.* London: Sainsbury Centre for Mental Health

SPN (2007) *Whose Recovery is it Anyway?* Paper 11. Notes from a Joint SPN/SCIE/SOGIAG/DRE Programme study day, 16 October

Stacey R (2005) 29th S. H. Foulkes Annual Lecture: Organisational identity: The paradox of continuity and potential transformation at the same time. *Group Analysis, 38(4)*: 477–498

Trivedi P (2008) Black user involvement – rhetoric or reality. In S Fernando & F Keating (Eds.), *Mental Health in a Multi-ethnic Society*, second edition. London: Routledge

Trivedi P (2002) Racism, social exclusion and mental health (pp. 71–82). In K Bhui (Ed.) *Racism and Mental Health*. London: Jessica Kingsley

Trivedi P (2004) Are we who we say we are or who you think we are? *Asylum*, *14*: 4–5

A deep sorrow and regret,
That we never met,
And yet,
I loved you still.
Thoughts, memories,
Of what could have been,
A strong belief in the unseen.
I longed to hear your soft voice,
To feel your warm embrace
Or a gentle kiss on the face.
You were always part of me,
There was no escaping that.
Creating a delusion,
Which in turn would
Cause more and more
Confusion.

Mariyam Maule, 'To What Could Have Been'

14

Stand to Reason

Jonathan Naess

Introduction

I wanted to contribute to more openness around mental health problems because the stigma is a big part of the problem. You know that the first step to recover is to talk to somebody about your situation so you can share your burden and not bear it alone. (Kjell Magne Bondevik, former Prime Minister of Norway, interview with Jeremy Paxman, BBC *Newsnight*, 22 January 2008)

Paxman was impressed:

I know we're supposed not to be partisan, or to pass judgement on those we interview. But I have to say that of all the many politicians it has been my (occasionally painful) duty to interview over the years, Mr Bondevik comes pretty near the top. It's so rare to find a man talking with such frankness and courage about such a charged and sensitive subject. Mr Bondevik's honesty in putting his cards on the table and telling the people of Norway what was going on in his mind and in his life is admirable. But the reaction of Norwegian voters is just as impressive. They voted him back into office. (BBC Newsnight blog, 2008)

Bondevik had, the day before, spoken in the House of Commons about his mental ill health and depression and how he handled this when he was prime minister. He was in the UK as a guest of Stand to Reason, an organisation of which I am the Director and which is committed to fighting discrimination and stigma, challenging stereotypes and changing attitudes. Stand to Reason is a service user-led

Voices of Experience: Narratives of Mental Health Survivors   Edited by Thurstine Basset and Theo Stickley ©2010 John Wiley & Sons, Ltd.

organisation that intends to work with and for people with mental ill health in the way that Stonewall has for gay people: raising the profile, fighting prejudice, establishing rights and achieving equality.

We also used this opportunity to conduct a survey of MPs, peers and general staff working in Parliament. A report was published in July 2008, based on a mental health questionnaire, which was completed by 94 MPs, 100 peers and 151 parliamentary staff. The survey found that 27 per cent of respondents had concerns about their mental health. It also revealed a real fear about speaking out about mental health issues despite a general agreement that greater openness and honesty could only be a good thing. In the report, Stand to Reason called for more openness and criticised the 1983 Mental Health Act requirement that an MP sectioned for more than six months automatically loses his or her seat.

Other key events for Stand to Reason in 2008 included a conference 'Mental Health and Emotional Wellbeing: A Call to London Employers', addressed by Lord Stevenson, Chair of HBOS, who spoke about his experience of living with depression. The conference was a catalyst for action and Stand to Reason has since been asked to act as adviser on mental health issues to business.

With its first ever meeting in late 2006, Stand to Reason had put itself firmly on the map and had somehow had the ability to reach out to an untapped and passionate resource base of capable people. These people, often in relatively high-status jobs and positions, had traditionally remained silent on issues of mental health. Stand to Reason has given them a voice.

By the end of a very eventful 2008, I had been fortunate to be awarded 'Person of the Year 2008' by RADAR. This award is made to 'an individual who has demonstrated an unswerving commitment to the furtherance of human and civil rights of disabled people'. I was proud to receive the award for myself but also on behalf of the many people who had worked with me in setting up and running Stand to Reason.

How, you might ask, did all this come about? As the founder of Stand to Reason, I shall attempt to trace my journey from being a patient on a psychiatric ward in the early 1990s to becoming RADAR's 'Person of the Year 2008'.

My Journey Begins

My 'mental health' journey started when I found myself as a young man on an acute ward in London. What little I knew about mental health problems had to this point been acquired through life in general. To say that I was poorly prepared for this new experience would be a massive understatement. I was scared – my breakdown had come out of the blue. In my search for an explanation, I hit a bit of a brick wall. The doctors and nurses seemed to offer no advice or guidance. Indeed, the nurses always seemed to be 'behind a glass wall' as they sat in their office and largely kept their distance from me and the other patients.

When I eventually left hospital, I felt that the whole experience have been a humiliating one. The message I internalised was that a shameful thing had occurred in my life and the best strategy for me was to get on with life and hope it never happened again. But it did!

It was over ten years later that I found myself on another acute ward after a very traumatic admission. I was older and hopefully wiser, but not about mental health. I wondered how this could be happening again. For some reason a 'handbag' analogy came to mind. Losing your handbag once was probably just bad luck, but to lose it twice was plain careless and very stupid! For me, the penny had dropped – I knew I had some kind of mental condition. I was determined to find out what it was. Perhaps, if I knew what it was, I could do something myself to manage it. Also, I felt a strong desire to improve things for my fellow patients.

I was more inquisitive on this admission, but even so it felt like I had to beg for information. Eventually, one of the doctors gave me a list of the symptoms of manic depression/bipolar disorder. I went thorough the list and ticked every one. This one initial act of collaboration between myself and the professionals set me off on a journey of discovery and learning.

Learning from Others

I have learned so much from others, in particular from people with similar experiences to mine and indeed sometimes from their families as well. My first stepping-stone was the Manic Depression Fellowship (now MDF: The BiPolar Organisation). I learned so much about managing my condition from them, mainly in their excellent support groups. I still am a member to this day. The amount of help that can be gained from this 'peer support' should not be underestimated. However, for me, there was another stage I wanted to move on to. I found the talk at these sessions to be almost completely, and indeed importantly, focused on coping and learning to live with the condition. There was little talk of the accompanying stigma and the discrimination in society that we must have all been facing.

By chance at this time I came across Mosaic Clubhouse in South London. I contacted them and eventually became a trustee. Clubhouse is an international mental health organisation with an emphasis on employment and with a philosophy that it is run by the members working alongside the staff. As a trustee I was bringing to them my expertise as a partner in a corporate finance house in the City of London. To my surprise, they also valued my expertise as somebody who had learned a bit about living with mental health problems.

It was while attending a Clubhouse conference in Finland that the idea for starting Stand to Reason first developed. Perhaps it helped to be in a Scandinavian country with a long tradition of social justice and away from England and its class structures, which so often inhibit social change. Maybe the fact that my culture is half-Norwegian and half-British influenced my thoughts. By then, I was also more confident in managing my own polarity and had read a great deal about bipolar disorder. All these things combined to encourage me to move into a more political dimension and to attempt to challenge stigma and discrimination in my own workplace – the City of London.

My Work and My Sabbatical

I had recently had a good experience of returning to work after my second episode of mental ill health, at the corporate finance house at which I was a partner. I was fortunate in having the support of a brave and outspoken office manager who advocated for me and helped arrange a stepped reintroduction to work. She was helpful in handing questions from more doubtful colleagues who might ask 'How will we know if Jonathan is well or not?' to which she replied, 'Don't worry, he'll tell you if he's not feeling well.'

My reintroduction went well and I began to think that something similar could be done in other companies in the City. I asked for a sabbatical and set myself the task of creating an organisation that could both help people like me and at the same time challenge stigma and discrimination at the top level of business and commerce.

Early on in my sabbatical, I was fortunate to meet Anne Beales, who had recently been appointed Director of Service-user Involvement at the national charity 'Together'. Anne was the first person I had met from the campaigning mental health world. She was very supportive, not least because she too was a service user. She came up with the expression 'service users in suits' – appropriate in some ways, although Stand to Reason has always avoided being seen as an elitist organisation for the well-off. We certainly acknowledge that, at root, we are fighting discrimination for all people who experience mental distress.

Stand to Reason started with an initial idea of 'networking breakfasts' and it snowballed on from there.

Stand to Reason

Our philosophy

In seeking to become a 'Stonewall' for mental health, Stand to Reason both was and is keen to use tried-and-tested approaches from a broadly civil rights back-ground in getting its message across. We also borrowed the slogan 'Breaking Glass Ceilings' from the women's movement as we have sought to draw attention to the stigma and discrimination that inhibits people with mental health problems from reaching their full potential in the workplace.

Our approach has always been at heart a positive one, built on an understanding that people with personal experience of mental health problems are able to offer very powerful and helpful peer support. The realisation that no previous organisation had sought to tackle stigma and discrimination in relation to mental health across the business and commerce sector gave us a strong sense of purpose. As its founders, we knew there were so many people who could potentially back us – people who had perhaps remained silent or kept their mental health problems hidden in the past. There was, and indeed still is, a powerful sense of an enormous, untapped resource of capable people. Once people had been reached out to, become involved, realised the benefits of talking about and sharing their day-to-day issues, they would see that they were not alone – far from it, there were colleagues everywhere who had both passion and a desire to change attitudes and combat discrimination.

Stand to Reason has always acknowledged the need to shake off the stigma that persistently clings to people with mental health problems. This idea of 'shaking off stigma' comes directly from my experience of being a psychiatric in-patient. I noticed that nurses going off their shifts sometimes went through a process of 'shaking off' as they left the ward and went out into the outside world. I remember seeing them physically shaking off the effects of their shift – not very nice to witness when you are a patient. Turning this on its head, I came up with the idea of patients needing to go through a similar process in shaking off the stigma that can follow them on their discharge from hospital. I hope this is typical of the positive approach in Stand to Reason, where negative experience is often turned into positive gain.

Testimonials and supporting comments

We have been fortunate in receiving support from a variety of places. Dr Liz Miller, Trustee of Stand to Reason, General Practitioner and Mind 'Mental Health Champion of the Year' in 2008 has written this visionary piece for us:

> We too have dreams. Not the dreams of normal people, but simple dreams. Dreams of a place where we are seen not as ill, but as damaged and healing fast. Dreams of a place where we are seen as who we are, not labelled by a doctor as different and separate from you.
>
> Dreams of a place where we are accepted for the contribution we can make, for the wisdom we learnt from our journey. Our journey has not been ordinary. We have seen things that you cannot even dream about. For us, heaven and hell did open and the way home has not been easy.
>
> We too have dreams, of being welcomed back, of making our contribution, of learning from our experience. We cannot do this without you. We no longer have your strength and stamina. Much has changed whilst we have been away. We took a few hits. We did not go down with the first blow, nor with the second, or even

the third. Our chance has come to heal. We dream that you will help us, that you will offer out your hand and help us stand up straight again. Proud of what we have done, wiser for where we have been and stronger for knowing who we are.

We too have dreams. Our minds have changed, and changed again. Yet though that experience makes us different it doesn't make us separate from you. It brings us closer to you, because we see what runs beneath your surface.' (www. standtoreason.org.uk)

Following the publication of 'Fit for Purpose' by Mary O'Hara in *Society Guardian*, (14 November 2007), Dr Larsen's was one of many letters published a week later:

This kind of courageous coming out does more for mental health than any psychiatrist can hope to achieve during the whole of a working life. Congratulations, Mr Naess. I have lost count of the number of times I have debated whether a successful career, or any career at all, was feasible for my mentally ill patients. Now, referring to you and your charity will make that argument easier. (in www.standtoreason.org.uk)

The Future

Building on its successes in its early life, Stand to Reason aims to continue its campaigning in Parliament. A particular interest is the implementation of the Equality Act (2010) and the need to ensure that mental health issues are kept in the frame in this legislation. Also a Stand to Reason trustee, Rachel Perkins, is working with me in advising the government's cross-departmental strategy on mental health and employment. Rachel is Director of Quality Assurance and User/Carer Experience at the South West London and St George's Mental Health NHS Trust. This Trust has a good record of employing people with mental health problems.

Stand to Reason will continue its work in relation to offering training to employers, with a number of key products being develop for this strand of work. It is also actively collecting stories from members and supporters with a particular eye to the effects of the economic recession in relation to employment and mental health issues.

Events, conferences and debates are planned looking at key issues, for example, creativity and mental health. High-profile supporters such as Stephen Fry and Alistair Campbell continue to assist in spreading the word. Physical activity and wellbeing were the topic for a conference, chaired by Stand to Reason, at Lord's Cricket Ground in April 2009.

Peer support remains high on the agenda, and recovery and employment workshops will be offered to members and supporters to discuss key issues within a supportive environment.

I feel we are winning the argument. We sometimes have to struggle with our self-stigma – we are in combat with both internal and external voices that make us wonder 'Are we good enough?' Because of this it is always necessary to cele-brate the talents and achievements of people with mental health problems and raise consciousness. We take pride in our achievements.

There is perhaps a tipping point. At Stand to Reason we are aware that for every one person who contacts us there are more than 20 who could, but don't. We want to mobilise these people. But we also want to work with businesses, which increasingly realise that mental wellbeing in their workforce is linked to increased creativity and productivity. Often they are keen to do something but not sure what their strategy should be. This is where Stand to Reason has an important role. Our message is that mental health promotion and wellbeing are central to a whole organisation. It is not just about being nice to the 'maddies', using the expression of Stephen Fry, one of our key supporters. It is about us all.

References

BBC Newsnight blog (2008) www.bbc.co.uk/blogs/newsnight/2008/01/bravery_in_the_face_of_mental_illness.html

O'Hara, Mary (2007) Fit for purpose. *Society Guardian* (14 November) www.guardian.co.uk/society/2007/nov/14/guardiansocietysupplement.mentalhealth

Stand to Reason website (www.standtoreason.org.uk)

I am me
I think
I see
I feel
I love

I wasn't me
My thoughts were wrong
I wasn't seeing properly
I didn't feel right
I didn't love me

I was sick
A sickness not understood
Except by me
And I was sick

Medication helped slowly
Oh so slowly
And time was a healer
And kindness helped
Kindness of strangers
Who accepted me
And seemed to understand
That I was sick

A long journey
Sick again
Sickness of the mind not the body
And medication helped
And an acceptance
And kindness of strangers
I wasn't alone

Take my hand
Love me
And I will love me
And the hurt
And the pain
And the memories
Will ease

See beyond the wall
To the brain
And the heart
And the love will help me
And the love will help you
And we can talk
And laugh
And be close
And the tears will wash away
the pain
And we can live
And laugh
And love again

Libby Jackson, 'I Am'

15

Walking with Dinosaurs

John Stuart Clark

There was no question about it, I had testicular cancer and was on my way out. Over the course of a year, the symptoms had progressed from throbbing through burning to horrific stabbing pains that made me shriek. My bollocks were being butchered by a pathological Norman Bates! If only to gain a decent night's sleep, I went to the doctor's to plead for the mercy of morphine. We had moved house. It was a new surgery. Three doctors examined me, conferred and sheepishly delivered a prognosis. Yep, I had a 'mental disorder' (and that's a quote!).

The doc I settled on gave me the illustrated lecture on malfunctioning serotonin receptors and banged me on 40 mg of something nasty called an SSRI. Within a fortnight brain functions had decelerated down to slow-mo, my faeces stank like an Eli Lilly research lab, and all about me had become a morphing psychedelia. An intrepid cyclist and fitness freak, I had never experienced colds or flu. Suddenly every virus on the block was moving in, welcomed by a drippy immune system that flung open the front door and just shrugged.

I had given up on work months earlier, devoting my time to being a dedicated waste of space. If not blanking them, I was rude and abusive to friends and acquaintances. I hurled profanities at the TV, spat venom at newspaper stands and chuntered expletives the length of supermarket aisles. When my long-suffering partner took off for a three-month residency in China, I stocked up on meds and tagged along as Sherpa. I had to escape the small-minded claustrophobia of Britain. And it was an escape. The People's Republic was like nowhere on earth I had journeyed. Exhilarating, challenging, endlessly fascinating, China and the Chinese brought me out of my miserable self. I flushed the meds and took up painting on *gal bai ne* porcelain, producing caricatures of street vendors who knew nothing of cartoons, let alone satire. I returned to the UK invigorated, hopefully cured.

Voices of Experience: Narratives of Mental Health Survivors   Edited by Thurstine Basset and Theo Stickley ©2010 John Wiley & Sons, Ltd.

Within a week, I had banished the world from my sight, assumed a foetal position under the duvet and was back on the Smarties. For weeks, I survived on scoops of peanut butter and roll-ups.

Physically, everything started going south. My tits ballooned to a Double-D, waistline spilled over like lava, and hair and teeth started falling out. Now home to a million cicadas, screaming tinnitus filled my skull. Real as the keyboard I type on, a giant lizard, white and cynical, sprang up before my eyes. 'Atro' was to become an unshakeable nuisance over the coming years; the nutter on my bus. He was the height of a door frame, walked on hind legs and had a mouth on him to challenge Alf Garnet. A fellow depresso and committed kleptomaniac suggested I keep a diary. I read hers. It was rambling, self-indulgent tosh but no doubt served the purpose. I started drawing a comic account of my demise (in both senses of comic). I drew every day, and if I couldn't I oozed panic. I signed on for a personal development course called 'Moving Out of Depression' or MOOD (geddit?). Straight off, the lecturer warned us that the most depressing thing about depression is how depressingly difficult it is to understand its causes. By week 2 course membership was down 60 per cent. Week 3 it was cancelled. A development course for depressos in January was never going to be a hot ticket.

Fourteen months after popping the first of three species of happy pills, I got to see somebody reputed to know more about minds than bodies. Patiently, the nurse listened to me rail against just about everything for an hour before handing me an A4 sheet flowcharting what every head case needs to know about 'mental distress', provided they know what 'dysfunctional assumptions' and 'somatic symptoms' mean. He filled me in on traumatised Amerindian 'grunts' returning from Nam and how they turned to their shaman and the sweat lodge when Medicare failed them, then sent me home to 'percolate'. It sounded a lot like 'wait', something I was becoming horribly skilled at.

By now the current account was blitzed, my career had spiralled down the sink and my partner was dusting off suitcases, putting out feelers for somewhere to crash. In desperation I went in search of a Navaho, Sioux, any tribe of medicine man, but Nottingham was clean out of shamans. I fell back on the city's Counselling Service. Five months and several domestics later I got to see a volunteer counsellor in a creepy attic similar to one that haunted my nightmares. She was obese and badly needed counselling. It was furnished from car boot leftovers. I didn't go back.

A friend I didn't know I had in turn had a friend who was a retired psychotherapist who was happy to take me on, fee negotiable. She was brilliant, incisive and worked my emotional socks off. Against best advice, I stopped the meds dead. Only on them for a couple of years, I had spasms and scratched, retched and hallucinated like the 'ardest of mainline junkies. Two weeks later some semblance of clear reason returned. I spent a year on a mind-blowing magical mystery tour my shrink said represented 'an emerging sense of mastery' before bad news hit the mat and shook the household. Our savings were spent. My head doctor offered to continue for free, but it would have been insulting. She was too damn good.

Besides, in the meantime, I was being evaluated by the NHS. Who was to say their witch doctors wouldn't be just as brilliant?

And in the meantime I was hauled into Jobcentre Plus, where a chirpy Welshman informed me that, should I feel able to return to work, I was a desirable proposition for potential employers. I could read and write, something Aldi the supermarket held in great awe. Then I was hauled into Medical Services, the bunch contracted to sniff out 'sicky pullers', and interrogated by a Greek doctor with O-level English charged with providing a second opinion (or in my case, sixth). Most of what I said flew over his head, but the verdict seemed to pivot on incisive questions like did I clean up after myself and could I use a vacuum cleaner. I told him, 'Thanks, but we've already got one.'

Over five months I was assessed by a state psychoterrorist, a graduate of the Nurse Ratchet School of Inter-personal Skills, whose granite features never expressed less than a deeply etched fear of me. Concluding I needed to see a shrink ('No, really!?'), I had only 12 months to wait until, a mere three years and four months after entering the system, I was assigned a psychodynamic Freudster. His pin-up hangs over her desk and is starting to irk me. I'm half-Austrian and know way too well the national character traits that were always going to throw up a Fritzl, Freud and Hitler.

Current status: still talking, still broke, still incapable of breathing life into the rigor mortis of my career, but still partnered.

Weaving through this flippant account is all the rage, bewilderment, despair and blind terror others in this tome will chronicle more eloquently, and a few curve balls the texts didn't prepare me for. While it should have vacated the premises, my libido went into hyper-drive. The cat feared for her cherry. Six months of medication miraculously transformed me from a life-long reluctant shopper to a compulsive consumer, strictly CDs, books, DVDs and comics. I had to have everything, became an obsessive completist. And I didn't once flirt with suicide. Instead, I craved the harshest wasteland strafed by the cruellest winds, sourcing maps of the Libyan Desert and flights to Al Khartum.

It is now three years since Atro latched on to my atrophy and barely two months since we parted company. Good riddance. I'm not out of the woods but like to think I'm hacking through the undergrowth on a firm compass bearing. I haven't the faintest idea who I am anymore or where the fix will lead me, but I'm pleased I'm not 'in recovery', as too many medics deign to call it. Wherever I was when the shutters came down, I sure as hell don't want to go back and pick up the pieces. Pinned on my wall is the Stevenson quote, 'To travel hopefully is better than to arrive, and the true success is to labour.' That'll do me for the time being, but I think I have been lucky.

I'm told I was lucky to fall between three GPs hesitant about how to handle a new patient whose records had yet to transfer. Had I bowled up at my old surgery clutching my bollocks, predicting the end is nigh, 25 years of caring for my maladies would have told them I had flipped. Chances are I would have been hospitalised. Two years into my demise I felt strong enough to search out fellow wackos to offload with. Their tales from the white ward made *Shock Corridor* look like *Finding Neverland*. It was news to me that men in white coats still wire folk up to the grid and zap them! Whatever happened to patient rights?

I've also been told that never being properly diagnosed was a big break. Baffling terms like 'dysthymic', 'dysphoric' and 'IEED' (y'wot!?) were bandied about in my presence, but by the time popping off to see a psychiatrist was mooted, I had adamantly said 'NO' to drugs and wasn't letting any pseudo-scientist near me. In some way or other I was off my rocker, out of my box, bonkers, loony, whatever the man on the Clapham omnibus wants to call the dribbler sat next to him. In a country where psychiatric diagnosis can confine a person to a life of illness and abject misery, any one of those stigmata was good enough for me. It upset friends that I referred to myself as a depresso. It upset me that the chattering classes were more concerned about language than realities.

In China I learned they had no word for mental illness, at least not until recently, not until our drug pushers started sniffing round. (Say what you will about the Central People's Government, you have to admire their embargoes on the pharmaceutical companies camped on their doorstep salivating at the prospect of turning 1.5 billion people on to the brave new world of the chemical cosh. If that's not striking a blow for human rights!) In a medical model that holistically integrates mind, body, soul and spirit, what we stigmatise as mental illness they accept as simply an integral part of being mammalian. They go to work on the *qi*, the vital unseen energy that imbues the very metal of the human machine, keeping the whole caboodle bouncing along sweetly. They employ acupuncture, moxibustion, traditional medicines and massage, but most of all they exploit the healing therapy of being cared for by family and friends, street and community.

Of course, this grossly simplifies an ancient approach that has been 'deconstructed' since 1949. It would take a small library to explain the principles of *Huang Di Nei Jing* and the cultural context in which it was born, developed and compromised down the centuries, but the guy who got me leafing was masseur No. 33 at the Big World Parlour beside Lotus Blossom Garden, Jingdezhen, Jiangxi Province. I had gone to him for a foot massage. It's what folk do at night in a filthy industrial city that has no GPs, only hospitals and herbalists, and no cinemas, theatres or concert halls. They call it preventive medicine, and they treat themselves as often as pockets allow, generally in groups of guys or gals.

Things were going soothingly, until No. 33 hit a spot on my sole that splattered me against the ceiling. 'You do not sleep?' he said, understating a problem that has plagued me since my teens. It's why I was an endorphin addict, physical exhaustion my only guarantee of quality zeds. A later session had me shooting through the roof. 'You have a sickness of the soul?' was a rough translation of his greeting on my return to earth. No. 33 thought he could improve my sleep patterns in the time I had left in Jingdezhen, but to heal my soul would take much longer.

Between the Chinese masseur and the British CPN babbling on about a shaman, I was spurred to pursue a literature trail that taught me a thing or two about madness in all its guises – historical, cultural, political, philosophical. I learned about witches and vision quests, Jung's shadow and Morita's therapy, even dipped into nutrition and voodoo. Many nutters make a point of becoming specialists in their disability, outstripping the 'experts' in their knowledge of drugs and treatments. I don't have the brain for words like tranylcypromine or isocarboxazid, particularly not in the depths of depression, but anything that threw into perspective the shortcomings of the West's approach to mad medicine I devoured. This can cause problems, f'sure, particularly for those susceptible to reading self-help manuals like some personalised Bible. For me the problem was feeding my brain while starving my soul, massaging the marbles at the expense of my emotions.

Whatever had hurled me into the dungeon had something to do with being an 'emotional retard', as my partner so delightfully put it. Beginning the painful process of clawing my way out of darkness, I struggled to find anything that might enrich my spirit. The simple, even childish activity of drawing cartoons appeased my frustration with the health service, providing somewhere to bury my anger, and writing the script helped me understand me a bit better. But it wasn't exactly uplifting, more essential. The old me would have jumped on a bike and set off on some ludicrous solo expedition, the pain of the effort masking the pain of inner turmoil, the uncomplicated wilderness enveloping me in a stark beauty that made me feel I belonged, the need to be calculating about food, water and shelter telling me I'm alive. Unfortunately, the new me was kind of sick of my own company.

Against everything I stood for, I dipped a toe in religion, thinking there might be something I was missing. In an effort to get a handle on belief and spiritual enrichment, I talked to born-agains and apprentice vicars. I took up yoga, which I know isn't a religion (it is banned from some church halls) but might as well be, given the conviction with which practitioners proselytise its spiritual benefits. Time and again with the orthodox I came up against the idea that madness was just reward for original sin. One deacon wasn't impressed when I explained I would never have made it this far in life without a whole lot of sinning, original and otherwise. I had known her for eight years and helped write some of the theological essays for her degree. She refused to talk to me ever again. So much for the benevolence of the Christian spirit. I still do the yoga, more as a stress-buster than the road to enlightenment.

I became a volunteer ranger at Bestwood Country Park, the most southerly tip of what remains of Sherwood Forest. Aside from going some way to satisfying a childhood desire to become a lumberjack, it was physical graft in a stunning environment working with a handful of others, some of them mental health casualties. The feel-good factor in conserving the forest was soul food. After a lifetime of insular self-employment in the media, it was pure joy co-operating with folk who weren't writers or artists or obsessive self-publicists striving for column inches in the *Guardian* reviews. I still take my regular Monday hit, and stroll through the woods almost daily, but the bummer about working with nature is how rapidly a man's efforts are obliterated by new growth. There is a lesson in that somewhere.

So I took on odd jobs for friends – fencing, repairing, slabbing – things I wasn't skilled at but weren't rocket science for a geezer who loves tools. I enjoyed the worry of them, the satisfaction of a job done well, the appreciation heaped by 'customers' who could afford the professionals but were doing us both a favour. For the first time in decades I felt valued, but it wasn't enough. What I needed was some kind of long-term therapy. What I got was a dog. Not just any old mutt, but an RSPCA rescue.

Suzi had been beaten. She was traumatised and neurotic, and fitted right in with our dysfunctional family. She was or rather is a Border Collie, which means no matter how shitty I'm feeling I have to drag my sorry butt round the woods at least once a day, twice when my partner's working. If we walk any distance of a weekend, we've got to be looking at 20 miles and a final furlong of chasing sticks before she's vaguely puffed. The payback in boundless love and almost suffocating devotion is just what the doctor ordered when your heart is black and mind awash with self-loathing.

Besides, after two and a half years of slobbing out, zonked on body-distorting chemicals, I needed to get back into shape. The bike was out and the graft had limited impact. The dog was helpful, but I was searching for some form of jerks that would tender a different perspective on the meaning of my life. Why was physical exertion so important to someone whose normal working routine was a 15-second commute and a day of flicking the right wrist (so to speak)? I smoke, so it certainly wasn't a desire to lengthen or improve the quality of my life.

The means came to me while walking the Beeston Canal. Watching moorhens shelter from the wake of a passing narrowboat, I spied a terrapin in the reeds, then a second, certainly not an indigenous species. Leaving the reader to make the leap, I blagged an open canoe, joined a club where nobody knew me from Adam, and learned the strokes. A whole new world of adventure travel opened up for me; new friends, new challenges, a different perspective on town and country at a pace that fitted my new rhythm of life. And there was space in the front for one other person and a dog. Without any prompting, my partner became my 'stoker', a role she had stoically borne throughout my years of uselessness. The one person who had really suffered during my illness was the last person I thought about while incarcerated in the dungeon of despair.

Lose a soul-mate, a friend or relation, and you grieve but move on, knowing they will live forever in your heart and memories. Lose your own soul, however, and you're buggered. Nothing to grieve with, no way to move on, no heart for anything. I haven't the foggiest if that's what befell me, but I certainly became the most selfish bastard on the planet, totally ignoring that I was in a partnership. Nothing mattered more than me, largely because I had vanished without trace. For almost a year I was myopic about just one thing – finding me, and fast, before something truly grizzly moved in and claimed squatters' rights. I was undoubtedly hell to live with, so there was a whole lot of maintenance and repair work to do on our relationship as I hacked my way towards the light. It wasn't easy, there were protracted rows and interminable heart-to-hearts, but paddling together on a stormy lake the size of Rutland in a Canadian wilderness park the dimensions of Belgium went a long way towards rebuilding the bond. We are not the same couple we were four years ago, thank God, but who *did* I talk to during the dead days?

I first saw the white lizard fleetingly disappearing round a corner of my dungeon. Soon after, he took up residence in my mind and leased a pied-à-terre in my nightmares. He introduced himself as my best friend, but it quickly became evident he was also my worst enemy, mutating from cute lizard to fiery dragon when I dared defy him. Back then, it was impossible to shake Atro, no matter how vociferously I badgered him to get lost. A number of times in China, when firecrackers exploded around us like incoming fire, he freaked out and went walkabout for a few weeks. (Firecrackers are lit to expel evil spirits. They evidently work.) Over the years, I learned to live with the involuntary dialogue that rattled between us, possibly because Atro had his uses. He was never reticent about challenging my encounters with the medics. He had a faultless take on how to live with insanity and stay sane, and was a reliable source of gags for my comic, but latterly he got in the way of what my therapists considered I needed to focus on. I was relieved when I felt strong enough to finally evict the annoying eejit, though I suspect he's still hovering on the doorstep. Like a number of other contributors, I am now in a position to share my grizzly journey with student nurses and practising professionals in so-called 'recovery training' sessions. I do so in the hope that some of what I disclose rings a bell with sufficient of their own, maybe not so traumatic experiences to reassure them that being bonkers is just part of being human. We are no more living with the alien than they are, but maybe ours isn't so bedded in. I do it in the hope they will never be cowed by what I perceive as the state's culture of containment rather than nurturing, and that they will never let the NHS behemoth reduce them to robotic target-tickers. I do it because what they reveal of themselves sometimes helps me make a little more sense of where the hell I've been, and because many of their patients need a lot more care and understanding than I got.

I still say I was lucky, if only because a career as a freelance political cartoonist embedded in me an indefatigable desire to be self-determining. Next to your average estate agent, bank teller or check-out operative I was always considered unusual, maybe exceptional. Society expected me to be a tad off-the-wall, long before I back-flipped off it. That buried resilience didn't make my journey any easier, but maybe I was better equipped than many to roll with the punches, more willing to blindly ride the wave of serendipity and see where it dumped me. Plainly it couldn't be anywhere worse than where I was.

Right now I find myself in the thick of a battle I don't need with the Department of Work and Pensions, fighting to retain the 80 odd quid a week

Incapacity Benefit they so generously bestow on me after 35 years paying taxes. At a time when state bankers and corrupt politicians are applying billion pound Band-Aids to a system that is suffering the mother of all breakdowns, you've got to say it's a mad, mad world we're expected to cope with. One in four seems a conservative estimate.

To find out more about my work as a cartoonist and read sample pages from my comic *DEPRESSO: or How I Learned to Stop Worrying and Embrace Being Bonkers* please go to: www.brickbats.co.uk

Negatives
Ill
drugged
self doubt
self hate
scared
insecure
fear
lazy
drain on the system
worthless
scrounger
But look at the **positives**
Sensitive
Perceptive
Strength to recover
Trusting
Loving
Overcome pain
and fear
Able to listen to others
And empathise
And care
And find success
and self-worth
And love oneself
In may be little things
Like a smile
or writing
or reading
or playing a game
or picking flowers
or cooking a meal
or cleaning
or brushing your teeth
To smile again
We are valuable
And our struggle
on life's journey
Is as valuable as our brothers and sisters

Libby Jackson, 'Negatives and Positives'

16

Conclusions, Discussion and Ways Ahead

Thurstine Basset, Joan Cook and Theo Stickley

In this book we have presented narratives of recovery and survival from a diversity of people. Each story and poem reflects the journey of every one of the contributors. As editors, we have not attempted to achieve uniformity or harmony in the text. Indeed, the central message of this book is that we each have our unique story to tell and it is by appreciating the diversity of people's experiences that an understanding of the proper focus of mental health care may emerge. The word 'recovery' has been used much throughout the text, but this concept itself will lapse with the passage of time. Nevertheless, the concept of recovery has had a remarkable journey, originating largely from and building on service user/survivor perspectives and eventually becoming part of mental health policy. What is significant about the concept is that it has both challenged the traditional medical construction and definition of mental illness and also introduced certain values that need to inform practice. These values, which are firmly based on the uniqueness and worth of the individual, are central to more positive approaches in mental health work. Recovery-oriented approaches are intrinsically optimistic and inspire hope for the person, their families and mental health workers too.

Historically, serious mental illness has been considered life-ruining. Stories are common of people being told by mental health professionals that they will never be able to work, form lasting relationships or live independently. The recovery paradigm challenges the very core of this miserable view of human nature. Recovery from serious mental health problems is not a new idea. Of course, there has been discussion about recovery in its more general sense for many years, as psychiatry and other mental health disciplines have sought to ascertain how best to help people to recover. The current recovery concept and approach can be traced back to the 1970s (Anthony, 1994; Young & Ensing, 1999). The backdrop to

---

the concept of recovery is the programme of deinstitutionalisation during the last three decades. The policies that facilitated these developments have also signified a shift in political power from the institutions of the asylum to the varied developments in community care. As more and more people found greater freedom in the community, so some found licence to challenge the domination of the medical model. For many, however, the effects of deinstitutionalisation were loneliness and a sense of abandonment as failings in community care became apparent.

In chapter 1, we explored how a 'recovery approach' became part of the policy agenda for mental health services in England and was increasingly adopted by NHS Trusts from 2005 onwards. We suggested that this approach was never part of mainstream policy, but emerged through the efforts and enthusiasm of some key people both within and outside the National Institute for Mental Health (NIMHE). NIMHE issued a guiding statement (NIMHE, 2005) and championed a recovery approach. In this document they published 12 guiding principles for the delivery of recovery-oriented mental health services, with the first principle being:

> The user of services decides if and when to begin the recovery process and directs it; therefore, service user direction is essential throughout the process.

Reading this, it is easy to see just how difficult it is for an NHS Trust to adopt a recovery-oriented approach. It is hard to imagine an NHS Trust adopting any approach which enables service users to decide if and when they will engage with it. Certainly, this has not been the model of delivering mental health services in the past. There remains the suspicion that a recovery approach has been bolted onto an existing mental health system that does not really value the input and expertise of those that use the service.

It is hoped that the impact of this book will broaden readers' understanding of what it means to experience mental health problems and continue to lead meaningful and fruitful lives. Contributors use a variety of words to describe their experiences and journeys. Some talk of recovery, others of discovery. Some speak of coping and survival. Self-management, self-help or peer support and strategies for living feature strongly as key parts of a toolkit for survival, growth and liberation. Understanding stigma and discrimination, in relation to mental health and more broadly, and combating it in a variety of both small- and large-scale ways, comes with the territory.

Pilgrim (2008: 297) suggests that there are three ways of viewing recovery:

1. recovery from illness, i.e. an outcome of successful treatment;
2. recovery from impairment, i.e. an outcome of successful rehabilitation;
3. recovery from invalidation, i.e. an outcome of successful survival.

Whilst there are some overlaps between these three strands, there are also major differences. It is not difficult to see how clashes might occur between and among mental health workers and service users where the word 'recovery' is interpreted very differently. It does not help that recovery is in common parlance in health and wider fields. Furthermore, for many people, recovery is as much about coming to terms with the social consequences of being diagnosed and treated as it is about recovering from an illness.

The Scottish Recovery Network has a useful definition:

> Recovery is being able to live a meaningful and satisfying life, as defined by each person, in the presence or absence of symptoms. It is about having control over and input into your own life. Each individual's recovery, like his or her experience of the mental health problems or illness, is a unique and deeply personal process (www.scottishrecovery.net)

This definition has the strength that it makes recovery accessible to and achievable by all, as well as controlled by the individual involved. Achievability by all is important, because a narrow perspective on recovery can lead to a service that includes only service users who are judged by professionals to be capable of recovery.

Chandler and Hayward (2009) give some useful pointers for modern-day mental health workers and services in how to apply a recovery approach:

> Recovery 'is' the collection of recovery pathways that make up a group of people at any given moment and can be enabled or disabled by the person's relationship with supporting services. (2009: 131–132)

Explanations, Beliefs and Strategies

Throughout this book, there is a strong sense of people seeking explanations for their life experiences. People want to make sense of the path that their lives have taken. These explanations may have a physical, medical, social, political, spiritual or philosophical basis, or indeed they may be a mixture of one or more of these elements (see Figure 16.1). People's beliefs are also very important and formed either early in life or developed as life moves on; these beliefs often underpin their explanations. Finally, these explanations and beliefs lead people to work out their own, often very personal strategies for living. These strategies are primarily about all aspects of life, with living with mental health problems as a part of a wider whole. These strategies, often devised and reframed through a long process of trial and error, are the bedrock on which people base their lives.

We also need to acknowledge the contested nature of mental health and mental illness. When we speak of people seeking explanations, we are aware that the mental health professions contribute to these explanations, but not with a single and clear voice. If you were new to the mental health field and decided to pick two recent and well-respected books to learn more about it, you might choose *Doctoring The Mind: Why Psychiatric Treatments Fail* (Bentall, 2009) or the *Oxford Handbook of Psychiatry* (Semple & Smyth, 2009).

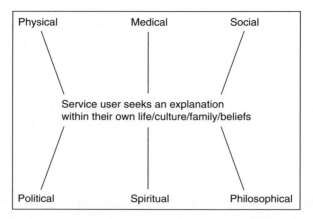

Figure 16.1   Explanations

If you were to read both, you could be forgiven if you ended up in a state of deep confusion. Different opinions and perspectives can be a strength but, in our keenness to cooperate and work with others in an increasingly complex and difficult world, we sometimes overlook the crucial fact that at root we may not agree on the basic principles.

Self-Help and Peer Support

Another key theme is the importance of self-help/peer support groups, with group members describing their value in chapter 12 and other contributors also referring to the important power of shared experience. It is clear that groups can provide a safe space where people share, reframe and make sense of their experiences, and with the combination of empathy, acknowledgement and ordinariness support each other in getting on with life. Another benefit is that not only may people find help and assistance, but also often new and lasting friendships are established. While some of the benefits of sharing and empathy can happen in groups run by workers, the extra power and real effectiveness of self-help groups comes through self efficacy, seeing the group being run and power held by its members, taking on roles in the group, and the affirmation of being able to help others as well as being helped.

As with recovery, self-help/peer support is done 'by', not 'to' or 'for' people, and again this poses dilemmas for services. It is hoped that commissioners will recognise the value of peer support groups and wish to increase their availability, either generally or for particular issues. However, with groups' self-defined identities often based on experiential rather than medical definitions, even the choice of 'subject' may differ – sometimes oppositionally – from groupings defined by mental health professionals or desired by commissioners.

The Role of the Mental Health Worker

We would like to conclude this book with an examination of the role of the mental health worker in working with individuals and groups. Although recovery has now become an important element of current mental health services in the UK, it is not something that can be done to another; rather, it is something that people may do for themselves with support from others (Repper, 2000). The worker needs to assume the position of *not* being the expert. In the process of recovery, the person is the expert in his or her own life process. In order for mental health professionals to help facilitate the individual's process towards recovery, they need to believe in the individual's capacity to recover and understand the debilitating effects of serious mental health problems and their social and psychological consequences. The most obvious way for the worker to find out about the person's experiences is to listen to the person's story. It is all too easy to read a person's case history in their notes and think that we know the individual. Unless mental health practitioners place significance and value on listening to the person's story, they stand little chance of promoting recovery. That said, we need to acknowledge the potential for recovery in spite of the care given by mental health services. Mental health workers may protest that an individual is not interested in recovery and lacks motivation. It is all too easy to blame the person and not look at the broader picture. Perhaps, however, the person is feeling hopeless because he or she has been told in thousands of different ways over many years that he or she is a hopeless case. The person may have developed profound learned hopelessness (Seligman, 1975). Before workers cast the first stone, they need to accept the possible damage done to the individual by the psychiatric system, recognise their own humanity and reach out to the hope that might lie buried deep within the person (Watkins, 2001).

The recovery paradigm demands basic human respect from mental health practitioners. It is hopeful and forward-looking and workers need to adopt a positive and optimistic approach in their work. Care plans need to be representative of what the person wants for their future according to their abilities and strengths. All too often care plans focus on need, disability, deficits and problems. In Western mental health education, workers are taught to be experts in their practice. The recovery model demands that practitioners recognise that the individual client is the expert in the subject of their own personal experience of mental suffering. They too are the experts in understanding the effects of stigma and discrimination. The worker's prime task is therefore not to provide treatment, but to facilitate the individual's journey of coming to terms with the psychological and social effects of mental illness. Service users and providers invariably have differing priorities. Whilst mental health workers focus their care planning on risk, medication, treatment and monitoring, people are often more interested in decent housing, money, social networks and having something meaningful to do.

Mental health policy in the UK has been confusing in recent years, as New Labour has delivered mixed messages. On the one hand, we have seen the growth of recovery policies, but on the other, the amendment to mental health law has introduced greater coercion. Another backdrop agenda has been the increased attention paid to risk. Risk management has become central to much of mental health policy since John Hutton, then junior minister with responsibility for mental health, stated at the MIND conference in 1998: 'Non-compliance is not an option in mental health.' Ron Coleman commented, 'This denies many of the fundamental requirements for recovery ... and denies basic rights of citizens' (1999: 51). Therapeutic risk-taking on the part of mental health professionals is essential for growth and recovery. If, as Coleman warns, the government agenda seeks to eliminate risk through social control (for example, community treatment orders), then it follows that opportunities for individual recovery may be limited.

Some useful tools have recently emerged to guide and inform mental health workers. Self Help Nottingham's top ten points to consider when working with groups are a helpful guide for mental health workers. The first four points address fundamental attitudes and understanding, and the latter six concern positive approaches and practical support.

1. *Recognising the importance of self-identification, choice, and initiation by the group:* If a group is established by workers, look for opportunities to create space for the group's self-identification to emerge later.
2. *NOT a service that workers can refer people to, and NOT a crisis service:* Provide information to people who will take their own decisions about approaching groups. Unless a group specifically offers a crisis service, suggesting a self-help group as somewhere people can go in a crisis is inappropriate, counter-productive and potentially dangerous for the service user and for the group.
3. *Empowerment and recovery are done by, not for or to:* However, workers can create space for and support these processes.
4. *Self-awareness by professionals:* Acknowledge any fears and conflicting feelings or beliefs, and recognise potential personal and professional rewards from working with groups – ensure that the primary gain is for the group and its members rather than for the worker.
5. *Clarity in staff roles:* Clarify workers' roles through discussion and negotiation with groups, and in formal work structures to highlight ambiguities such as staff supporting groups in their own time, sustainability and any professional code of conduct issues. Boundaries between offering support and creating dependency are fluid and roles need to be reviewed as group members gain confidence or health fluctuates.

6. *Transition from support groups to self-help groups:* Unexpected or enforced transition due to staffing or service changes is traumatic, and best avoided by being clear from the outset about workers' roles and other support, and their likely duration. It is possible to take a positive, gradual, planned approach to transition, negotiated with the group.
7. *Support for development of self-help groups:* At its best this offers groups information and choice about levels of support, and advice about funding, constitutions and publicity. It takes a facilitative approach, modelling group members' ability to solve problems and building confidence through open discussion of risk.
8. *Organisation and resilience of mental health self-help groups:* Groups often develop attitudes and practical arrangements for resilience, encouraging shared roles and back-up for the work of running the group. Groups may develop ground rules and 'what if?' agreements in addition to constitutions.
9. *Ongoing support and services for self-help groups:* These include assistance with problem-solving, training, contact with other groups, access to facilities and (ideally) small amounts of funding, with workers able to support groups in ways that recognise and leave control with the group. Support also includes providing the public and other organisations with up-to-date information that understands the context of groups.
10. *Sources of support for groups:* Specialist self-help organisations are rare, but support may be offered by mental health and other health workers and organisations, local Councils for Voluntary Services, and other community development and voluntary organisations.

In essence the role of the mental health worker is as an enabler and facilitator, working with service users and their families as a co-worker, using their own expertise, but also drawing on the expertise of the service user.

Figure 16.2 shows the grass-roots tasks for service users and workers in a number of interrelated arenas.

Some final and simple lessons for workers that emerge from reading the accounts in this book can be summarised as follows:

- Listen and learn from both service user and their families – acknowledge their experience and expertise.
- Use your own expertise as a helpful addition to that of the service user.
- Respect people and their perspectives – try to put yourself in their shoes to understand their view.
- Be hopeful and remind people of their achievements – see their potential.
- Accept that there will be times when people go backwards.
- Know when to be 'hands-on' and when to be 'hands-off' – in general, take an enabling and facilitative approach.
- Understand that tasks are easier to achieve when broken down into small units.

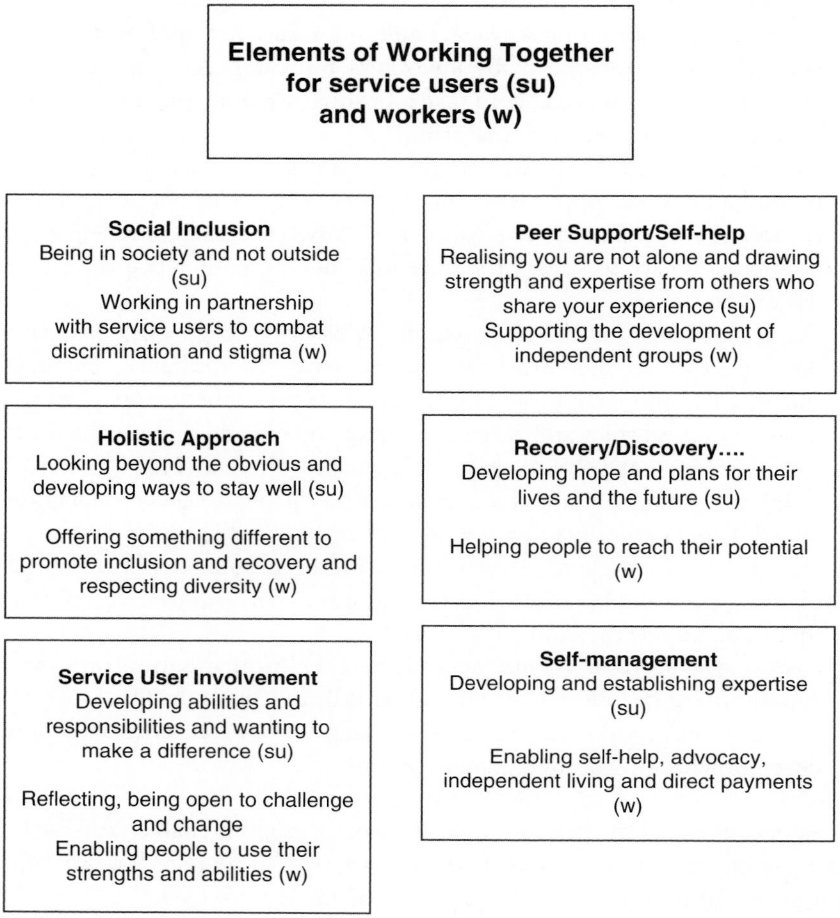

```
┌─────────────────────────────────┐
│   Elements of Working Together  │
│      for service users (su)     │
│         and workers (w)         │
└─────────────────────────────────┘
```

Social Inclusion
Being in society and not outside (su)
Working in partnership with service users to combat discrimination and stigma (w)

Peer Support/Self-help
Realising you are not alone and drawing strength and expertise from others who share your experience (su)
Supporting the development of independent groups (w)

Holistic Approach
Looking beyond the obvious and developing ways to stay well (su)

Offering something different to promote inclusion and recovery and respecting diversity (w)

Recovery/Discovery....
Developing hope and plans for their lives and the future (su)

Helping people to reach their potential (w)

Service User Involvement
Developing abilities and responsibilities and wanting to make a difference (su)

Reflecting, being open to challenge and change
Enabling people to use their strengths and abilities (w)

Self-management
Developing and establishing expertise (su)

Enabling self-help, advocacy, independent living and direct payments (w)

Figure 16.2   Elements of Working Together

- Keep in touch with and encourage local self-help/peer support groups.
- Join the battle against stigma and discrimination.

Concluding Comment

This book has celebrated the voices, opinions and expertise of people who have experience of living with mental health problems. We are grateful to the individuals who contributed their personal stories. We also acknowledge the contributions of two independent service user organisations: CAPITAL and Making Waves. We hope these and similar organisations continue to grow and flourish.

The expertise from the contributors offers a guide to anybody who may be struggling with living and surviving in the twenty-first century. People who have struggled with the complexities of existence and found their own unique ways of surviving, learning and moving on can teach us all a great deal about how to live in our modern, or postmodern, world. They are part of a long tradition of people of wisdom who tell their stories. This tradition will always survive.

References

Anthony W (1994) Recovery from mental illness: the guiding vision of the mental system in the 1990's (Chapter 7). In L. Spaniol et al. (Eds.) *An Introduction to Psychiatric Rehabilitation*. International Association of Rehabilitation Services, Columbia, and USA

Chandler R & Hayward M (2009) *Voicing Psychotic Experiences – A Reconsideration of Recovery and Diversity*. Brighton: OLM-Pavilion

Coleman R. (1999) *Recovery: an Alien Concept*. Gloucester: Handsell

National Institute for Mental Health in England (2005) *NIMHE Guiding Statement on Recovery*. London: Department of Health

Pilgrim D (2008) 'Recovery' and current mental health policy. *Chronic Illness 2009, 4*: 295–304

Repper J M (2000) Adjusting the focus of mental health nursing: Incorporating service users' experiences of recovery. *Journal of Mental Health, 9(6)*: 575–587

Scottish Recovery Network: (www.scottishrecovery.net)

Seligman M (1975) *Helplessness: on Depression, Development and Health*. San Francisco: Freeman

Semple D & Smyth R (2009) *Oxford Handbook of Psychiatry*, second edition. Oxford: Oxford University Press

Watkins P (2001) *Mental Health Nursing: The Art of Compassionate Care*. Oxford: Butterworth Heinemann

Young S L and Ensing D S (1999) Exploring Recovery from the perspective of people with psychiatric disabilities. *Psychiatric Rehabilitation Journal, 22(3)* (Winter): 219–231

In the beginning it was one
The world, with no borders, definition or difference
With the heart-shaped land mass in the centre
Afrika
Afrika
The heart of humankind
Giving the means of life to the world
Circulating the essence
For humankind's will to live in harmony
The nucleus of humanity
A legacy of peace love and understanding
Afrika
Mother of humankind
Tenderly watching over the sons and daughters of man
The cradle of civilisation
Then an almighty earthquake shook the earth
Splitting the heart of humankind
Into many separate veins running through continents
A shift of consciousness occurred
Causing pain anguish and great suffering
The heart was displaced, fractured
Usurped by the mind
An exodus flowed outwardly
Blood ties broken
The loving union divided
Signalling a schism
Creating nation states and partition
The hair now torn from the roots
Of the nourisher
The umbilical cord disconnected from humankind
The children separated from the birth mother
O rainbow citizens of the world
Look to the beginning
Look to the roots
Look to the self
Afrika
Mother Afrika
Her heart never stops beating
Yearning for all her children to return home

Mariyam Maule, 'The Heart of Humankind'

Index

Compiled by Indexing Specialists (UK) Ltd